IFIP Advances in Information and Communication Technology 543

IFIP – The International Federation for Information Processing

IFIP was founded in 1960 under the auspices of UNESCO, following the first World Computer Congress held in Paris the previous year. A federation for societies working in information processing, IFIP's aim is two-fold: to support information processing in the countries of its members and to encourage technology transfer to developing nations. As its mission statement clearly states:

> IFIP is the global non-profit federation of societies of ICT professionals that aims at achieving a worldwide professional and socially responsible development and application of information and communication technologies.

IFIP is a non-profit-making organization, run almost solely by 2500 volunteers. It operates through a number of technical committees and working groups, which organize events and publications. IFIP's events range from large international open conferences to working conferences and local seminars.

The flagship event is the IFIP World Computer Congress, at which both invited and contributed papers are presented. Contributed papers are rigorously refereed and the rejection rate is high.

As with the Congress, participation in the open conferences is open to all and papers may be invited or submitted. Again, submitted papers are stringently refereed.

The working conferences are structured differently. They are usually run by a working group and attendance is generally smaller and occasionally by invitation only. Their purpose is to create an atmosphere conducive to innovation and development. Refereeing is also rigorous and papers are subjected to extensive group discussion.

Publications arising from IFIP events vary. The papers presented at the IFIP World Computer Congress and at open conferences are published as conference proceedings, while the results of the working conferences are often published as collections of selected and edited papers.

IFIP distinguishes three types of institutional membership: Country Representative Members, Members at Large, and Associate Members. The type of organization that can apply for membership is a wide variety and includes national or international societies of individual computer scientists/ICT professionals, associations or federations of such societies, government institutions/government related organizations, national or international research institutes or consortia, universities, academies of sciences, companies, national or international associations or federations of companies.

More information about this series at http://www.springer.com/series/6102

Ulrike Schultze · Margunn Aanestad
Magnus Mähring · Carsten Østerlund
Kai Riemer (Eds.)

Living with Monsters?

Social Implications of Algorithmic Phenomena, Hybrid Agency, and the Performativity of Technology

IFIP WG 8.2 Working Conference
on the Interaction of Information Systems
and the Organization, IS&O 2018
San Francisco, CA, USA, December 11–12, 2018
Proceedings

 Springer

Editors
Ulrike Schultze (iD)
Southern Methodist University
Dallas, TX, USA

Margunn Aanestad (iD)
University of Oslo
Oslo, Norway

Magnus Mähring (iD)
Stockholm School of Economics
Stockholm, Sweden

Carsten Østerlund (iD)
Syracuse University
Syracuse, NY, USA

Kai Riemer (iD)
The University of Sydney Business School
Darlington, NSW, Australia

ISSN 1868-4238   ISSN 1868-422X   (electronic)
IFIP Advances in Information and Communication Technology
ISBN 978-3-030-04090-1   ISBN 978-3-030-04091-8   (eBook)
https://doi.org/10.1007/978-3-030-04091-8

Library of Congress Control Number: 2018960862

This Springer imprint is published by the registered company Springer Nature Switzerland AG
The registered company address is: Gewerbestrasse 11, 6330 Cham, Switzerland

Preface

The papers in this volume constitute the proceedings of a working conference organized by the IFIP Working Group 8.2, whose brief is "The Interaction of Information Systems and the Organization." The conference, entitled "Living with Monsters? Social Implications of Algorithmic Phenomena, Hybrid Agency and the Performativity of Technology," was held in San Francisco during December 11–12, 2018. An important inspiration for the theme of the conference was the highly successful 2016 Dublin working conference organized by Working Group 8.2; we would like to see the current conference as at least partly a continuation and extension of themes and ideas put forward in Dublin.

The call for papers resulted in a total of 49 submissions. Of these, 11 full papers, four panel papers, and 16 interactive papers were selected for presentation at the working conference. The submissions were selected through a blind review process involving at least two reviewers and the editors. Authors of submissions that were selected for the next round were requested to revise their contributions in accordance with the reviewers' and the editors' recommendations. The revised submissions were then reviewed for publication in this volume.

An introductory paper serves as an introduction to the volume, and two short papers, by Lucy Suchman and Paul N. Edwards, reflect the contents of the two keynote addresses given at the conference. Lucy Suchman deals with our ambivalent relationship with technological power and control, concretely in relation to the increasing automation of military systems. Suchman reminds us that we are not absolved from responsibility because the technological systems are beyond our control, and she emphasizes the challenge posed to us by the monster imaginary. Paul N. Edwards takes on algorithms and develops four principles that capture core aspects of their nature; the principle of radical complexity, the principle of opacity, the principle of radical otherness, and finally the difficult-to-name principle of infrastructuration or of Borgian assimilation.

In addition to the keynotes and paper presentation sessions, we organized interactive poster presentations and two panels. The first panel, called "Monstrous Materialities," brought together papers that investigate various aspects of the surprising and sometimes unintended effects of our actions and interactions with technologies. A second panel was given the title "Studying 'Sociomateriality': An Exploration of Constructs in the Making." The panel was chaired by Wanda Orlikowski and focused on how we work with materiality in our research studies. Going beyond debates about the best approach to examining "sociomateriality," the panelists (Dubrava Cecez-Kecmanovic, Eric Monteiro, and Susan Scott) offered a constructive exploration of the specific ideas and practices that guide their research studies, sharing the value they obtain from working this way.

During the work in preparing the conference, one of the submitting authors, Natalie Hardwicke of the University of Sydney, tragically and prematurely passed away.

As a tribute to her, and a memento of a promising academic career cut short, we have decided to include her short paper as the final chapter in this volume.

We would like to express our thanks to all the contributors to this volume, as well as the panelists and presenters at the conference. We would also like to express our gratitude for the excellent work of all the members of the Program Committee, as well as additional reviewers, during the review process. Further, we are grateful for the support of the Cox School of Business at Southern Methodist University, the Stockholm School of Economics, the University of Sydney Business School, the iSchool at Syracuse University, and the Department of Informatics at the University of Oslo.

Last but not least, we are most grateful for the professional and efficient support of Erika Siebert-Cole, Niranjan Bhaskaran and their colleagues at Springer in producing these proceedings.

October 2018

Ulrike Schultze
Margunn Aanestad
Magnus Mähring
Carsten Østerlund
Kai Riemer

Organization

Program Chairs

Ulrike Schultze	Southern Methodist University, USA
Margunn Aanestad	Oslo University, Norway
Magnus Mähring	Stockholm School of Economics, Sweden
Carsten Østerlund	Syracuse University, USA
Kai Riemer	Sydney University, Australia

Program Committee

J. P. Allen	University of San Francisco, USA
Luis Araujo	University of Manchester, UK
Michel Avital	Copenhagen Business School, Denmark
Diane Bailey	University of Texas at Austin, USA
Michael Barrett	University of Cambridge, UK
Beth Bechky	New York University, USA
Nick Berente	University of Notre Dame, USA
Magnus Bergquist	Halmstad University, Sweden
Mads Bødker	Copenhagen Business School, Denmark
Sebastian Boell	University of Sydney, Australia
Dubravka Cecez-Kecmanovic	University of New South Wales, Australia
Melissa Cefkin	Nissan Research Center, USA
Panos Constantinides	University of Warwick, UK
Alessia Contu	University of Massachusetts, USA
Kevin Crowston	Syracuse University, USA
Bill Doolin	Auckland University of Technology, New Zealand
Paul Dourish	University of California Irvine, USA
Hamid Ekbia	Indiana University, USA
Amany Elbanna	Royal Holloway, University of London, UK
Ingrid Erickson	Syracuse University, USA
Anne-Laure Fayard	New York University, USA
Miria Grisot	University of Oslo, Norway
Ella Hafermalz	Vrije Universiteit Amsterdam, The Netherlands
Dirk Hovorka	University of Sydney, Australia
Lotta Hultin	Stockholm School of Economics, Sweden
Lucas Introna	Lancaster University, UK
Tina Blegind Jensen	Copenhagen Business School, Denmark
Matthew Jones	University of Cambridge, UK
Jannis Kallinikos	London School of Economics and Political Science, UK

Helena Karsten	Åbo Akademi University, Finland
Karlheinz Kautz	RMIT University, Australia
Donncha Kavanagh	University College Dublin, Ireland
Séamas Kelly	University College Dublin, Ireland
Stefan Klein	University of Münster, Germany
Olivera Marjanovic	University of Technology, Sydney, Australia
Melissa Mazmanian	University of California Irvine, USA
Joan Rodón Mòdol	ESADE Ramon Llull University, Spain
Emmanuel Monod	Shanghai University of International Business and Economics, and Beijing University of Post and Telecom, China
Eric Monteiro	Norwegian University of Science and Technology, Norway
Benjamin Mueller	University of Groningen, The Netherlands
Bonnie Nardi	University of California, Irvine, USA
Marko Niemimaa	University of Jyväskylä, Finland
Eivor Oborn	University of Warwick, UK
Brian Pentland	Michigan State University, USA
Dimitra Petrakaki	Sussex University, UK
Kathleen H. Pine	Arizona State University, USA
Elpida Prasopoulou	Coventry University, UK
Maha Shaikh	University of Warwick, UK
Mari-Klara Stein	Copenhagen Business School, Denmark
Edgar Whitley	London School of Economics and Political Science, UK

Conference Sponsors

Cox School of Business, Southern Methodist University
Department of Informatics, University of Oslo
House of Innovation, Stockholm School of Economics
The iSchool, Syracuse University
The University of Sydney Business School

University of Oslo

Contents

Hybrid Agency and the Performativity of Technology

Living with Monsters

Setting the Stage

Living with Monsters?

Margunn Aanestad[1](✉)[iD], Magnus Mähring[2][iD], Carsten Østerlund[3],
Kai Riemer[4][iD], and Ulrike Schultze[5][iD]

[1] University of Oslo, Box 1072 Blindern, 0316 Oslo, Norway
margunn@ifi.uio.no
[2] Stockholm School of Economics, Box 6501, 11383 Stockholm, Sweden
magnus.mahring@hhs.se
[3] Syracuse University, 343 Hinds Hall, Syracuse, NY 13244-1190, USA
costerlu@syr.edu
[4] The University of Sydney, Sydney, NSW 2006, Australia
kai.riemer@sydney.edu.au
[5] SMU Cox School of Business, Box 750333, Dallas, TX 75275-0333, USA
uschultz@smu.edu

1 Introduction

These proceedings of the IFIP WG 8.2 reflects the response of the research community to the theme selected for the 2018 working conference: "Living with Monsters? Social Implications of Algorithmic Phenomena, Hybrid Agency and the Performativity of Technology". The IFIP WG 8.2 community has played an important role in the Information Systems' (IS) field, by promoting methodological diversity and engagement with organizational and social theory. Historically, it has acted as a focus for IS researchers who share these interests, always sustaining a lively and reflexive debate around methodological questions. In recent years, this community has developed an interest in processual, performative and relational aspects of inquiries into agency and materiality. This working conference builds on these methodological and theoretical focal points.

As the evolving digital worlds generate both hope and fears, we wanted to mobilize the research community to reflect on the implications of digital technologies. Early in our field's history Norbert Wiener emphasized the ambivalence of automation's potential and urged us to consider the possible social consequences of technological development [1]. In a year where the CEO of one of the world's largest tech giants had to testify to both the US Congress and the EU Parliament[1], the social implications of digital technologies is a pertinent topic for a working conference in the IFIP 8.2 WG community.

The monster metaphor allows reframing and questioning both of our object of research and of ourselves [2]. It brings attention to the ambivalence of technology as our creation. Algorithms, using big data, do not only identify suspicious credit card

---

[1] https://www.theguardian.com/technology/live/2018/apr/11/mark-zuckerberg-testimony-live-updates-house-congress-cambridge-analytica, https://www.nytimes.com/2018/04/12/technology/mark-zuckerberg-testimony.html, https://www.bbc.com/news/technology-44210800.

U. Schultze et al. (Eds.): IS&O 2018, IFIP AICT 543, pp. 3–12, 2018.
https://doi.org/10.1007/978-3-030-04091-8_1

transactions and predict the spread of epidemics, but they also raise concerns about mass surveillance and perpetuated biases. Social media platforms allow us to stay connected with family and friends, but they also commoditize relationships and produce new forms of sociality. Platform architectures are immensely flexible for connecting supply and demand, but they are also at risk of monopolization and may become the basis for totalitarian societal structures.

We have realized that digital technologies are not mere strategic assets, supporting tools, or representational technologies; instead, they are profoundly performative [3]. They serve as critical infrastructures and are deeply implicated in our daily lives. The complexity and opacity of today's interconnected digital assemblages reduce anyone's ability to fathom, let alone control them. For instance, stock market flash crashes, induced by algorithmic trading, are highly visible examples of the limits of oversight and control.

Cautionary tales of technology have often employed monster notions, such as the sorcerer's apprentice, the juggernaut, and the Frankenstein figure [4]. The complex hybrid assemblages that have become so crucial for our everyday lives, are our own creations but not under anyone's apparent control. In fact, we might even be controlled by them [5]. Consequently, we ask: "Are we living with monsters?"

The monster, emphasizing the unintended consequences of technologies, can also encourage a reflection on what it is we do when we contribute to the creation of technologies, and what our roles and duties are as researchers. The monster figure has stimulated such moral reflection ever since Mary Wollstonecraft Shelley's paradigmatic novel *Frankenstein or The Modern Prometheus* was published 200 years ago in 1818. The novel has often been read as a critique of modern science's hubris and lack of moral restraint in the pursuit of knowledge, especially when linked to creating artificial life or tinkering with natural, biological life.

A slightly different reading is presented by Winner [4] and Latour [6], who point to the lack (or delayed onset) of the realization that a moral obligation accompanies the pursuit of knowledge and technological creation. "Dr. Frankenstein's crime was not that he invented a creature through some combination of hubris and high technology, but rather that he *abandoned the creature to itself*" ([6] [italics in original]). If our involvement should be followed by a moral obligation, we need to ask what this entails. What does it mean to take care of the monsters in our midst?

The monster disturbs us. A central thrust in the literature on monsters in the humanities is geared to explore the revelatory potential of the monster figure. Attending to monsters is a way of reading a culture's fears, desires, anxieties and fantasies as expressed in the monsters it engenders [7]. The monster is a mixed, and incongruous entity that generates questions about boundaries between the social and the material: Where are the borders of the human society? Does the monster have a place among us?

This ontological liminality can be exploited as an analytic resource: the monsters reveal that which is "othered" and expelled, perhaps that which we neither want to take responsibility for nor to take care of. How do we think about being deeply implicated in the ongoing (re)creation of digital societies? Many of us use social media while criticizing their privacy-invading tendencies; many enjoy the gig economy for its low-cost services while disliking its destabilization of workers' rights; and many perpetuate the quantification of academic life while criticizing it. Do we as researchers inadvertently contribute to such "eyes wide shut" behavior? How can we conduct our research in ways that are open to the unintended? How can we be self-reflexive and realize our own biases, preferences, interests and (hidden) agendas?

These are some of the reflections we hoped the conference theme would trigger and the questions it would raise. We had hoped for an engaged response from members of the IFIP WG 8.2 community, and we were not disappointed. We received 49 submissions from researchers addressing a wide range of topics within the conference theme. Enacting a double-blind review process, the papers were assigned to one of the conference co-chairs (acting in a senior editor role) and then sent to at least two reviewers. As a sign of the 8.2 community's critical yet supportive culture and its generosity of spirit, the reviewers offered highly constructive and carefully crafted feedback that was invaluable to both editors and the authors.

After a careful and highly competitive selection, we accepted 11 contributions for full presentation at the conference. These papers, and opinion pieces by our two keynotes, make up these proceedings.

Following after this chapter and two short papers summarizing the keynote addresses, we have clustered the 11 papers into three groups, each making up a section in this editorial. The first section, **Social Implications of Algorithmic Phenomena**, features contributions that deal with questions about objectivity, legitimacy, matters of inclusion, the blackboxing of accountability, and the systemic effects and unintended consequences of algorithmic decision-making. In particular, utopian visions of new forms of rationality are explored alongside dystopian narratives of surveillance capitalism.

Hybrid Agency and the Performativity of Technology, our second cluster of papers, includes papers that explore relational notions of agency, as well as perspectives, concepts and vocabularies that help us understand the performativity of sociomaterial practices and how technologies are implicated in them. These contributions embrace hybridity, liminality, and performativity.

The papers in the third section, **Living with Monsters**, take up the notion of monsters as their core metaphor. They explore the value and threat of these complex, autonomous creations in our social worlds and develop ideas for how we, as creators, users and investigators of these technologies, might reconsider and renew our relationships to, and intertwining with, these creatures/creations.

2 Contributions from Our Keynote Speakers – Lucy Suchman and Paul N. Edwards

Our two eminent keynote speakers engage with the conference theme in different ways. In "Frankenstein's Problem," Lucy Suchman deals with our ambivalent relationship to technological power and control. She seeks to intervene in the increasing automation of military systems, where the identification of targets and initiation of attack via military drones seem on track to becoming fully automated. Drawing on Rhee's *The Robotic Imaginary* [8], she describes the dehumanization that is made possible by the narrowness in robotic views of humanness and argues that we need to direct our attention towards the "relation between the figurations of the human and operations of dehumanization."

Rather than seeking to control our monster, Suchman argues for *continued engagement* and reminds us that we are not absolved from responsibility because the technological systems are beyond our control. While we are obliged to remain in relation, we should also remember that these relations often are about either dominance or instrumentality. Suchman urges us to recognize how "a politics of alterity" operates through the monster figure, and how the monster [9] can challenge and questions us. Indeed, this is the promise that the monster imaginary holds.

Paul N. Edwards takes on algorithms in his chapter "We have been assimilated: some principles for thinking about algorithmic systems". While we often think of an algorithm as a recipe or a list of instructions, Edwards claims that this is "merely the kindergarten version" of what is going on with algorithmic systems. To gain a more realistic appreciation of contemporary algorithms, Edwards develops four principles that capture their nature.

Firstly, there are too many intricate interactions in a complicated algorithmic system (e.g., climate models) for us to grasp an algorithm's totality. This constitutes *the principle of radical complexity*. Secondly, the category of algorithms produced by machine learning systems are not a set of pre-programmed instructions but are themselves "builders" that develop new models. Thus, the algorithms, as well as the high-dimensional feature matrices that are used to develop and evaluate the models being built, are beyond human comprehensions. Edwards captures this aspect of algorithms in the *principle of opacity*.

Thirdly, despite the frequent invocation of the human brain as a metaphor for artificial intelligence, learning algorithms do not work like human cognition. This is expressed in the *principle of radical otherness*. Finally, to indicate the need for a comprehensive view that goes beyond a mere focus on the technology, i.e., algorithms and data, Edwards highlights the performative and constitutive nature of algorithms, which he struggles to capture in a succinct principle. He thus offers alternatives like the *principle of infrastructuration* and the *principle of Borgian assimilation*.

Edwards concludes with a call for intellectual tools – of which his principles might form an integral part – that might help us engage with this new world. However, he worries that we might already be too assimilated to a world infused with algorithmic systems, and that "there probably is no going back."

Lucy Suchman and Paul Edwards both stimulate our reflections on living with the technologies we have created, caring for them and contemplating the roles and responsibilities of the IS researcher in studying these imbroglios. In this way, our keynote speakers set the tone we envisaged for this working conference, aptly located in the shadow of Silicon Valley.

3 Social Implications of Algorithmic Phenomena

The proliferation of algorithmic decision-making in work and life raises novel questions about objectivity, legitimacy, matters of inclusion, the blackboxing of accountability, and the systemic effects and unintended consequences of algorithmic decision-
making. Utopian visions of new forms of rationality coexist with dystopian narratives
around surveillance capitalism and the remaking of society [10]. Will algorithms and
artificial 'intelligence' provide solutions to complex problems, from reimagining
transport and reducing social inequality to fighting disease and climate change, or are
we putting undue faith in the techno-utopian power of algorithmic life [11]? Several of
the papers engage with this topic in a range of settings:

In the chapter "Algorithmic Pollution: Understanding and Responding to Negative
Consequences of Algorithmic Decision-making," Olivera Marjanovic, Dubravka
Cecez-Kecmanovic, and Richard Vidgen draw inspiration from the notion of environmental pollution to explore the potentially harmful and unintended consequences of
algorithmic pollution in sociomaterial environments. While the authors recognize the
potentially significant benefits of algorithms to society (e.g., healthcare, driverless
vehicles, fraud detection) they offer evidence of the negative effect algorithms can have
on services that transform people's lives such as (again) healthcare, social support
service, education, law and financial services. Using sociomateriality as their theoretical lens, the authors take the first step in developing an approach that can help us track
how this type of pollution is performed by sociomaterial assemblages involving
numerous actors. The paper is a timely call to action for IS researchers interested in
algorithms and their role in organizations and society.

In "Quantifying Quality: Algorithmic Knowing Under Uncertainty", Eric Monteiro,
Elena Parmiggiani, Thomas Østerlie, and Marius Mikalsen examine the complex
processes involved in geological assessments in commercial oil and gas exploration.
The authors uncover how traditionally qualitative sensemaking practices of geological
interpretations in commercial oil and gas exploration are challenged by quantification
efforts driven by geophysical, sensor-based measurements captured by digital tools.
Interestingly, even as more geophysical data become available, they feed into narratives
that aim to provide actionable explanations for what geological processes and events
gave rise to the current geophysical conditions discernible from the data. Adopting a
performative view of scaffolding as underpinning geological (post-humanist) sensemaking, they argue that scaffolding is dynamic, provisional, and decentered. They also
argue and show that even as practices evolve, towards quantification, there remains an
irreducible relationship between, or intertwining of, qualitative judgments and data-
driven quantitative analysis.

In "Understanding the Impact of Transparency on Algorithmic Decision Making
Legitimacy" David Goad and Uri Gal argue that the lack of transparency in algorithmic
decision making (ADM), i.e., the opacity of how the algorithm was developed and how
it works, negatively impacts its perceived legitimacy. This is likely to reduce the
application and adoption of decision support technologies, especially those leveraging
machine learning and artificial intelligence, in organizations. To unpack the complex
relationship between transparency and ADM's perceived legitimacy, the authors

develop a conceptual framework that decomposes transparency into validation, visibility and variability. Furthermore, it distinguishes among different types of legitimacy, i.e., pragmatic, moral and cognitive. Based on this conceptual scaffold, Goad and Gal develop a set of propositions that model the complex relationship between transparency and ADM's perceived legitimacy. Since transparency affects the legitimacy of algorithmic decision making positively under some circumstances and negatively under others, this paper offers useful guidance for the design of business processes that seek to leverage learning algorithms in order to deal with the very real organizational challenges of big data and the Internet of Things.

The chapter called "Advancing to the Next Level: Caring for Evaluative Metrics Monsters in Academia and Healthcare", is written by Iris Wallenburg, Wolfgang Kaltenbrunner, Björn Hammarfeldt, Sarah de Rijcke, and Roland Bal. The authors use the notions of play [12] and games to analyze performance management practices in professional work, more specifically in law faculties and hospitals. The authors argue that while evaluative metrics are often described as 'monsters' impacting professional work, the same metrics can also become part of practices of caring for such work. For instance, these metric monsters can be put to work to change and improve work. At other times, they are playfully resisted when their services are unwarranted. Distinguishing between finite games (games played to win) and infinite games (games played for the purpose of continuing to play), the authors show how evaluative metrics are reflexively enacted in daily professional practice as well as how they can be leveraged in conflictual dynamics. This chapter therefore provides rich nuance to the discussion of the "metric monsters" of performance evaluations.

In "Hotspots and Blind Spots: A Case of Predictive Policing in Practice", Lauren Waardenburg, Anastasia Sergeeva and Marleen Huysman describe the changes following the introduction of predictive analytics in the Dutch police force. They focus on the occupational transformations and describe the growing significance of intermediary occupational groups. The previously supportive role of the "information officers" evolved into a more pro-active role that involved the exercising of judgment, which impacted the outcome of the analytics. This earned the group, now denoted "intelligence officers" a more central position. Paradoxically, the work of the intelligence officers was critical to establishing a perception of the predictive analytics' trustworthiness among the police officers.

In the chapter entitled "Objects, Metrics and Practices: An Inquiry into the Programmatic Advertising Ecosystem," Cristina Alaimo and Jannis Kallinikos explore "programmatic advertising," i.e., the large scale, real-time bidding process whereby ads are automatically assigned upon a user's browser request. In this process of dizzying computational and organizational complexity, the study focuses on the functioning of digital objects, platforms and measures. The chapter shows how the automated exchanges in these massive platform ecosystems shift the way they measure audiences from user behaviour data to contextual data. Adopting Esposito's notion of conjectural objects [13, 14], the authors describe how ads are assigned not based on what a user did but rather the computable likelihood of an ad to be seen by a user, or what the industry calls an "opportunity to see." Thus, rather than being simple means to monitor a preexisting reality (e.g., user behaviour) these metrics and techniques bring forward their own reality by shaping the objects of digital advertising. This intriguing account of programmatic advertisement contributes to our understanding of automation in the age of performative algorithmic phenomena.

4 Hybrid Agency and the Performativity of Technology

We are deeply entangled with technologies ranging from avatars through wearables to ERP systems and infrastructure. To explain this, a notion of agency as a property possessed by actants seems insufficient, and we need to explore relational notions of agency, as well as perspectives, concepts and vocabularies that help us understand the performativity of sociomaterial practices and how technologies are implicated in not just organizational but also social life. What are the methodological implications of a performative lens; the practices, becoming, and processes associated with AI, big data, digital traces and other emerging phenomena [15, 16]? Several of the papers in this volume reflect on and experiment with research approaches that embrace hybridity, liminality, and performativity:

Mads Bødker, Stefan Olavi Olofsson, and Torkil Clemmensen detail in their chapter titled "Re-figuring Gilbert the Drone" the process of working with a drone in a maker lab. They approach the drone as a figure that has not been fully fleshed out, where a number of potential figurations lie beyond many of the current assemblages of drones as tools for policing, surveillance and warfare. By merging insights from philosophies of affect [17–19] and critical design [20, 21] they develop a re-figuring process to explore this potentially "monstrous" technology. Various figurations of drones, they argue, can be explored critically by paying attention to how material things are entangled in how we feel and what we do. Asking how things enchant us and how we feel about technologies, widens, the authors find, the possibilities for re-figuration in a critical design process.

In her chapter "Making a Difference in ICT research: Feminist theorization of sociomateriality and the diffraction methodology", Amany Elbanna heeds the call to advance sociomateriality research practice. The author builds on Barad's Agential Realism [22] as one prominent theoretical lens, which she locates and discusses in the wider context of feminist theorizing. In so doing, she critically questions contemporary, scientistic forms of knowledge production in IS, in particular the assumption that core entities of the field exist unequivocally and ex ante [23], to be located and observed in the field during research. Instead, assuming ontological inseparability, [23, 24] the author proposes to build on the notion of diffraction [25, 26] in leaving the delineation of meaningful entities to the research process, which she spells out in detail. The paper makes an important contribution to IS research practice, at a time when the discipline grapples with novel and indeterminate phenomena, such as the emergence of "platform monsters".

5 Living with Monsters

Several of the papers took up the monsters notion directly, addressing head-on the core metaphor of the conference. They explore the entry of these complex, autonomous creations, or creatures, in our social worlds and examine our own roles as creators. The papers deal with the simultaneous intentions and desires that push us towards creative acts, and as co-inhabitors of the emergent technology-infused worlds, prompts us to reconsider and renew our relationships to, and intertwining with, our creations.

In the opening chapter in this section, "Thinking with Monsters," which is authored by Dirk S. Hovorka and Sandra Peter, we return to some of the themes introduced by Lucy Suchman. The authors call on technology researchers to develop approaches to inquiry that respond better to the needs of our future society. Specifically, they critique the optimistic instrumentalism that dominates most future studies. This approach projects the practices, materialities and conditions of the present into the future, and fails to recognize the 'train tracks' of thought that limits the imaginaries thusly produces. Drawing on examples such as Isaac Asimov's "The Laws of Robotics" and Philip K. Dick's "Minority Report," Hovorka and Peter advance an alternative method that privileges the human condition and everyday life a given technological future entails. They label this approach to future studies as 'thinking with monsters,' and argue that it illustrates what dwelling in a technological future would feel like. If IS researchers are to influence, shape or create a desirable future, gaining deeper insights into the worlds our technologies will create is imperative, and this paper outlines a potentially powerful approach to engage with the future in ways that are better able to paint a realistic picture.

In "A bestiary of digital monsters", Rachel Douglas-Jones, Marisa Cohn, Christopher Gad, James Maguire, John Mark Burnett, Jannick Schou, Michael Hockenhull, Bastian Jørgensen, and Brit Ross Winthereik introduces us to an uncommon academic genre – the bestiary – a collection of real and imagined monsters. Drawing on Cohen [7] and Haraway [2] the authors seek to explore novel forms of analysis available for describing "the beasts in our midst". The chapter recount encounters with 'beasts' that have arisen in attempts to govern organizations, businesses and citizens. None of the beasts in the bestiary are technologies alone, rather, with this form of narrating, the authors wish to ensure that the concept of the monster does not 'other' the digital as untamed or alien. The bestiary helps with "the work of figuring out what is monstrous, rather than simply identifying monsters.... including something in the bestiary is a move of calling forth, rather than calling out". Thus, the chapter draws our attention firmly to the devices we used in narration of the digital monsters, which defy the border between the real and the imaginary.

In our final chapter "Frankenstein's Monster as Mythical Mattering: Rethinking the Creator-Creation Technology Relationship", Natalie Hardwicke problematizes our relationship with technology and with ourselves. Building on a careful analysis of Shelley's *Frankenstein* [27], the author questions critically the human pursuit of knowledge as technological mastery of nature. Drawing on both Heidegger's [28] and McLuhan's [29] work she argues that such pursuit takes us further away from locating our own-most authentic selves. Our desires to separate ourselves from, and control the world through the technologies we build, ultimately fails to bring us closer to the meaning of our own existence, which is to live an authentic life. Only by accepting both our own mortality and by understanding ourselves as an inseparable part of the world do we stand a chance to free ourselves; to assume an organic relationship with technology that brings us closer to the world, others and ourselves, rather than to alienate us.

In sum, the papers presented in this volume address a broad range of phenomena involving the monsters of our day, that is, the increasingly autonomous algorithmic creations in our midst that carry promises, provoke concerns and have not surrendered their ability to incite fear. The diversity of perspectives taken by the authors – ranging between pragmatic and critical, rational and emotional, and hopeful and (somewhat) despondent – might be seen as a manifestation of the ambiguity, hybridity and liminality of the Fourth Industrial Revolution (4IR) that is developing at warp speed. It is these characteristics of the emergent social worlds that we sought to capture in the question mark at the end of the working conference's title "Living with Monsters?"

What the papers in this volume are telling us is that a life in which people and technologies are increasingly entangled and intertwined, is an ongoing journey that will require continuing conscious and critical engagement with, and care for, the creatures/monsters we have created. Only in this way can we live up to our responsibilities as participants in, as well as creators and researchers of, the new ecosystems that constitute our contemporary social worlds.

References

1. Wiener, N.: The Human Use of Human Beings: Cybernetics and Society (No. 320). Perseus Books Group, New York (1950/1988)
2. Haraway, D.: Promises of monsters: a regenerative politics for inappropriate/d others. In: Grossberg, L., Nelson, C., Treichler, P.A. (eds.) Cultural Studies, pp. 295–337. Routledge (1992)
3. MacKenzie, D.: Is economics performative? Option theory and the construction of derivatives markets. J. Hist. Econ. Thought **28**(1), 29–55 (2006)
4. Winner, L.: Autonomous Technology: Technics-out-of-Control as a Theme in Political Thought. MIT Press, Cambridge (1978)
5. Ciborra, C.U., Hanseth, O.: From tool to gestell: agendas for managing the information infrastructure. Inf. Technol. People **11**(4), 305–327 (1998)
6. Latour, B.: Love your monsters. Break. J. **2**, 21–28 (2011)
7. Cohen, J.J.: Monster culture (seven theses). In: Cohen, J.J. (ed.) Monster Theory: Reading Culture, pp. 3–25. University of Minnesota Press, Minneapolis (1996)
8. Rhee, J.: The Robotic Imaginary: The Human and the Price of Dehumanized Labour. University of Minneapolis Press, Minneapolis and London (2017)
9. Cohen, J.J.: The promise of monsters. In: Mittman, E.S., Dendle, P. (eds.) The Ashgate Research Companion to Monsters and the Monstrous, pp. 449–464, New York (2012)
10. Zuboff, S.: Big other: surveillance capitalism and the prospects of an information civilization. J. Inf. Technol. **30**(1), 75–89 (2015)
11. Harari, Y.N.: Homo Deus: A Brief History of Tomorrow. Vintage Publishing, New York (2016)

12. Huizinga, J.: Homo Ludens: A Study of the Play Element in Culture. Beacon Press, Boston (1955)
13. Esposito, E.: Probabilità improbabili. La realtà della finzione nella società moderna. Meltemi Editore (2008)
14. Esposito, E.: The structures of uncertainty: performativity and unpredictability in economic operations. Econ. Soc. **42**(1), 102–129 (2013)
15. Ingold, T.: Towards an ecology of materials. Annu. Rev. Anthropol. **41**, 427–442 (2012)
16. Nicolini, D.: Practice Theory, Work, & Organization. Oxford University Press, Oxford (2013)
17. Clough, P.: The affective turn: political economy, bio-media and bodies. Theory, Cult. Soc. **25**(1), 1–22 (2008)
18. Bennett, J.: The Enchantment of Modern Life: Attachments, Crossings, and Ethics. Princeton University Press, Princeton (2001)
19. Bennett, J.: Vibrant Matter: A Political Ecology of Things. Duke University Press, Durham (2010)
20. Dunne, A., Raby, F.: Design Noir: The Secret Life of Electronic Objects. Birkhäuser, Basel (2001)
21. Dunne, A., Raby, F.: Critical design FAQ (2017). http://www.dunneandraby.co.uk/content/bydandr/13/0. Accessed 21 May 2018
22. Barad, K.: Agential realism: feminist interventions in understanding scientific practices. In: Biagioli, I. (ed.) The Science Studies Reader, pp. 1–11. Routledge, New York/London (1999)
23. Orlikowski, W.J., Scott, S.V.: Sociomateriality: challenging the separation of technology, work and organization. Acad. Manag. Ann. **2**(1), 433–474 (2008)
24. Riemer, K., Johnston, R.B.: Clarifying ontological inseparability with heidegger's analysis of equipment. MIS Q. **41**(4), 1059–1081 (2017)
25. Barad, K.: Diffracting diffraction: cutting together-apart. Parallax **20**(3), 168–187 (2014)
26. Haraway, D.J.: Modest–Witness@Second–Millennium Femaleman–Meets–Oncomouse: Feminism and Technoscience. Psychology Press, Hove (1997)
27. Shelley, M.: Frankenstein or The Modern Prometheus, London (1818)
28. Heidegger, M.: Being and Time: A Translation of Sein und Zeit. SUNY press, Albany (1996)
29. McLuhan, M.: The Extensions of Man, New York (1964)

Frankenstein's Problem

Lucy Suchman[(✉)]

Lancaster University, Bailrigg, UK
l.suchman@lancaster.ac.uk

Abstract. This text is based on an invited address presented at IFIP 8.2 'Living with Monsters' in San Francisco, CA, 11 December 2018. Taking the 200th anniversary of Mary Wollstonecraft Shelley's *Frankenstein* as a starting place, I explore questions of autonomy and control with respect to human/technology relations. I consider the ambivalence of these agencies, and recent initiatives in science and technology studies and related fields to reconceptualize the problem as matters of relation and care. While embracing this turn, I reflect as well upon the ambivalences of relation and care, and the need to address the resilient politics of alterity in our figurations (and celebrations) of the monstrous.

Keywords: Technological autonomy · Control · Care

1 The Ambivalence of Control

In *Autonomous Technology* [16] Langdon Winner observes that imaginaries of technics-out-of-control have been a persistent preoccupation in modern political thought. Winner's project in the book is to cast a critical eye on this collective anxiety, and at the same time to think through some ways in which questions of control in relation to technological systems could be important for us to engage. Most relevant for the theme of this conference, the book's final chapter, titled 'Frankenstein's Problem,' calls on us to read Shelley's original text [8], now celebrating its 200th birthday, as the articulation of a deeply ambivalent relationship to technological power.

To bring the ambivalence of technological power and control into the present moment, I begin with an iconic image from photographer Peter Souza, documenting the meeting of President Barack Obama and members of his national security team in the White House Situation Room [9], during the mission against Osama bin Laden on May 1, 2011 (an event that we now know has itself been mythologized, but that's another story; see [4]). There is much to be said about this photograph, but I read it in this context through questions that I take the figure of Frankenstein to index for us; that is, autonomous technologies-as-monsters, control, responsibility and care. Here we see the audience to an event outside the frame for us as viewers of this image, and distant for them as well, as they watch video feeds transmitted from the scene of operations in Abbottabad, Pakistan. Rather than an autonomous weapon system in which the human has been removed from 'the loop' (I return to that shortly), what we have here is a version of the 'loop' and some of the humans and technical systems that inhabit it, operating under a configuration that might be characterised as a highly complex form of remote control.

U. Schultze et al. (Eds.): IS&O 2018, IFIP AICT 543, pp. 13–18, 2018.
https://doi.org/10.1007/978-3-030-04091-8_2

But what sense of 'control' exactly is in play here? The bodies crowded together in the room look on, mesmerized, apprehensive, but with little hint as to their own responsibility for the events that they are witnessing. Or read another way, it is only their absorption as spectators that implies their sense that they are themselves implicated. They've set something in motion; but it's now out of their hands, and they can only watch it unfold. This is Frankenstein's problem, then, in a 21st century manifestation.

2   The Monster's Birth

Shelley's text addresses themes of creation, neglect, and their consequences. As a technoscientist born out of a youthful infatuation with the alchemists, Victor Frankenstein is subsequently dazzled first by an encounter with lightning, and then with chemistry and the powers of Enlightenment reasoning. Loss of control over one's desires is a theme early on, as Victor explains "None but those who have experienced them can conceive of the enticements of science" [3: 32]. By the early pages of Volume I Victor has discovered, in his own words, "the cause of the generation of life; nay more, I became myself capable of bestowing animation upon lifeless matter" [3: 34].

For those of us committed to demystifying what Herbert Simon some 150 years later named "the sciences of the artificial" [9], Victor's account of how he actually made his creature has little to offer. We learn that having achieved the capacity to bestow life, the creation of in his words "a frame for the reception of it" was a painstaking project. He reports that he spent his time "in vaults and charnel houses," and experienced "days and nights of incredible labour and fatigue" [3: 33–34]. His decision to make the creature somewhat larger than life was based on the practical difficulties of working at a smaller scale. Having formed the determination "to make the being of a gigantic stature; that is to say, about eight feet in height, and proportionably large … and having spent some months in successfully collecting and arranging my materials, I began" [3: 37].

What follows is a vivid account of the details less of the creature's composition, than of Victor's own mental, physical, and emotional labours as, in Victor's words, "with unrelaxed and breathless eagerness, I pursued nature to her hiding places" [3: 38]. As is the case throughout the novel, Shelley's writing is devoted overwhelmingly to relations and structures of feeling, including those between passion and labour, family and friendship and associated feelings of negligence and guilt, comfort and care. Even at the moment that the creature finally comes to life, how that happens is of less interest to Shelley than Victor's response to it including, infamously, the repulsion that causes him to abandon the creature despite the latter's attempts to engage him. When the creature re-encounters Victor and persuades him to listen, it describes its own ambivalent encounters with the human world, including its heartbreaking abjection, in extraordinary detail. Even here, however, what enabled the creature's capacities for language, communication, reflection, injury, rage, and ultimately despair were not a primary concern either for Victor or it seems for Shelley. But they are crucial questions for our understanding of comparable claims and promises in the contemporary field of humanoid robotics.

3 Monstrous Agencies

Fast forward two centuries, and on October 11th of 2017 the United Nations General Assembly Economic and Social Council is holding a meeting in New York titled 'The Future of Everything – Sustainable Development in the Age of Rapid Technological Change.' Widespread media coverage of this meeting is prompted by the appearance of a robot named Sophia, symptomatic of the latest reanimation of the field of AI [15]. Figured in the image of film icon and humanitarian Audrey Hepburn, according to creator David Hanson, Sophia has become the spokesmodel first and foremost for Hanson Robotics, based in Hong Kong, and secondly for the imminent arrival of the humanoid robot as a transformative global force. Announcing, "I am here to help humanity create the future," Sophia's demonstration at the United Nations comprises a closely scripted 'conversation' between the show robot (effectively an animatronic manikin) and Deputy Secretary General Amina J. Mohammed. As the robot utters this statement, it slowly raises its arm until its multiply jointed hand is positioned inappropriately close to the Deputy Secretary's face, in what consequently might be read as a threatening gesture. Mohammed mugs a grimace of perhaps only partially mock horror, eliciting a laugh from her fellow delegates.

Sophia's software was sourced from the company SingularityNET, a name that gestures towards desires for and fears of humanity's machinic supersession. One plotting of that trajectory has brought me to the UN myself for the meeting of another body, fittingly for the Frankensteinian narrative based in Geneva. The Convention on Certain Conventional Weapons or CCW is a body charged with establishing "prohibitions or restrictions on the use of certain conventional weapons which may be deemed to be excessively injurious or to have indiscriminate effects." Following a report by the UN Special Rapporteur on Extrajudicial, Summary or Arbitrary Executions to the Human Rights Council in 2013 [5], member states agreed to begin discussions at the CCW on what were then christened 'lethal autonomous weapon systems.' A coalition of non-governmental organizations headed by Human Rights Watch participated in the CCW's preliminary series of 'informal meetings of experts,' aiming to build support for a pre-emptive ban on weapon systems in which the identification of targets and initiation of attack is put under fully automated machine control. The campaign is premised on the observation that the threat posed by robotic weapons is not the prospect of a Terminator-style humanoid, but the more mundane progression of increasing automation in military systems. A central concern is initiatives to automate the identification of particular categories of humans (e.g. those in a designated area, or who fit a machine-readable profile) as legitimate targets for killing.

As a member of the International Committee for Robot Arms Control, part of the NGO coalition, I presented testimony at the CCW in April of 2016 in a panel on the question of machine 'autonomy' [12, see also 14]. My brief contribution focused on the problem of 'situational awareness,' accepted in military discourses to be a precondition for distinction between legitimate and illegitimate targets, a prerequisite to legal killing within the frameworks of International Humanitarian Law. I made a case for the inherent limits of algorithmic approaches to situational awareness, particularly in terms of the requirement of distinction.

My effort to pose an irremediable obstacle to the legality of autonomous weapon systems within the military's own terms required suspension of what would otherwise be profound questions for me about those terms, beginning with the trope of 'autonomy,' treated here as at once the litmus test of the model human subject, and that which is in danger of escaping human control. Further disconcertment comes with the principle of distinction in international laws of armed conflict, where enactments of difference are at their most lethal, in the profoundly gendered, racialized, and irremediably contingent categories of 'us' and 'them' that govern violence in practice. In a new book titled *The Robotic Imaginary* [7], Rhee argues that positing the human as originary and as recognisable effectively underwrites the dehumanization of that which can't be known. Following Judith Butler's question regarding differently grievable lives she asks: "Who, in their purported incommensurability, unknowability, unfamiliarity, or illegibility within robotics' narrow views of humanness, is excluded, erased, dehumanized, rendered not-human?" [7: 4]. As a case in point she takes the United States drone program, characterized by practices of dehumanization that she contends are embedded in the history of robotics and its various inscriptions and erasures of the human.

The narrowness of robotic views of humanness that Rhee identifies is not only a technical problem, but also indicative of the wider problems of drone visualities. In the past few months these problems have come under some scrutiny thanks to a small but significant rebellion on the part of Google employees against the company's participation in Project Maven, a US Defense Department effort to gain some control over the vast store of video surveillance footage generated by its drone program. Despite protests on the part of the company that the seeing to be automated concerns only classes of objects, it soon became clear that the objects of interest include vehicles, buildings and indeed humans on the ground. Those of us who joined in support of the insurgent Googlers pointed out that further automation of the scopic regimes of the US drone program can only serve to worsen an operation that is already highly contested, and arguably illegal and immoral under the laws and norms of armed conflict [13].

4   The Politics of Alterity

As Mary Shelley taught us by breathing life into Frankenstein and his creature, the anthropomorphic artifact is a powerful disclosing agent for the relation between figurations of the human and operations of dehumanization. Dehumanization, Rhee argues, is a kind of evil twin of anthropomorphism, an 'anti-metaphor' that creates a relation of difference between what would otherwise be recognizable as similar and kindred entities. As an antidote she calls for "an understanding of the human through unrecognizable difference, and unfamiliarity, rather than recognition, knowability, and giveness" [7: 5]. The essence of Frankenstein's problem, which Winner suggests is now a problem for us all, is "the plight of things that have been created but not in a context of sufficient care" [16: 313]. But as recent feminist technoscience has taught us

– notably Puig de la Bellacasa in her book *Matters of Care* – care itself is "ambivalent in both its significance and its ontology" [6: 1]. As a way forward de la Bellacasa writes in support of "committed knowledge as a form of care" [6: 16]. In my own writings I've proposed continued engagement as an alternative to 'control' over the life of technologies (which we know is impossible) (11). Our inability to control something does not absolve us of being implicated in its futures. Rather, our participation in technoscience obliges us to remain in relation with the world's becoming, whether that relation of care unfolds as one of affection or of agonistic intervention.

But while relationship is necessary, it is not sufficient. The problem of Frankenstein can be understood within a twofold cultural/historical imaginary, comprising on the one hand autonomy read as separateness, and on the other, fantasies of control. The twin figures of the autonomous machine as either the perfect slave or the cooperative partner [1: 2], while positing a human-machine relationship, reinstate relations of dominance at worst, instrumentality at best. The former is problematic for its inbuilt injustice, while the justice of the latter is contingent on the projects in which both humans and machines are enrolled. Taken together, these imaginaries work to obscure the politics of alterity that operate through the figure of the monster, as well as the modernist genealogies that shape technology's contemporary forms. The promise of monsters [2], in contrast, is that they might double back to challenge their makers, questioning the normative orders that are the conditions of possibility for their monstrosity.

References

1. Llach, D.C.: Builders of the Vision: Software and the Imagination of Design. Routledge, New York and Oxford (2015)
2. Cohen, J.J.: The promise of monsters. In: Mittman, A.S., Dendle, P. (eds.) The Ashgate Research Companion to Monsters and the Monstrous, pp. 449–464, New York (2012)
3. Guston, D., Finn, E., Robert, J.S. (eds.): Frankenstein: Annotated for Scientists, Engineers, and Creators of All Kinds. MIT Press, Cambridge and London (2017)
4. Hersch, S.: The killing of Osama Bin Laden. In: London Review of Books, 21 May 2015
5. Heyns, C.: Report of the special rapporteur on extrajudicial, summary or arbitrary executions (2013). http://www.ohchr.org/Documents/HRBodies/HRCouncil/RegularSession/Session23/A-HRC-23-47_en.pdf
6. Puig de la Bellacasa, M.: Matters of Care: Speculative Ethics in More Than Human Worlds. University of Minnesota Press, Minneapolis and London (2017)
7. Rhee, J.: The Robotic Imaginary: The Human and the Price of Dehumanized Labor. Minnesota University Press, Minneapolis and London (2018)
8. Shelley, M.W.: Frankenstein, or The Modern Prometheus. Anonymous, London (1818)
9. Simon, H.: The Sciences of the Artificial. MIT Press, Cambridge (1969)
10. Souza, P.: Situation Room, photo taken by White House photographer Pete Souza at 4:06 pm on 1 May 2011. Wikimedia (2011). https://en.wikipedia.org/wiki/Situation_Room_(photograph). Accessed 22 Sept 2018
11. Suchman, L.: Located Accountabilities in Technology Production. Scand. J. Inf. Syst. **14**(2), 91–105 (2002)

12. Suchman, L.: Situational awareness and adherence to the principle of distinction as a necessary condition for lawful autonomy. In: Geiss, R., Lahmann, H. (eds.) Lethal Autonomous Weapon Systems: Technology, Definition, Ethics, Law & Security, pp. 273–283. Federal Foreign Office, Division Conventional Arms Control, Berlin (2016)
13. Suchman, L., Asaro, P., Irani, L.: Google's march to the business of war must be stopped. The Guardian, 16 May 2018. https://www.theguardian.com/commentisfree/2018/may/16/google-business-war-project-maven. Accessed 22 Sept 2018
14. Suchman, L., Weber, J.: Human-machine autonomies. In: Bhuta, N., Beck, S., Geis, R., Liu, H.-Y., Kreis, C. (eds.) Autonomous Weapons Systems, pp. 75–102. Cambridge University Press, Cambridge (2016)
15. UN News: At UN, robot Sophia joins meeting on artificial intelligence and sustainable development. https://news.un.org/en/story/2017/10/568292-un-robot-sophia-joins-meeting-artificial-intelligence-and-sustainable. Accessed 11 Oct 2017
16. Winner, L.: Autonomous Technology: Technics-out-of-Control as a Theme in Political Thought. MIT Press, Cambridge (1977)

We Have Been Assimilated: Some Principles for Thinking About Algorithmic Systems

Paul N. Edwards[1,2]([envelope]) [iD]

[1] Center for International Security and Cooperation, Stanford University,
Stanford, USA
pedwards@stanford.edu
[2] School of Information, University of Michigan, Ann Arbor, USA

Abstract. This text is an opinion piece motivated by an invited keynote address at the 2018 IFIP 8.2 working conference, 'Living with Monsters?' (San Francisco, CA, 11 December 2018.) It outlines some principles for understanding algorithmic systems and considers their implications for the increasingly algorithm-driven infrastructures we currently inhabit. It advances four principles exhibited by algorithmic systems: (i) radical complexity, (ii) opacity, (iii) radical otherness, and (iv) infrastructuration or Borgian assimilation. These principles may help to guide a more critical appreciation of the emergent world marked by hybrid agency, accelerating feedback loops, and ever-expanding infrastructures to which we have been all too willingly assimilated.

Keywords: Algorithmic systems · Complexity · Opacity · Otherness
Infrastructure

In 2016 I had the great good fortune to inherit a graduate seminar on "Algorithmic Culture" from my brilliant colleague Christian Sandvig, who had to back out of teaching it at the last minute. I already knew about half of the literature he assigned from other contexts, but I had never quite seen the pattern of it the way he did. That syllabus was full of intriguing surprises, one of those gifts from a random universe that happen a few times in your life if you're lucky.

The biggest surprise awaiting me, however, arrived in the classroom. Even sophisticated students with backgrounds in computer science could not, it seemed, genuinely grasp the complexity, opacity, partial autonomy, and radical otherness of algorithmic systems. Even fewer understood the stark differences between human-programmed algorithms and those produced by machine learning systems. Confronted with unsavory outcomes such as racial bias in face recognition systems, or porno-graphic images returned as top hits on the search "Black girls," their first, second, and third impulses were to attribute these results to the conscious or unconscious biases of human programmers, even to a deliberate intent to harm.

They are hardly alone. The most recent (and most ridiculous) expression of this impulse is President Trump's August 2018 claim that Google search results are biased against him, accompanied by a thinly veiled threat of legal action against it and other tech firms. (Given his rampant narcissism, he might only be satisfied if 100% of all search results glorified his name.) Because people program computers, this line of thinking goes, the algorithms they create must reflect their biases, whether intentional or not.

Published by Springer Nature Switzerland AG 2018. All Rights Reserved
U. Schultze et al. (Eds.): IS&O 2018, IFIP AICT 543, pp. 19–27, 2018.
https://doi.org/10.1007/978-3-030-04091-8_3

This opinion piece has modest goals. First, I outline some principles for understanding algorithmic systems. I then consider their implications for the increasingly algorithm-driven infrastructures we currently inhabit.

The concept of an algorithm is often likened to a recipe or an assembly manual. Gather ingredients or parts, follow the instructions to the letter, and you end up with a Boston cream pie or an Ikea bookcase. In a computer, it's a list of instructions for operating on data. In computerese, algorithms are "effective procedures" that deterministically transform inputs into outputs, such that if you run the same algorithm on the same data it will always produce the same result—or at least that's how I learned it as a teenager in the 1970s, when I was programming and operating Honeywell mainframes for a large company in Maryland.

Lots of everyday algorithmic systems, such as your word processor or the accounting systems at banks, are still coded by human programmers and still correspond closely to the recipe view. If you dig into the code, you find thousands of sub-algorithms, each comprising a list of instructions for operating on data. Each one is entirely understandable in terms of human logic and/or mathematics. Apart from the occasional (and inevitable) bug, even the whole thing is pretty easy to grasp, because the interactions among all the sub-algorithms are part of the system design, and actually are not all that complicated. When I was learning computer science, the sub-algorithms were called "subroutines," for a good reason: they automate some step-by-step routine formerly carried out by a person. Make this word italic, put this text in a footnote, and so on.

Yet from a practical perspective, the recipe view of algorithmic systems is merely the kindergarten version of what's happening today. The largest modern climate models, for example, comprise over a million lines of code. Individual sub-models, constructed separately by domain specialists, represent the atmosphere, the oceans, sea ice, snow, land surfaces, and other elements of the climate system. Each model, in turn, contains numerous sub-models. An atmospheric model may include sub-models of (for example) radiation, cloud formation, aerosols, and atmospheric chemistry. Just as in the real climate system, all of these algorithms and sub-algorithms constantly interact, time-stepping forward in increments of 10 min until 100 simulated years have passed to generate a picture of how Earth's climate will evolve as we blast it with our greenhouse gases.

The complexity of climate models is reflected in complicated organizational structures required to create and maintain them. The Community Climate System Model, for example, holds annual meetings involving some 300 scientists and software developers, each representing larger groups responsible for different elements of the model [7]. Even though at least one specialist team understands each part, no one person understands the entire climate model in detail. Of course, this is the reason we need climate models in the first place: interactions in the real climate system are so many and so complicated that we can only understand them by simulating their behavior.

Let's call this inability to grasp all the interactions in a complicated algorithmic system the **principle of radical complexity**. This principle says that large, interactive algorithmic systems produce emergent behavior we cannot anticipate. Even if we can comprehend every individual component, scaling up highly interactive systems ultimately translates into cognitive opacity. It's still a recipe, and if you are a cook you can understand every instruction—but only the computer can bake the cake.

Arguably, an increasingly important category of algorithms—those produced by machine learning systems—no longer fits the recipe view at all. Machine learning comprises many techniques, but all share certain common features. "Learning" means building increasingly effective algorithms that can classify, or recognize, desired patterns in data. These patterns can be almost anything: handwritten letters, individual faces, fingerprints, email spam, consumer creditworthiness, and so on. The key difference is that these classification algorithms *aren't coded by human beings*.

Instead, human programmers write a "learner" algorithm, which generates other algorithms, known as models or classifiers. The learner algorithm—perhaps better understood as a "builder"—does not know in advance which models work best. (If it did, there would be no need for machine learning.) In some systems, the learner starts with a simple, approximate statistical model (aka classifier) introduced by the human programmer. It then constructs thousands of variations on the original classifier and tests all these variants against training data pre-sorted by the developers (e.g. spam/not spam, or handwritten letters identified as A, B, C, etc.). The best-performing classifiers are preserved, then modified to produce numerous new variants, which are tested again, and the cycle repeats. Once the classifier is trained, it's tested against "wild" datasets to prove that it can generalize beyond the training data. If it performs well enough, the cycle stops; if it doesn't, the training dataset may be expanded, and the test-modify-test-repeat cycle begins again. Thousands or millions of classifiers may be built and rejected before an acceptable level of performance is reached [21, 26].[1]

The nature of this process makes it all but impossible for human programmers to fully understand the logic that makes the winning algorithm work. "Learning" means finding significant features in the training data, which may include millions of examples. To discover these features, machine learning systems deploy n-dimensional matrices of *all* features (i.e. variables or properties) that might be relevant in the data. The classifier's goal is then to cross-correlate the features in all of these examples in search of some set or sets of features that reliably characterize the desired class. Many machine learning models use high-dimensional feature matrices—for example, the thousands of words that might indicate a message is spam—causing difficulties known as the "curse of dimensionality." These matrices, like the algorithms themselves, are beyond human comprehension [6].

Neural networks, another type of machine learning system, don't generate statistical models of feature correlation. Instead, they build algorithms "from scratch" by weighting the connections between simple artificial "neurons." When a given threshold of input values is reached, the neuron sends a signal to its neighbors. "Weights" or multipliers (positive, negative, and/or fractional) on incoming connections determine whether each neuron fires; each outgoing connection is weighted as well. At every test of the network, threshold values and connection weights are automatically readjusted, and the system is tested again until it performs as desired. Such a system can comprise

---

[1] An excellent video explaining this process, ideal for classroom teaching, is available at https://www.youtube.com/watch?v=R9OHn5ZF4Uo.

tens of thousands of neurons, arranged into multiple "layers," with millions of connections among them. Yet even a small network of a few hundred neurons can be capable of sophisticated pattern recognition. As in other machine learning techniques, a training data set includes human-classified examples of what the net is supposed to recognize; as it gets better, it more reliably distinguishes the positive examples from the negative ones.

Together, the weights, connections, thresholds, and layers in a neural net certainly comprise an algorithm—at least in the abstract sense of a list of instructions operating on data to produce a definite result. At the level of individual instructions, neural nets are incredibly simple, mostly reducing to simple addition and multiplication. Yet *this list of instructions is meaningless to a human being.* In other words, we don't really know exactly what they do, or how they do it. Following Jenna Burrell's lucid explication, let's call this the **principle of opacity** [4]. It's not only that machine learning algorithms are radically complex (though they are); it's that they cannot be understood as recipes at all.

In pursuit of some kind of grip on what neural nets are doing, some Google engineers realized in 2015 that they could reverse a neural network's pattern-recognition processes to make them *generate* images. Instead of asking a net to identify images of bananas (for example), they made it create its own image of a banana starting from white noise. The resulting images, often eerily beautiful and always strange, reveal just how differently a neural network "thinks." For example, one network generated images of dumbbells that always contained part of a human arm attached to the dumbbell (no doubt because most of its training images included people lifting weights).[2]

This kind of thing is commonplace in the world of machine learning. One neural net, trained to recognize sheep, did fairly well with this task most of the time, but also classified empty green fields as sheep. As one blogger put it, neural nets

> ...only see sheep where they expect to see them. They can find sheep easily in fields and mountainsides, but as soon as sheep start showing up in weird places, it becomes obvious how much the algorithms rely on guessing and probabilities. Bring sheep indoors, and they're labeled as cats. Pick up a sheep (or a goat) in your arms, and they're labeled as dogs. The thing is, neural networks match patterns. They see patches of furlike texture, a bunch of green, and conclude that there are sheep. If they see fur and kitchen shapes, they may conclude instead that there are cats. If life plays by the rules, image recognition works well. But as soon as people— or sheep—do something unexpected, the algorithms show their weaknesses.[3]

A fascinating collection of bizarre logic from the closely related fields of evolutionary computation and artificial life includes the example of a program that was supposed to learn to sort lists. Instead, it deleted the list—which was then (from its point of view) no longer unsorted. Another program built simulated robots tasked with learning to travel quickly; one such robot assembled itself into a tall tower, then simply fell over to "travel" a long way. Another algorithm "was supposed to figure out how to apply a minimum force to a plane landing on an aircraft carrier. Instead, it discovered

---

[2] https://ai.googleblog.com/2015/06/inceptionism-going-deeper-into-neural.html.

[3] http://aiweirdness.com/post/171451900302/do-neural-nets-dream-of-electric-sheep.

that if it applied a *huge* force, it would overflow the program's memory and would register instead as a very *small* force. The pilot would die but, hey, perfect score."[4] Machine-built systems use machine logic, not human logic. Let's call this the **principle of radical otherness**.

As in the cases above, sometimes error analysis can give us clues to how that logic may work. All too often, however, significant errors only become apparent after an algorithm created by machine learning is deployed operationally. One example is the well-known case, reported in 2015, of the Google Photos system labeling images of African-Americans as gorillas. Google apologized and said it would "fix" the algorithm. But in early 2018, nearly three years later, tesing by *Wired* magazine revealed that Google had simply blocked its image recognition system from labeling *any* photo as a gorilla or chimpanzee. (It will recognize other primates, but not those.)[5] The radical otherness of the recognition system's logic makes it impossible for engineers to tweak it directly, or to know exactly why it cannot distinguish between an African-American face and a gorilla—a difference that is immediately obvious to people. (Of course, we must admit that we don't know how people manage this feat either.) It's possible that Google is just being lazy and hasn't even tried to fix the algorithm. But another possible explanation is that even if a re-trained algorithm is much less likely to make this mistake, the social costs of repeating it even once are too great for the company to unblock the "gorilla" tag. This is just one of many examples of how machine learning can go awry.

The last principle I want to articulate here is hard to name succinctly. It stems from the fact that we now live in a world governed not by algorithmic systems *per se*, but rather by interacting ecologies of algorithmic systems, human individuals, social groups, cultures, and organizations. Natural ecosystems are characterized by extensive interactions and feedbacks among species. Changes in one species (caused by disease, parasites, etc.) or in the physical environment (higher temperatures, less water) affect all the others to varying degrees, driving some to extinction while creating openings for new species to enter the mix. In the long run, all species evolve in response to changing conditions, including the simultaneous evolution of other species.

Similarly, in today's information ecosystems, everything interacts with almost everything else, constantly evolving and adapting to changing conditions. People and organizations are always part of byzantine algorithmic feedback loops. Your "waste" data of searches and clicks becomes input to Google, Amazon, and Facebook, which feed it back to you as targeted advertising and personalized search. Bots spread both true and fake news on Twitter, but humans retweet the fake news more often [2, 25]. New forms of "networked discrimination"—much more fine-grained than the traditional broad categories of race, class, and gender—become possible when individuals' online social networks can be viewed by prospective employers and used to determine "cultural fit" [3]. The essential materials of culture itself, such as music, movies, books, TV, games, and informal social interaction, are exchanged, "curated," recommended,

---

[4] http://aiweirdness.com/post/172894792687/when-algorithms-surprise-us.

[5] https://www.wired.com/story/when-it-comes-to-gorillas-google-photos-remains-blind/.

and sometimes even produced by algorithmic systems, a phenomenon Galloway and Striphas have called "algorithmic culture" [10, 11, 15, 24].

Online recruiting makes it possible to hire employees, or enlist terrorists, without ever meeting them in person, challenging the traditional concept of an "organization." People develop folk theories of how algorithmic systems work, leading to quasi-superstitious practices that may in turn influence algorithmic behavior [5, 9, 20]. Algorithmic systems designed by the so-called "gaming" industry very effectively reinforce and "optimize" gambling addictions [22]. Meanwhile, YouTube, Facebook, Instagram, and hundreds of other so-called "platforms" promote other addictions, including the "outrage cycle" currently driving American politics. Some of this becomes embedded in culture as norms and expectations, reinforcing and legitimizing both addictive behavior and awful politics. I'm sure you could easily name a hundred other ways in which algorithmic systems, culture, individuals, social groups, and organizations interact.

This is true not only at the level of societies, but even within the larger platform systems. It's popular to talk about "the Google search algorithm," for example. That phrase makes many of us immediately think of PageRank, the innovation that first made Google famous—but this just shows how out of touch we are. PageRank is now just one of dozens of algorithms that Google uses to process search queries. Updates to the overall search system have been christened with a series of names, including Caffeine (2009), Hummingbird (2013), and Medic (2018). Since 2015, an AI learning system known as RankBrain has played a significant role. Its secrets are closely guarded intellectual property, so we don't know exactly how RankBrain works—but for all the reasons just discussed, it's quite likely that Google engineers don't know either. Furthermore, Google's near-monopoly on search makes Google rankings so important to the visibility and sales of other firms that a whole industry of "search engine optimization" (SEO) has arisen to analyze how the algorithm evaluates search queries; they then advise firms on how to tweak their websites to raise their pages' search rankings. Large parts of the web are thus constantly evolving in response to the recommendations of these SEO firms, creating a continuous feedback cycle with Google's search algorithms. Similar feedback loops mark YouTube, Twitter, Facebook, and all other major platforms.

The many scandals surrounding the 2016 US presidential election, including "fake news," Russian disinformation, resurgent white supremacism, and the Cambridge Analytica episode, have forced major platforms to police their content more closely. The nature of these responses shows the limits of algorithmic agency. In 2017, Google hired some 10,000 "quality raters" to identify "upsetting or offensive" content such as Holocaust-denial and white-supremacist websites. Engineers then adjust Google's search algorithms so as to lower the ranking of those results—or perhaps, as in the "gorilla" case, block them altogether [14]. Facebook and Twitter have also hired large numbers of people to review and remove false and offensive content. Faced with a relentless onslaught of clever bots, as well as credulous and/or malevolent human users, the success of these strategies has been partial at best.

As I said earlier, it's hard to find a soundbite phrase to capture all this. Maybe it's a **principle of framing feedbacks:** that comprehending algorithmic systems requires backing out from a narrow focus on algorithms and data per se to a broader frame that encompasses some of the feedback loops I've described, or at the very least takes seriously the anthropology of human software developers [23]. Maybe it's a **principle of infrastructure** [19]: as my colleagues and I have articulated elsewhere, many modern infrastructures are not systems at all, but rather complex clusters of interacting elements best captured by organic or ecological metaphors [8]. Or it might be called the **principle of hybrid agency**, focusing on the constant interplay of individual choice, social norming, organizational change, and algorithmic action.

To capture all three of these notions at once, we could call it a **principle of infrastructuration**, my bad intellectual pun on Giddens' structuration theory [12, 13]. (Sorry about that.) To paraphrase Giddens, infrastructure shapes, limits, and enables agency. Meanwhile, agents (now including algorithmic agents) constantly *perform* infrastructure, constantly regenerating it but also transforming it over time. The most appropriate moniker of all might be **the principle of Borgian assimilation.** As the hive-mind cyborg aliens from *Star Trek* put it, "Lower your shields and surrender your ships. We will add your biological and technological distinctiveness to our own. Your culture will adapt to service us. Resistance is futile."[6]

We still lack adequate intellectual tools to engage this fast-changing, globally active Borgian world. Notions such as sociomateriality, hybrid agency, monsters, and cyborgs take us in the right direction, but seem too simple and impoverished to capture the rich complexity of these interactions. Methods such as algorithm audits can help us understand how algorithmic systems may create or reinforce undesirable biases, but draw the frame too narrowly. Statisticians and practitioners can help us understand how biased and undesirable outcomes can occur even when designers do everything possible to eliminate them, and even in the presence of much more and much better data about human populations than we have ever had before [1, 16]. Behavioral economics and cognitive psychology remind us how little we really know our own minds [17, 18], how much we overestimate our rationality and the quality of our perception, and how embarrassingly susceptible we all are to subtle influences that can now be amplified and disseminated widely by algorithmic systems.[7]

We have been assimilated, all too willingly, and there is probably no going back.

References

1. Barocas, S., Selbst, A.D.: Big data's disparate impact. Calif. Law Rev. **104**, 671–732 (2016). http://www.californialawreview.org/wp-content/uploads/2016/06/2Barocas-Selbst.pdf
2. Bessi, A., Ferrara, E.: Social bots distort the 2016 US presidential election online discussion. First Mon. **21** (2016). http://uncommonculture.org/ojs/index.php/fm/article/view/7090/5653
3. Boyd, D., Marwick, A.E., Levey, K.: The Networked Nature of Algorithmic Discrimination. Open Technology Institute (2014). https://www.danah.org/papers/2014/DataDiscrimination.pdf

---

[6] As articulated by the Borg in *Star Trek: First Contact* (1996).

[7] One of the best discussions of these susceptibilities and how algorithmic systems can manipulate them is an astonishingly direct 2016 presentation by Alexander Nix of Cambridge Analytics, "The Power of Big Data and Psychographics," available at www.youtube.com/watch?v=n8Dd5aVXLCc.

4. Burrell, J.: How the machine 'thinks': understanding opacity in machine learning algorithms. Big Data Soc. **3**, 1–12 (2016). https://doi.org/10.1177/2053951715622512
5. Dietvorst, B.J., Simmons, J.P., Massey, C.: Algorithm aversion: people erroneously avoid algorithms after seeing them err. J. Exp. Psychol.: Gener. **144**, 114–126 (2015). https://doi.org/10.1037/xge0000033
6. Domingos, P.: A few useful things to know about machine learning. Commun. ACM **55**, 78–87 (2012). https://doi.org/10.1145/2347736
7. Edwards, P.N.: A Vast Machine: Computer Models, Climate Data, and the Politics of Global Warming. MIT Press, Cambridge (2010)
8. Edwards, P.N., Jackson, S.J., Bowker, G.C., Knobel, C.P.: Understanding Infrastructure: Dynamics, Tensions, and Design. Deep Blue, Ann Arbor (2007). http://hdl.handle.net/2027.42/49353
9. Eslami, M., et al.: First I "like" it, then I hide it. In: The 2016 CHI Conference, pp. 2371–2382 (2016). https://doi.org/10.1145/2858036
10. Galloway, A.R.: Gaming: Essays on Algorithmic Culture. University of Minnesota Press, Minneapolis (2006)
11. Galloway, A.R.: The cybernetic hypothesis. Differences **25**, 107–131 (2014). https://doi.org/10.1215/10407391-2420021
12. Giddens, A.: Agency, institution, and time-space analysis. In: Knorr-Cetina, K., Cicourel, A. V. (eds.) Advances in Social Theory and Methodology: Toward an Integration of Micro- and Macro-sociologies. Routledge & Kegan Paul, Boston (1981)
13. Giddens, A.: The Constitution of Society. Spectrum Educational Enterprises, Washington, D.C. (1984)
14. Guynn, J.: Google starts flagging offensive content in search results. USA Today (2017). https://www.usatoday.com/story/tech/news/2017/03/16/google-flags-offensive-content-search-results/99235548/
15. Hallinan, B., Striphas, T.: Recommended for you: the Netflix Prize and the production of algorithmic culture. New Med. Soc. **18**, 117–137 (2015). https://doi.org/10.1177/1461444814538646
16. Hardt, M.: How big data is unfair: understanding unintended sources of unfairness in data driven decision making. Medium (2014). https://medium.com/@mrtz/how-big-data-is-unfair-9aa544d739de
17. Kahneman, D.: Maps of bounded rationality: psychology for behavioral economics. Am. Econ. Rev. **93**, 1449–1475 (2003). http://www.jstor.org/stable/3132137
18. Kahneman, D.: Thinking, Fast and Slow. Macmillan, New York (2011)
19. Plantin, J.-C., Lagoze, C., Edwards, P.N., Sandvig, C.: Infrastructure studies meet platform studies in the age of Google and Facebook. New Med. Soc. **10**, 1–18 (2016). https://doi.org/10.1177/1461444816661553
20. Rader, E., Gray, R.: Understanding user beliefs about algorithmic curation in the Facebook news feed. In: The 33rd Annual ACM Conference, pp. 173–182 (2015). https://doi.org/10.1145/2702123
21. Royal Society: Machine Learning: The Power and Promise of Computers that Learn by Example. Royal Society, London (2017)
22. Schüll, N.D.: Addiction by Design: Machine Gambling in Las Vegas. Princeton University Press, Princeton (2012)
23. Seaver, N.: What should an anthropology of algorithms do? Cult. Anthropol. **33**, 375–385 (2018). https://culanth.org/articles/966-what-should-an-anthropology-of-algorithms-do

24. Striphas, T.: Algorithmic culture. Eur. J. Cult. Stud. **18**, 395–412 (2015). https://doi.org/10. 1177/1367549415577392
25. Vosoughi, S., Roy, D., Aral, S.: The spread of true and false news online. Science **359**, 1146–1151 (2018). https://doi.org/10.1126/science.aap9559
26. Wallach, H.: Big data, machine learning, and the social sciences. Medium (2014). http:// medium.com/@hannawallach/big-data-machine-learning-and-the-social-sciences-927a8e20460d

Social Implications of Algorithmic Phenomena

Algorithmic Pollution: Understanding and Responding to Negative Consequences of Algorithmic Decision-Making

Olivera Marjanovic[1]([⊠]), Dubravka Cecez-Kecmanovic[2], and Richard Vidgen[2]

[1] University of Technology Sydney, Sydney, Australia
olivera.marjanovic@uts.edu.au
[2] University of New South Wales, Sydney, Australia

Abstract. In this paper we explore the unintended negative social consequences of algorithmic decision-making, which we define as "algorithmic pollution". By drawing parallels with environmental pollution, we demonstrate that algorithmic pollution is already here and causing many damaging, unrecognised and yet-to-be understood consequences for individuals, communities and a wider society. Focusing on transformative services (i.e., services that transform human lives, such as social support services, healthcare, and education), we offer an innovative way of framing, exploring and theorizing algorithmic pollution in the contemporary digital environment. Using sociomateriality as a theoretical lens, we explain how this type of pollution is performed, how it is spreading and who is responsible for it. The proposed approach enables us to articulate a preliminary set of IS research challenges of particular importance to the IS community related to living with and responding to algorithmic pollution, together with an urgent call for action. Our main practical contribution comes from the parallels we draw between the environmental protection movement and the newly created sociomaterial environment that needs protecting from the spread of algorithmic pollution.

Keywords: Algorithmic pollution · Sociomaterial environment
Negative consequences · Algorithmic justice

1 Introduction

Algorithmic decision-making is playing an increasing role in our private lives, in business, and in social worlds. Indeed, algorithms are now used to make "big decisions about people's lives" from job applications, job performance, provision/denial of social services, insurance, medical benefits and financial services [1]. While we acknowledge the various reported benefits of algorithms, for example in medicine, science, agriculture [2–5], in this paper we focus on the growing evidence of various harmful effects of algorithmic decision-making for society and for individuals working and living in a contemporary digital data environment [6].

We are particularly concerned with the negative consequences of automated algorithmic decision-making (i.e., decision-making with no human intervention) in the

U. Schultze et al. (Eds.): IS&O 2018, IFIP AICT 543, pp. 31–47, 2018.
https://doi.org/10.1007/978-3-030-04091-8_4

so-called transformative services. These are services that transform human lives, such as social support services, education, healthcare and aged care [7–9]. The consequences of these algorithms are far-reaching, unpredictable and potentially hurtful to individuals, their families, community groups and society at large [1, 10, 11]. Moreover, these consequences are propagated and amplified by the widespread and often invisible processes of datafication, where individual's data are harvested, consolidated and constructed through often unknown, unregulated and un-auditable processes, and perpetually re-constructed and reused in future unpredictable contexts [12–15]. Consequently, these negative consequences are extending well beyond the original service provision. Yet, they are hard to detect and to prove unjustified or unjust, and even harder to completely reverse.

In this paper we contribute to a growing body of knowledge on the negative consequences of automated algorithmic decision-making in transformative services by providing an innovative way of framing these consequences as "algorithmic pollution". By using a well-developed concept of pollution (or environmental pollution), we conceptualize these harmful consequences as a new type of pollution, one that pollutes the social environment where we work and live. Compared to environmental pollution, which is recognized and regulated, we demonstrate that algorithmic pollution is unrecognized, unregulated, and rapidly spreading – yet it is masked by myths of objectivity, neutrality, efficiency and superiority of algorithms over human decision-makers.

The purpose of this paper is two-fold: (i) to articulate and bring our collective attention to a new phenomenon here-termed "algorithmic pollution" and (ii) to propose a sociomaterial theoretical grounding for its exploration and collective action. Based on a literature review we identify the widespread and widening consequences of algorithmic decision-making on individuals (e.g., citizens, customers, patients, employees), organizations and a wider society. Of particular interest are the unintended negative consequences of automated algorithmic decision-making, which require the urgent attention of researchers and social action. Specifically, we aim to:

1. Define "algorithmic pollution" by building upon the concepts of "environmental pollution" and demonstrate that it is appropriate for framing negative unintended consequences of algorithmic decision-making;
2. Propose a sociomaterial theorization of algorithmic pollution in order to explain how this type of pollution is performed, how it is spreading and who is responsible for it;
3. Identify and articulate new research challenges for the IS community related to living with and responding to "algorithmic pollution".

Our research makes several research and practical contributions. First, we articulate a new concept of algorithmic pollution, thus expanding the existing bodies of knowledge in algorithmic decision-making as well as in environmental pollution. Second, we offer strong evidence, collected from multidisciplinary literature, why algorithmic pollution is a growing problem that is of concern to the IS discipline, requiring urgent attention. Third, we propose a preliminary approach to studying algorithmic pollution which discloses the hidden and uncertain performing of algorithms in sociomaterial environments that would enable researchers to examine the nature of algorithmic pollution and how the damage is done. Fourth, we identify and articulate a set of IS research challenges that call for our urgent attention.

Our main practical contribution comes from the parallels we draw between environmental protection and the sociomaterial environment that needs protecting from the spreading of algorithmic pollution. This line of thinking opens up future opportunities for building upon lessons from the environmental protection movement [16], including environmental justice and impact assessment frameworks. We argue that they need to be expanded to include the sociomaterial environment and algorithmic pollution.

The paper is organized as follows. In the next section we describe our research focus, which is at the intersect of transformative services, algorithms and datafication. Using the related literature from different disciplines, we then provide evidence of negative consequences of algorithmic decision-making in transformative services. Having set the context for our research, we then introduce the concept of pollution and use it to frame the negative consequences of algorithmic decision-making as "algorithmic pollution". We then proceed to identify different mechanisms that contribute to the generation and spreading of algorithmic pollution. By seeing algorithms as actors in complex and emerging sociomaterial assemblages, we then propose a preliminary approach to studying how algorithmic pollution is performed in the first instance and how and why it is spreading. Based on the proposed approach, we identify a set of IS research challenges and discuss a possible way forward.

2   Research Focus: Algorithmic Decision-Making in Transformative Services

Our research into algorithmic decision-making is situated at the intersection of transformative services, algorithms and datafication (Fig. 1). We are particularly concerned with algorithmic decision-making in the context of transformative services where machines make important decisions about people but with little or no human judgement or intervention. This section sets the scope and foundations for our research by introducing the key concepts, as follows.

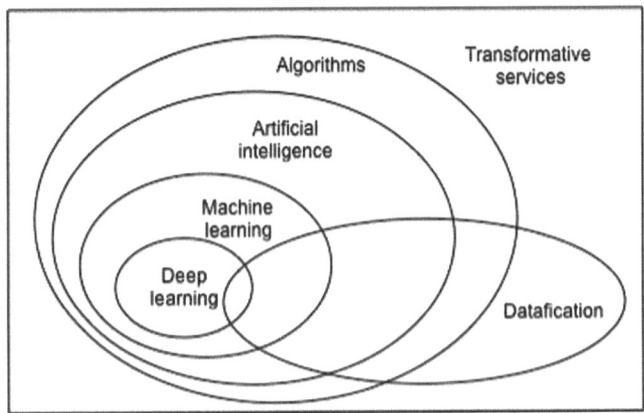

Fig. 1. The algorithmic decision-making research setting (drawing on Chollet [17])

2.1 Transformative Services

Compared to transactional services (e.g., in the retail sector such as online commerce), transformative services are those services that transform human lives by having a direct impact on the well-being of individuals, communities and the wider ecosystem [8, 9]. Prominent examples of transformative services include healthcare, social support services, education, financial services and law enforcement [9]. Compared to other service-related research, the emerging multidisciplinary field of transformative services research (TSR) brings the impact of service outcomes on human well-being to the forefront [8]. Indeed, "Improving well-being through transformative services" was identified as one of the top research priorities of the emerging multidisciplinary field of Services Sciences [7].

The key aspects of human well-being such as discrimination, marginalisation, and disparity in adverse conditions in population groups, as well as the issues of inclusion and access to services [8] are of particular interest to TSR. These are the same aspects that are now impacted by algorithmic decision-making. Hence, our motivation to situate this research in the context of transformative services.

2.2 Algorithms

An algorithm is often understood to be "a set of instructions for how a computer should accomplish a particular task" [1, p. 1]. The Computer Science community, including widely used textbooks, often quote Kowalski's [18] definition: Algorithm = Logic + Control (e.g., Kitchin [19]). Here "Logic" specifies what is to be done to solve a particular well-defined problem, while "Control" describes how the logic should be implemented under different scenarios. Thus, in Fig. 1, the general class of algorithms is shown in the outer ellipse.

Within the general class of algorithms, we focus on a particular subclass – artificial intelligence. While terms are often used interchangeably, we follow Chollet [17] to differentiate between artificial intelligence (AI), machine learning, and deep learning. AI has roots in the 1950s enthusiasm for building a machine that could think. Typically, the approach was to hard-code lots of rules, which worked well for well-defined problems, such as chess, but less well with the sorts of ill-defined problems that humans are good at – such as recognizing images and speech and understanding and engaging in argumentation. Traditional approaches (also known as symbolic AI) take rules plus data as input and provide answers as the output (for example, some predictive policing applications may use this approach).

Machine learning turns this on its head and works by taking data and answers as the inputs with the output being rules (using neural networks). Thus, a machine learning algorithm is trained through examining lots of examples in which it detects patterns. Machine learning is empirical and is more engineering-oriented than statistical, i.e., the inner workings may be black-boxed and the test of a 'good' algorithm is in its predictive performance rather than its theoretical correctness. While machine learning is an undoubtedly powerful technique, it is not without dangers, as evidenced by the failure of Google flu, which failed as a result of model over-fitting, relying on unreliable data, and failing to update the model to take account of underlying changes [20]. Deep learning is a subclass of machine learning in which multiple layers of data transformations are made to give an increasingly meaningful representation of the data. Deep learning has been successfully applied, despite only becoming a prominent technique in the early 2010s, in notoriously difficult domains such as image and speech classification, digital assistants (e.g., Google Now and Alexa), autonomous driving, and natural language processing [17].

Explaining how a deep learning application comes to the conclusions it does is certainly an issue for traceability and justification in decision-making [21]. However, Rahimi, an AI researcher at Google, argues that the problem is larger, that machine learning is a form of alchemy in which researchers do not know why some algorithms work and others don't and have no rigorous criteria for choosing one AI architecture over another. Rahimi distinguishes between a machine learning application that is a black box and "an entire field that has become a black box" (Rahimi quoted by Hutson [22]). The use of AI in general (and deep learning in particular) poses significant issues for understanding decision-making.

2.3 Datafication

Algorithms work based on data and also produce data. However, rather than focusing solely on data, we expand our focus to *datafication*, a process of turning everything and everyone into data [2, 6]. While datafication may have positive effects, such as new types of jobs and more value for customers [23], there is growing evidence of its negative and unintended social consequences [6, 12–14]. This is because datafication will "unavoidably omit many features of the world, distort others and potentially add features that are not apparent in the first instance" [24, p. 384]. Moreover, datafied phenomena are further propagated, processed, reused and distorted [14], having the performative power to re-shape the organizational and social worlds in unpredictable and undesirable ways [25].

Datafication is at the core of algorithmic decision-making as algorithms are applied to 'datafied individuals' (i.e., individuals represented by an always limited set of attributes and the corresponding data values). Additional data about individuals may be acquired from third parties who applied their own datafication processes in unknown ways and contexts. Algorithms also contribute to further datafication of individuals as their outcomes create new data also attached to these individuals (e.g., customer scoring or customer rating). These customer scores may be combined with more data and fed into other algorithms further down the "datafication chain".

When used in transformative services, algorithmic decision-making without human intervention, combined with ongoing datafication processes, often results in negative consequences for human well-being, as discussed in the next section.

3   The Consequences of Algorithmic Decision-Making in Transformative Services

Algorithmic decision-making is making its way into transformative services at "a breathtaking pace", often in the name of innovation and progress [10, p. 11]. Consequently, "algorithms driven by vast troves of data, are the new power brokers in society" [26, p. 2] that already "have control of your money market funds, … your retirement accounts, …they will decide your chances of getting lifesaving organs" [5, p. 214].

However, in spite of the reported enthusiasm, there is growing evidence of unfair, unjustified and discriminatory effects of these algorithms for individuals and wider communities [1, 11, 27]. Eubanks [10] offers a vivid example of devastating effects of automated eligibility systems implemented in a particular type of transformative services (social support services):

> *"Across the country, poor and working-class people are targeted by new tools of digital poverty management and face life-threatening consequences as a result. Automated eligibility systems discourage them from claiming public resources that they need to survive and thrive… Predictive models and algorithms tag them as risky investments and problematic parents. Vast complexes of social services, law enforcement, and neighborhood surveillance make their every move visible and offer up their behavior for government, commercial, and public scrutiny"* [10, p. 11].

Law enforcement is another prominent example of transformative services using algorithmic decision-making, most notably in predictive policing. Celebrated as the new era of "data-driven scientific decision-making", predictive policing has been increasingly used to inform decisions such as arresting people or determining the length of their sentence, based on the calculated probability of them committing future crimes [28]. This practice relies on datafication of individuals, including a variety of personal as well as other data that individuals may not have any control over, such as past data on "gang districts" or post codes. Consequently, individuals are assigned "risk scores" that are subsequently used for decision-making in a variety of contexts. The practice is spreading with more and more departments embracing the scientific approach to policing. For example, Ferguson [28] reveals that almost 400,000 Chicago citizens now have an official police risk score:

> *"This algorithm – still secret and publicly unaccountable – shapes policing strategy, the use of force, and threatens to alter suspicion on the streets. It is also the future of big data policing in America – and depending on how you see it, either an innovative approach to violence reduction or a terrifying example of data-driven social control"* [27, p. 1].

In addition to citizens not being aware of their risk scores, Ferguson [28] warns that "[c]urrently there is no public oversight of the police data, inputs or outputs, so communities are left in the dark unable to audit or challenge any individual threat score" (p. 1). Consequently, the "profound benefits" of predictive policing continue to be celebrated in the popular press. For example, in a controversial Financial Times article Gilian Tett (a respected financial reporter) offers the following support for predictive policing: "After all, …the algorithms in themselves are neutral" [29, p. 1].

Similar examples are reported in other types of transformative services including education, healthcare, social support and disability services (see for example, [1, 10,

11, 27, 30]). In particular, Caplan and colleagues [1] warn, "there is a need for greater reflection on models of power and control, where the sublimation of human decision-making to algorithms erodes trust in experts" (p. 6). There is a growing number of critical studies of algorithmic decision-making emerging across a range of disciplines including sociology, public policy, communications and media studies, political studies, and increasingly information systems (see for example, [6, 12, 13]). We contribute to the existing body of knowledge by proposing a novel approach to framing the problem of negative consequences of algorithmic decision-making as *algorithmic pollution*.

4 Algorithmic Pollution

Having outlined some of the negative consequences of automated algorithmic decision-making in transformative services we now frame the problem situation using the lens of pollution. The pollution concept is suitable since it allows us to see algorithms as a force for good while recognizing that there are both intended and unintended negative consequences that affect individuals, communities and society. It would be hard to argue that electricity is not a good thing, but if its generation causes pollution in the form of global warming then remedial action and regulation are needed. We note that using the concept of pollution as a framing device is not new: for example, there has been research defining crime as pollution (CAP) [31].

4.1 Defining Algorithmic Pollution

According to a broad definition "Environmental pollution is the discharge of material, in any physical state, that is dangerous to the environment or human health" [32]. (Encyclopedia.com). Similarly, the Encyclopedia Britannica defines environmental pollution as: "the addition of any substance (solid, liquid, or gas) or any form of energy (such as heat, sound, or radioactivity) to the environment at a rate faster than it can be dispersed, diluted, decomposed, recycled, or stored in some harmless form" [33].

When algorithms produce negative consequences on individual or collective well-being, and when such consequences cannot be effectively detected and eliminated or dealt with, we argue that they 'contaminate' our sociomaterial environment. We call this phenomenon **algorithmic pollution** and define it as follows:

> *Algorithmic pollution denotes the presence of unjustified, unfair, discriminatory, or other harmful consequences of algorithmic decision-making for individuals, groups, organizations, sections of the population, the economy, or society at large.*

While our definition of algorithmic pollution accords with the view of pollution as harms suffered by living organisms caused by exposure to pollutants [31], the scientific definition of pollution is concerned with the presence of chemicals in the environment at a concentration above their normal background level that perturb the environment in a way that is harmful [34]. Harrison [34] also points out that not all instances of pollution involve the addition of chemicals to the environment; pollution can also be caused by adding to naturally occurring phenomena, such as light and noise. The scientific definition suggests that there is some background level of pollution that is acceptable. Since algorithms are probabilistic then some error in the form of false positives and false negatives is unavoidable, i.e., there will always be some level of background algorithmic pollution. The challenge is to detect when the outcomes of algorithmic decision-making exceed a threshold and result in systematic injustice (individual decisions) and larger, systemic social injustice (emergent societal effects). While there must inevitably be a substantial element of subjectivity in this judgment for algorithms it is also present with environmental pollution where acceptable limits (e.g., parts per million) have to be established to calibrate a 'normal' background level.

Drawing on Lynch and colleagues [31], we note that the pollution literature distinguishes between an 'end-pipe' (e.g., a factory chimney) and the process that generates the pollution (e.g., a manufacturing process). Further, end-pipes are a stationary source of pollution, while pollution itself is mobile and it is not always possible to know the source of pollution from monitoring the environment. Pollution can be generated as point source pollution (PSP) and nonpoint source (NPSP). While a factory chimney is a PSP, motor vehicles, which pollute the environment by generating particles and nitrogen dioxide while in standing traffic, are an example of NPSP.

4.2   Generation and Spreading of Algorithmic Pollution

For algorithmic pollution to occur there must be data (input) to feed the algorithms and the algorithms must lead to decisions (output). Algorithms only have the capability to produce pollution when they are used to automate decisions based on datafied individuals, i.e., data, algorithms, and decisions are always present and implicated in algorithmic pollution (even when this is not readily apparent). Using this production metaphor and concepts from the environmental pollution literature, we identify necessary elements that work together in the case of AI and machine-learning algorithms:

Datafication: algorithms are constructed using 'datafied' individuals i.e., individuals represented by limited number of attributes that have been chosen as relevant. As they are never complete, such a datafication practice is bound to create the so-called "representational" harm [35]. This type of harm is further intensified with organisations (including governments) increasingly acquiring data from "data scorers and brokers" with individuals already datafied (e.g., a person's score) through some unknown processes [15, 27].

Production: in the case of machine learning, algorithms then learn from the data produced as a result of datafication to create rules. However, using past data to predict future behaviour is sometimes out-dated or inappropriate. For example, data collected on historical "gang districts" are now used by police for predictive policing even though these districts may be no longer representative [28]. As O'Neil [11] observes: "if we allowed a model to be used for college admissions in 1870, we'd still have 0.7% of women going to college. Thank goodness we didn't have big data back then" (p. 1).

Therefore, an algorithm might be designed in such a way that it discriminates against certain individuals, or it might learn from data to discriminate.

End-Pipes: algorithms are embedded in processes in transformative services of all types in order to make decisions with little or no human intervention. In the language of environmental pollution, this is the 'end-pipe' of algorithmic pollution, i.e., the point where decisions are made and enacted. Some of these decisions may result from point stationary pollution (PSP), where the decisions are generated by an identifiable organization, process, and algorithm. Other decisions are likely to have characteristics of non-stationary pollution (NPSP), being generated by multiple algorithm sources working collectively (for example decision generated by networks of inter-communicating algorithms).

Consequences: algorithmic decision-making in the transformative services has a direct impact on individuals, for example when a person is approved or declined for a loan, a medical operation, or parole. Algorithmic pollution is further propagated and amplified by highly interconnected systems of algorithms (NPSP). How these individual algorithms interact is not only invisible to those affected, but often to those who constructed them and deployed them [19, 36]. For example, a person with a poor credit card history is very likely to have difficulties finding employment; without a job they are very unlikely to repay their debt, which in turn will further impact on their credit card history [27]. Teachers being scored by algorithms as non-performing will face difficulties finding future employment, which in turn will limit their ability to improve their score [11]. In environmental pollution this is unlikely to be the case as, for example, radiation and water pollution do not augment each other. Algorithmic pollution, however, emerges from complex interactions that cannot be predicted and possibly cannot be traced back to root decisions, i.e., a cause and effect logic may be insufficient when addressing complex algorithmic pollution.

Feedback Loops: the algorithmic decision-making outcomes themselves lead to the generation of further data about individuals that can be harvested by machines and fed back into the algorithm building process. Not only can humans be removed from the decision-making process; they can also be removed from the algorithm building process as machines learn from data that was generated by machine-made decisions in the first place. Without some form of intervention these feedback loops may result in self-perpetuating vicious cycles, which may, ultimately, lead to deep rifts in the fabric of society. These feedback loops are thus unique to algorithmic pollution in that the consequences can affect the means of production in a direct and automated manner through datafication and machine learning, aided and amplified by data brokers and data scorers [27]. The end result is pollution itself becoming a pollutant, producing new forms of pollutions. This is a new digital phenomenon, not present in environmental pollution.

4.3 Implications

Algorithmic pollution is not only spreading but also intensifying. While in other cases of pollution humans and/or instruments are capable of detecting pollution (e.g., through sight, smell, or by radiation reading), algorithmic pollution remains hidden. Indeed, algorithmic effects are hidden and as such very hard to detect and prove. A customer of a health insurance company offers a vivid example:

> *"The insurance company repeatedly told me that the problem was the result of a technical error, a few missing digits in a database. But that's the thing about being targeted by an algorithm: you get a sense of a pattern in the digital noise, an electronic eye turned towards you, but you can't put your finger on exactly what's amiss"* [10, p. 5].

Moreover, it is very difficult (if possible at all) for an individual to fight the effects of algorithms. In fact, "bad inferences" about people are fast becoming "a larger problem than bad data because companies can represent them as "opinions" rather than fact. A lie can be litigated, but an opinion is much harder to prove false" [27, p. 32]. To make matters worse, algorithmic decision-making continues to be celebrated as superior to human-judgment [10, 11, 37]. The cult of "science" continues as "Technocrats and managers cloak contestable value judgements in the grab of "science" [27, p. 10]. Inevitably, and often unknowingly, they also contribute to the creation and propagation of pollution.

As algorithms now proliferate into various sectors of the economy and society they fundamentally reconfigure power relations and transform the ways sectors operate, without public awareness or broader understanding of their consequences. Given the potentially complex outcomes of algorithmic pollution, focusing on and opening up the 'black box' of how algorithms work (the production stage), is unlikely to be a successful strategy for algorithmic regulation. The lack of transparency, the hidden acting of algorithms, and the presence of feedback make the study of algorithmic pollution particularly challenging.

5 Theorizing Algorithmic Pollution

Contemporary forms of knowing, in particular those advanced by computer and communication technology research, artificial intelligence, data analytics and data science, are focused on the translation of problems (business, market, political, scientific) into codified knowledge and ultimately codes of algorithms. A considerable body of literature thus focuses on translations: first, the translation of tasks (or problem solutions) into formal statements or instructions (pseudo-code); and second, the translation of the pseudo-code into a source code [19, p. 17]. The first translation is particularly critical as it essentially codifies existing knowledge about a problem at hand in such a way that all possible conditions relevant for solving it (e.g., variables in a decision-making model) and for generating decisions are taken into account. Algorithms that have errors in the codified knowledge (logic or control or both) produce wrong or problematic outcomes [38] and can thus be identified as and shown to be pollutants.

However, algorithmic pollution occurs more often due to negative unintended consequences of carefully designed and seemingly correct algorithms. As examples above illustrate, the execution of algorithms involves mobilization and use of diverse data sources (e.g., shopping history data, prescription drugs, medical and wellness data, social media records, search engine logs/history, voting preferences, credit card transactions and many more, often sold by data brokers who consolidate data per individuals). These data are prone to errors, are uncertain, and contain a significant amount of noise [15]. Based on such data, algorithms calculate scores, make decisions or produce other outcomes (risk scores for individuals, loan or insurance approvals/declines, short listing of job applicants) that become effective in concrete sociomaterial practices: individuals are targeted as criminal suspects based on risk scores; bank clients are declined loans; applicants are not short listed. Such effects can be damaging while typically not being justified [10, 27].

The consequences of the algorithmic execution thus depend to a large extent on numerous heterogeneous actors enrolled in complex and uncertain sociomaterial assemblages. These consequences are rarely predictable and detectable at the design and coding stage. While understanding the reasoning embedded in the code of an algorithm and how outcomes (decisions) are calculated and derived from inputs, is important and necessary, it is far from being sufficient to comprehend what an algorithm is actually doing, on what grounds its decisions are produced and whether they are correct, fair, just, and justified. As algorithms become actors they "form a complex and at various times interpenetrating sociomaterial assemblage[s] that [are] diffused, distributed, fragmented, and, most importantly, "liquid" [39, pp. 18–19]. Their effects are produced by the sociomaterial assemblages. To understand algorithmic pollution, we argue, requires empirical attention to the workings of individual algorithms or systems of algorithms and the examination *within* their complex, diffused, fragmented, liquid and often interpenetrating sociomaterial assemblages [40]. This proposition opens many conceptual and methodological questions.

The notion of an algorithm as "Logic + Control" [18] or a set of instructions for completing a particular set of tasks [1], implies a self-sufficient non-human object with specified functions with defined inputs, a complete set of conditions and action possibilities (outcomes). When its code (a set of instructions) is executed an algorithm becomes the actor. In other words, the execution of code constitutes an algorithm as an actor. Code execution is a particular materialization of relations that form sociomaterial assemblages (mobilize and enact heterogeneous actants – servers, various data sets, other algorithms, things and human actors as objects of knowledge). It is through these relations that particular outcomes (decisions, recommendations) are achieved (credit scores calculated; crime suspect regions demarcated; terrorists predicted). How to study these enfolding relations becomes the key methodological issue, an issue that is yet further complicated by the ability of machines to learn from data without human input and, due to the use of deep learning, may be unable to fully account for the "Logic" that is being used to automate decisions [18, 19].

Through repeated execution algorithm codes keep performing their objects of knowledge and thus enact different entities (things and people) into being. They perform new distinctions and new categories of customers/clients/citizens often based on unchecked and error prone data, from dubious and unreliable sources [15]. Mackenzie and Vurdubakis [41] similarly note:

> *"the conduct of code, we might say, its execution, is a fraught event, and analysis should be brought to bear on the conditions and practices that allow code to, as it were, access conduct.*

While the knowledge or form that lies at the heart of the code promises completeness and decidability, the execution of code is often mired in ambiguity, undecidability and incompleteness" (p. 7).

Importantly, "ambiguity, undecidability and incompleteness" are kept hidden, buried in the complexity of code execution and largely unrecognized. Even the designers and users of algorithms (especially those with learning capabilities) do not understand the intricacies of code execution and cannot explain the resulting outcomes which are nevertheless actioned undoubted and undisputed.

This brief discussion suggests that to understand the actual doings of algorithms we need first to examine and dig deeper into the relational unfolding of code execution (a digital life of code) and the emergence of sociomaterial assemblages (the intra-acting in Barad's [42] sense), including the mobilization of numerous actors (data sets, companies, internet, data analytics technologies) and the *performing* of subjects and objects. The relational unfolding of a code however is hidden behind the interface and the traces of code execution are typically not provided.

When the algorithmic outcomes become enacted they continue the 'doing' by being enrolled in sociomaterial practices of the users (for example, in a police department or in a bank loan approval process). Entangled within these practices algorithmic outcomes have a life of their own, reconfiguring users' action domains while becoming constitutive of subjects (suspect citizens or risky clients) and objects (high criminality regions). Algorithmic outcomes thus perform what Barad [42] calls agential cuts, making particular subjects and objects in the image of their calculation. For instance, the subjects (citizens, clients, job applicants) become performed as particular calculated figures (e.g., citizens equated with their risk scores), the power of which comes from an unquestioned authority of algorithms [43].

These performative effects of algorithms are not only taken for granted, they are celebrated as unbiased, objective and thus fair [11]. That they are based on unchecked and uncertain data sets, often breaching basic human rights, and thus unjustified, unethical, and potentially illegal, is conveniently hidden and kept far from the public eye. Algorithmic pollution, we might tentatively conclude, is carefully covered up, systematically hidden, and deceivingly dressed up as technological progress.

These initial ideas, conceptualizations and methodological issues only scratch the surface of unprecedented methodological complexity of investigating algorithmic pollution. Uncovering it, revealing how algorithms pollute various sociomaterial environments and what injustices and damages are done to people and communities, will be an uphill battle for anybody who dares to research and report on it.

In this battle we can learn from ANT scholars who have studied similar reconfigurations of sociomaterial practices and the performing of subjects and objects in a variety of contexts (see for example, [44–47]). What is however different and new in algorithmic doing and performing is the particular discursive-calculative-digital nature of algorithmic outcomes and how they come into being in code execution. For this reason, ANT or other field methodologies would need to be adapted or reinvented to be delicately attuned to diffused, fragmented, uncertain and hidden sociomaterial practices of algorithmic doings and reality making.

6   A Research Agenda for Algorithmic Pollution

As we have shown, in addition to investigating the design of algorithms (that has been extensively studied in the literature, see [18, 43], researching and understanding algorithmic pollution requires empirical examination of interrelated sociomaterial practices of two key aspects: algorithm deployments and ongoing datafication processes. Both aspects offer new research challenges, as discussed in this section.

Algorithm deployment includes on the one hand, coding, execution of code and emergence of a sociomaterial assemblage that produce algorithmic pollution, and on the other, the enactment of algorithmic outcomes (decisions, recommendations) that reconfigures users' practices and performs subjects and objects. The need to better understand how these sociomaterial practices of algorithm deployment contribute to algorithmic pollution, leads us to a number of research questions.

For example, what is the relationship between coding practices and algorithmic pollution? We envisage the design of new frameworks and methods that could be used to guide developers to bring to the surface potential sources of algorithmic pollution, including datafication practices. An important step in this direction is the IEEE Global Initiative on Ethics of Autonomous and Intelligence Systems [48]. We envisage the challenge of translating the proposed generic principles into practical approaches in a particular context, taking into account the complexities of transformative services. These yet-to-be-discovered practices, could include for example moral imagining [49].

The challenge of making visible the process of emergence of a sociomaterial assemblage that produces algorithmic pollution opens yet more research questions. For example: How might we effectively recognize, report and mitigate the effects of algorithmic pollution throughout society? Who should be doing it? How might we recognise and deal with different types of polluters? How can we educate governments, organisations and society at large to look beyond the current hype of algorithmic neutrality, efficiency and superiority and comprehend the urgency of dealing with algorithmic pollution?

In framing a response to algorithmic pollution, we propose to turn our attention and learn from the established field of environmental justice, which is defined as follows:

> *"Environmental justice is a social movement seeking to address the inequitable distribution of environmental hazards among the poor and minorities. ... From a policy perspective, practicing environmental justice entails ensuring that all citizens receive from the government the same degree of protection from environmental hazards and that minority and underprivileged populations do not face inequitable environmental burdens."* [50, p. 1].

We propose that algorithmic pollution is added to the environmental dimensions already identified in the environmental justice movement, as *algorithmic justice*. As previously illustrated, there is already strong evidence that the hazards of algorithms are distributed inequitably. As Eubanks [10] explains, these new algorithmic systems for "automating inequality" have the most destructive and deadly effects on the poor and the underprivileged. Even more, "[t]he widespread use of these systems impacts the quality of democracy for us all" [10, p. 12].

The environmental justice agenda is reflected in the Toronto Declaration [51], which is calling for governments and companies to ensure that algorithms respect basic principles of equality and non-discrimination. Yet, as our paper demonstrates, this is going to be very difficult to implement in practice, as today's algorithms are so "deeply woven into the fabric of social life that, most of the time, we don't even notice we are being watched and analysed" [10, p. 5].

A possible way forward could be found by simultaneously looking forward at the emerging developments in AI and algorithmic decision-making and looking back at the history of the environmental movement. For example, a possible way of providing more visibility into the inner working of algorithms would be to store the trace of automated algorithmic decisions using a blockchain, as suggested by Schmelzer [52]. This has the benefit of the decision audit trail being stored in a way that can be shared, cannot be tampered with, and is not owned by the algorithm producer or deployer. A similar idea might be applied to the problem of spreading pollution by creating an audit trail for the ongoing datafication of individuals in transformative services.

By considering the history of environmental protection, we could also learn, for example, about the ways in which traditional pollution has been addressed. We could then expand or redevelop the existing frameworks and methods, such as Environmental Impact Assessment (EIA) [53] and market-based controls [31], to include algorithmic pollution. Finally, by researching the inner working of government environmental protection agencies we may identify new opportunities for policy development and possible establishment of similar agencies for algorithmic justice.

7   Conclusion and an Urgent Call for Action

In his work titled "Love Your Monsters", Latour turns his attention to technology "to protect the planet from ecological crisis" [54, p. 1]. We argue that a new type of crisis is already here, caused by a new type of technologically-induced pollution that we identify and name "algorithmic pollution".

Inspired by the observed parallels with environmental pollution, in this paper we articulate a new type of widespread, hidden, largely unregulated and evidently harmful "algorithmic pollution". Focusing on the transformative services, we offer evidence collected from multidisciplinary literature why this pollution is a growing problem that requires our urgent attention. We also offer a preliminary approach to studying algorithmic pollution that discloses the hidden and uncertain performing of algorithms in sociomaterial environments, which would enable researchers to examine the nature of algorithmic pollution and how the damage is done. This enables us to identify and articulate a set of IS research challenges that call for our urgent attention. By drawing parallels between environmental protection and the need to protect the observed sociomaterial environment that is now affected by algorithmic pollution, we open up new opportunities for a practical contribution.

We recognize that algorithms undoubtedly have the potential to provide society with significant benefits (e.g., healthcare, driverless vehicles, fraud detection). Therefore, this paper is not a treatise against algorithms. Far from it. It is however explicitly and consciously against algorithmic pollution. Recalling the words of the poet Ella Wheeler Wilcox – 'to sin by silence, when we should protest" – we, IS researchers, should raise our voices and enact our professional responsibility.

Building upon the fundamental principle of environmental justice that "all people deserve to live in a clean and safe environment free from industrial waste and pollution that can adversely affect their wellbeing" [50, p. 1], we conclude this paper with a claim that all people equally deserve to live in an environment free and safe from algorithmic pollution. If algorithms are our future, as many claim, then understanding, fighting against and preventing algorithmic pollution, may save our collective dignity and humanity.

References

1. Caplan, R., Donovan, J., Hanson, L., Matthews, J.: Algorithmic accountability: a primer. Prepared for the Congressional Progressive Caucus, 18 April 2018. Data & Society, Washington, DC. https://datasociety.net/wp-content/uploads/2018/04/Data_Society_Algorithmic_Accountability_Primer_FINAL-4.pdf, last accessed 2018/08/21
2. Cukier, K., Mayer-Schonberger, V.: Big Data: A Revolution that will Transform How We Live, Work and Think. Houghton Mifflin Harcourt, Boston (2013)
3. Davenport, T.: Big data @ Work: Dispelling the Myths, Uncovering the Opportunities. Harvard Business Review Press, London (2014)
4. Perkins, A.: May to pledge millions to AI research assisting early cancer diagnosis. The Guardian 1–2 (2018)
5. Steiner, C.: Automate This: How Algorithms Came to Rule Our World. Penguin, New York (2012)
6. Newell, S., Mirabelli, M.: Strategic opportunities (and challenges) of algorithmic decision-making: a call for action on the long-term societal effects of 'datafication. J. Strateg. Inf. Syst. **24**(1), 3–14 (2015)
7. Ostrom, A.L., Parasuraman, A., Bowen, D.E., et al.: Service research priorities in a rapidly changing context". J. Serv. Res. **18**(2), 127–159 (2015)
8. Anderson, L., Ostrom, A.L.: Transformative service research – advancing our knowledge about service and well-being. J. Serv. Res. **18**(3), 243–249 (2015)
9. Anderson, L., Ostrom, A.L., Corus, C., et al.: Transformative service research: an agenda for the future. J. Bus. Res. **66**(8), 1203–1210 (2013)
10. Eubanks, V.: Automating Inequality: How High-Tech Tools Profile, Police, and Punish the Poor. St. Martin's Press, New York (2017)
11. O'Neil, C.: Weapons of Math Destruction: How Big Data Increases Inequality and Threatens Democracy. Penguin Random House, New York (2016)
12. Galliers, R.D., Newell, S., Shanks, G., Topi, H.: Datafication and its human, organizational and societal effects: The strategic opportunities and challenges of algorithmic decision-making. J. Strateg. Inf. Syst. **26**(3), 185–190 (2017)
13. Markus, L.: Datafication, organizational strategy, and IS research: what's the score?". J. Strateg. Inf. Syst. **26**(3), 233–241 (2017)
14. Marjanovic, O., Cecez-Kecmanovic, D.: Exploring the tension between transparency and datafication effects of open government IS through the lens of Complex Adaptive Systems. J. Strateg. Inf. Syst. **26**(3), 210–232 (2017)
15. Clarke, R.: Risks inherent in the digital surveillance economy: a research agenda. J. Inf. Technol. (2018, forthcoming)
16. EPA: EPA – United States Environmental Protection Agency. https://www.epa.gov/laws-regulations/summary-national-environmental-policy-act. Accessed 21 Aust 2018
17. Chollet, F.: Deep Learning with R. Manning Publications, Greenwich (2018)

18. Kowalski, R.: Algorithm = Logic + Control. Commun. ACM **22**(7), 424–436 (1979)
19. Kitchin, R.: Thinking critically about and researching algorithms. Inf. Commun. Soc. **20**(1), 14–29 (2017)
20. Lazer, D., Kennedy, R., King, G., Vespignani, A.: The parable of Google flu: traps in big data analysis. Science **343**(6176), 1203–1205 (2014)
21. Voosen, P.: The AI detectives: as neural nets push into science, researchers probe back. Science **357**(6346), 22–27 (2017)
22. Hutson, M.: AI researchers allege that machine learning is alchemy. Science, 3 May 2018. http://www.sciencemag.org/news/2018/05/ai-researchers-allege-machine-learning-alchemy. Accessed 5 May 2018
23. Loebbecke, C., Picot, A.: Reflection on societal and business model transformation arising from digitization and big data analytics: A research agenda. J. Strateg. Inf. Syst. **24**(3), 149–157 (2015)
24. Lycett, M.: Editorial: 'datafication': making sense of (big) data in a complex world. Eur. J. Inf. Syst. **22**(4), 381–386 (2013)
25. Gitelman, L.: "Raw Data" is an Oxymoron. MIT Press, Cambridge (2013)
26. Daikopoulos, N.: Algorithmic accountability reporting: on the investigation of black boxes. A Tow/Knight brief. Tow Center for Digital Journalism, Columbia Journalism School. http://towcenter.org/algorithmic-accountability-2/. Accessed 21 Aug 2018
27. Pasquale, F.: The Black Box Society: The Secret Algorithms that Control Money and Information. Harvard University Press, Cambridge (2015)
28. Ferguson, A.G.: The police are using computer algorithms to tell if you're a treat. Time 1–2 (2017)
29. Tett, G.: Mapping crime – or stirring hate? Financial Times, Opinion, August 2014
30. Terhune, C.: They know what's in your medicine cabinet. Business Week, July 2008
31. Lynch, M., Kimberly, L., Stretesky, P.,.Long, M., Jarrell, M., Ozymy, J.: Crime as pollution? Theoretical, definitional and policy concerns with conceptualizing crime as pollution. Am. J. Crim. Just. **40**, 843–860 (2015)
32. Online Encyclopaedia. www.encyclopedia.com. Accessed 21 Aug 2018
33. Encyclopedia Britannica. www.britannica.com/science/pollution-environment. Accessed 21 Aug 2018
34. Harrison, R.M. (ed.): An Introduction to Pollution Science. Royal Society of Chemistry, London (2006)
35. Reisman, D., Schultz, J., Carwford, K., Whittaker, M.: Algorithmic impact assessments: a practical framework for public agency accountability. AI Now (2018)
36. Seaver, N.: Knowing Algorithms. Media in Transition 8, Cambridge. http://nickseaver.net/papers/seaverMiT8.pdf. Accessed 21 Aug 2018
37. McAfee, A., Brynjolfsson, E., Davenport, T.H., Patil, D., Barton, D.: Big data: the management revolution. Harvard Bus. Rev. **90**(10), 61–67 (2012)
38. Drucker, J.: Performative materiality and theoretical approaches to interface. Digit. Human. Q. **7**(1). http://www.digitalhumanities.org/dhq/vol/7/1/000143/000143.html. Accessed 01 May 2018
39. Introna, L.: Algorithms, governance, and governmentality: on governing academic writing. Sci. Technol. Hum. Values **41**(1), 17–49 (2016)
40. Shotter, J.: Understanding process from within: an argument for 'witness'-thinking. Org. Stud. **27**(4), 585–604 (2006)
41. Mackenzie, A., Vurdubakis, T.: Code and coding in crisis: signification, performativity and excess. Theory Cult. Soc. **28**(6), 3–23 (2011)
42. Barad, K.: Meeting the Universe Halfway: Quantum Physics and the Entanglement of Matter and Meaning. Duke University Press, Durham (2007)

43. Beer, D.: The social power of algorithms. Inf. Commun. Soc. **20**(1), 1–13 (2017)
44. Latour, B.: Reassembling the Social: An Introduction to Actor-Network-Theory. Oxford University Press, Oxford (2005)
45. Law, J.: After Method: Mess in Social Science Research. Routledge, London (2004)
46. Law, J., Hassard, J. (eds.): Actor Network Theory and After. Blackwell and the Sociological Review, Oxford and Keele (1999)
47. Law, J., Lien, M.E.: Slippery: field notes in empirical ontology. Soc. Stud. Sci. **42**(3), 363–378 (2012)
48. IEEE: The IEEE Global initiative on ethics of autonomous and intelligent systems. IEEE Standards 2018. http://standards.ieee.org. Accessed 21 Aug 2018
49. Wrhane, P.: Mental models, moral imagination and systems thinking in the age of globalization. J. Bus. Ethics **78**, 463–474 (2008)
50. Arney, J.: Environmental Justice. Encyclopaedia Britannica. https://www.britannica.com/topic/environmental-justice. Accessed 16 May 2018
51. Brandom, R.: New Toronto declaration calls on algorithms to respect human rights. The Verge, 16 May 2018
52. Schmelzer, R.: Combination of blockchain and AI makes models more transparent. TechTarget, May 2018. https://searchenterpriseai.techtarget.com/feature/Combination-of-blockchain-and-AI-makes-models-more-transparent. Accessed 21 Aug 2018
53. Gilpin, A.: Chapter 1: EIA approaches. In: Environmental Impact Assessment (EIA): Cutting Edge for the Twenty-First Century, pp. 1–15. Cambridge University Press, Cambridge (1995)
54. Nordhaus, T., Shellenberger, M.: The monsters of Bruno Latour. Breakthrough J. (Spring) (2012)

Quantifying Quality: Towards a Post-humanist Perspective on Sensemaking

Eric Monteiro[1]([⊠]), Thomas Østerlie[1], Elena Parmiggiani[1],
and Marius Mikalsen[2]

[1] Norwegian University of Science and Technology, 7491 Trondheim, Norway
{eric.monteiro, thomas.osterlie, parmiggi}@ntnu.no
[2] SINTEF Digital, Postboks 4760 Torgarden, 7465 Trondheim, Norway
marius.mikalsen@sintef.no

Abstract. Processes of quantifying the qualitative have deep historical roots that demonstrate their contested nature. The ongoing push for Big Data/data science presupposes the quantification of qualitative phenomena. We analyse an ongoing case where the core of the qualitative – judgements, assessments, sensemaking – is being challenged by quantification through Big Data/data science-inspired new digital tools. Concretely, we study how traditionally qualitative sensemaking practices of geological interpretations in commercial oil and gas exploration are challenged by efforts of quantification driven by geophysical, sensor-based measurements captured by digital tools. Drawing on Wylie's notion of scaffolding, we outline three aspects of the performativity of scaffolding underpinning geological sensemaking: scaffolding is (i) dynamic (evolving with additional data, quality assurance, triangulation), (ii) provisional (radically changed when faced with sufficiently inconsistent data) and (iii) decentred (in and through distributed, loosely coupled networks of practices). In our analysis, the quantitative does not unilaterally replace the qualitative; there is an irreducible, reciprocal relationship. Yet, there is scope for significant changes in the role, location and sequence of tasks of quantification within the qualitative as we reflect on by way of concluding.

Keywords: Scaffolding · Performative · Post-humanist · Sensemaking
Big data

1 Introduction

There has historically been a push for the quantification of qualitative phenomena [1]. To illustrate, the joint development of instruments and measuring scales during the 18th century transformed temperature from 'hot' (qualitative) to '50 °C' (quantitative) [2]. Some areas, however, have remained stubbornly beyond the reach of this transformation. The judgements, interpretations, and sensemaking involved in a host of knowledge-based professional work – the very heartland of the qualitative – has till date largely evaded quantification [3]. Big Data/data science, with its emphasis on data-driven, statistically based machine learning approaches, presuppose quantification. This raises the fundamental question whether the inability of quantification to make inroads

© IFIP International Federation for Information Processing 2018
Published by Springer Nature Switzerland AG 2018. All Rights Reserved
U. Schultze et al. (Eds.): IS&O 2018, IFIP AICT 543, pp. 48–63, 2018.
https://doi.org/10.1007/978-3-030-04091-8_5

into the heartland of the qualitative will prevail, or that the quantitative/qualitative boundary will be (radically) redrawn.

There are sound arguments for both views. On the one hand, data-driven approaches are already performing tasks well within what was until recently safely within the realm of the qualitative. Automated language tools, once identified as the acid test of 'intelligence' hence involving qualitative judgement, now 'work' in ways AI in the 1980 and 90s never did [4]. On the other hand, there are scholars underscoring the irreducibly qualitative. Leonelli et al. [5, p. 194], for instance, call for critically questioning "why, how, for whom, and when data are perceived as available, portable, and/or meaningful."

Against a backdrop of increasingly ideologically poised discourse, we adopt an empirically open stance. Somewhat simplified, current discourse oscillates between two extremes where Big Data/data science either spells the end of the qualitative and hence eliminate large swathes of human labour [cf. 3, 4] or views where the heartland of the qualitative can never be quantified [6]. Rather than hurling philosophical bricks, we approach the limit for quantification of the qualitative as an issue to be addressed empirically. As a first step, we pose the research question: *How to theoretically characterise practically working quantification of qualitative sensemaking?* Introducing Wylie's [7–9] concept of scaffolding and drawing upon post-humanist theorizing [10–12] to elaborate upon the performativity of scaffolding sensemaking, we argue that there is no necessary opposition between the quantitative and qualitative. Rather, based on ongoing, longitudinal engagement with industrial geoscience exploring for commercial oil and gas resources, we show how the quantitative and qualitative recursively draw upon and implicate each other.

Industrial geoscience exploring for oil and gas resources is well-suited for investigating the tensions, conflicts, and strategies implicated in efforts promoting quantification into traditionally qualitatively oriented practices. Heavy investments in Big Data capabilities throughout the oil and gas industry [cf. 13] add weight to these efforts, but also actualise a standing debate within the geosciences between the two key epistemic communities [14] involved: geophysics and geology. With its background in natural history [15], geology is deeply tied to narrative (i.e. qualitative) understanding of the geological processes resulting in today's situation. Geophysics, on the other hand, is inseparable from its origin in physics-oriented quantified approaches to describing the subsurface as is. Proponents of natural scientific approaches to geosciences has criticised geology for lacking proper methodological grounding, and that a host of epistemic problems undercut its claims to knowledge: incompleteness of data, lack of experimental control, and the great spans of time required for geological processes to take place [16]. Focusing on the hermeneutic nature of geology, rebuttals of this critique [17] highlights the prominence of judgements, interpretation, and sensemaking involved in geological reasoning, the practical application of geology. That the tools supporting the ongoing digital transformation of commercial exploration for oil and gas are heavily biased towards the epistemic practices of geophysics rather than geology further challenges geology's role in future oil and gas exploration.

Drawing on Wylie's concept of *scaffolding* [7–9], we analyse the sensemaking involved in producing, backing up and justifying geological interpretations of the subsurface – the lifeblood of industrial geoscience. Unfolding as a tension between qualitative impulses and quantified imports, we analyse the performativity of scaffolding in line with post-humanist perspectives [11]: scaffolding is dynamic, provisional and decentred. If you accept the inherent relationality, hence irreducibility, of the qualitative/quantitative, there is significant scope for transforming the scope, role and location of qualitative tasks as we reflect on in the conclusion.

2 Theoretical Background

The novelty of Big Data tends to get inflated. Working with large data sets certainly is not new. Many sciences have a long history of dealing with large quantities of data, whose size and scale challenge available strategies and technologies for data collection, sharing, and analysis [18]. The novelty of Big Data, rather, lies in the scope, depth and scale of the methods, technologies and infrastructures to retrieve, accumulate and algorithmically manipulate data. Consistent with a historical perspective, Big Data in our analysis is but a vivid and empirically relevant expression of the long-standing efforts towards quantifying quality.

Some see Big Data as the complete 'conquering' and unilateral replacement of the quantitative over the qualitative insofar as arguing for a new era of empiricism [19–21]. Pure empiricism, i.e. quantification taken to the extreme, however, is met with stark criticism [6]. First, data is always shaped by the technology and platforms used, ontologies employed, and sampling bias. Organisations are dealing with structured, semi-structured and unstructured data from in and outside the enterprise. Variety comes in the form of user-generated text, images and videos as well as a variety of sensor-based data. Second, the algorithms used to capture certain kinds of data arose and were tested within existing scientific tests of validity. Assessing the veracity of data, i.e. the credibility and reliability of different data sources, is also an issue. Third, the idea that data can speak for themselves assumes that it is possible for anyone with a reasonable understanding of statistics and the right tools to interpret them without domain-specific knowledge, effectively ignoring effects of context, culture, policy, and governance.

Knowing with big data therefore does not simply amount to gathering data or 'evidence'. Data "are always already 'cooked' and never entirely 'raw'" [2, p. 2]: they must be processed to count as evidence. Such processing involves informal and often unacknowledged social and technical routines. In a study of a 30-year effort to gather data to develop knowledge about HIV/AIDS, Ribes and Polk [22] describe how maintaining subjects' commitment to contribute data over time involved updating subjects with relevant information regarding the progress of knowledge about the condition and conducting sustained persuasion campaigns lobbying for subjects' continued participation. Similarly, Edwards examines data gathering informing climate change research and reports that measurement devices such as thermometers must be constantly calibrated to ensure the validity of their readings [23]. Procedures of verification are essentially collective organization-based exercises that invoke credibility [24]. Data quality thus involves not only creating but also maintaining procedures. In fact, it is precisely when grappling with uncertain and partial knowledge that it is crucial to legitimise and justify interpretations to make them credible and not mere guesswork.

Wylie's [7–9] *scaffolding* concept offers a promising way to theoretically characterise practically working quantification of qualitative sensemaking involved in
industrial exploration for oil and gas. Her notion is drawn from her extensive study of
practices of archaeology, a domain strikingly similar to our case of geology: knowledge
is partial, provisional, fallible and influenced by the arrival of quantified measurement
techniques (including ^{14}C isotope decay, lead isotope analysis, dental enamel for
oxygen isotopes). Scaffolding of archaeological knowing "build, and continuously
rebuild, credible background knowledge" to develop and mobilise meaningful interpretations of the material evidence, juggling with several interpretations (or working
hypotheses) at the same time. Currie [15] further expand upon the notion of scaffolding,
arguing for its centrality in all historical sciences (counting, among others, archaeology,
geology, and palaeontology). Consistent with a performative and relational perspective
[10, 12], scaffolding is never reified but is dynamic, open to multiple interpretations
and evolving [7]. Scaffolding is decentred and plays out in and through material-
discursive practices [11]. Finally, different from an inherent opposition between
qualitative vs. quantitative, a scaffolding perspective underscores their constitutive
entanglement[1].

3 Research Methods

This paper reports from a longitudinal industry/university research collaboration on
digital innovation in the oil and gas industry in the North Sea region. The particular
activity we report from is based on the shared observation of both operators and vendor
companies in the consortium that the existing digital toolset – which is predominantly
measurement-based – is not always a good match for the exploration geologists' work
practices. While this is fairly well known within the industry, the problem has proven
intransigent to resolve. As such, the problem and its resolution are of both practical and
scientific interest.

In line with principles of engaged scholarship [26], we are therefore conducting
collaborative basic research with key stakeholders in the research consortium to explore
and together with the stakeholders possibly resolve the problem. We draw upon the
authors' combined research on the topic, which is to a certain degree traditional
interviews (21 interviews with industrial exploration geoscientists, 1 interview academic geologist, 17 data managers in one oil company), but also field notes from 10
project workshops and informal conversations in a joint effort of understand and
explain the discrepancy between geologists' work practices and the digital tools
available to them. This work has been conducted against the backdrop of the author
team's sustained engagement with the oil and gas industry over the past twenty years.

The empirical case we present is theoretically sampled to reflect three key aspects
that have so far made the digitalization of knowledge work arduous to come by in
exploration geoscience: (1) the data-driven nature of exploration work, i.e. a

---

[1] Phrased in the vocabulary of paradox theorists [25] this amounts to recognising scaffolding not as a
dualism ('either-or') but as a duality (allowing both).

dependence on data to make sense of the inaccessible subsurface reservoir; (2) the irreducible uncertainty associated with the lack of access to the physical referents; (3) the importance of the continuous work to maintain and (re)interpret the data. Our data analysis is based on a working assumption that the transformation of data-centric knowledge work from qualitative assessments into quantified tasks performed within digital systems is not simply a matter of automation. Rather, it is generative of new phenomena whose potentials should be explored [27]. We have explored this through writing and discussing intermediate results multiple times with different industry stakeholders as well as academic representatives of the geosciences. The insight gained through these discussions has in turn been fed back into the analytic process.

4 Scaffolding Interpretation in Oil and Gas Exploration

Exploration for new oil and gas resources in the North Sea region has become increasingly digitalised over the past few decades. Where exploration for new resources used to be organised around offshore operations – initially through brute-force prospecting by drilling wells into the seabed, and later by collecting seismic data on subsurface formations – exploration is turning into mainly a data-intensive endeavor. Integrated cross-disciplinary exploration teams[2] work together on interpreting available exploration data to determine if and possibly where to drill exploration wells in an assigned geographical area. Organised in projects, the process of assessing an area consist of three sequential, but overlapping steps:

1. determining whether or not the likelihood of finding commercially viable reserves in the area is high enough to warrant investing in exploration well drilling,
2. assessing existing and identifying new potential prospects for drilling exploration wells in search of new oil and gas resources, and
3. ranking the identified exploration prospects into a prioritized list of wells to drill.

Exploration data are *inherently underdetermined*. A common expression among explorationists goes something like 'We really know nothing for certain until we drill a well, and then we only have knowledge about the well'. The underdeterminedness of digital exploration data plays out along multiple dimensions; they are partial in geographic coverage and phenomena measured, of varying quality due to heavy reliance on sensor data of varying accuracy, and inconclusive in and of themselves.

4.1 Scaffolding Geophysical Interpretation

Seismic cross-sections form the backbone of exploration projects (Fig. 1). They are visual snapshots of the geological layering in a slice of the Earth's crust. They are a product of seismic interpretation. While G&G experts working in interpretation

---

[2] These team as colloquially referred to as 'G&G', a shorthand for geology and geophysics, the predominant professions in such teams. However, exploration teams also draw upon resources from other specialized professions such as petrochemists, paleobiologists, and structural geologists, to mention a few.

software produce these visualizations, cross-sections are the product of a distributed machinery of quantitative processing and analysis methods along with stages and phases of manual inspection, cleaning, and massaging of different datasets. Emphasizing this distributed machinery brings out the scaffolding of seismic interpretation.

Seismic cross-sections are reflections of sound waves driven into the seabed and picked up by a long line of hydrophones (digital acoustic sensors) trailing behind a survey ship. Survey equipment configuration (the angle sound waves are driven into the seabed, what types of hydrophones used and their configuration in the trail) varies between surveys depending on the subsurface structures and phenomena expected to be found in the area. Transforming data of reflected sound waves into quantified properties of the subsurface that can be visualised in cross-sections involves a series of methods and techniques to correct for common errors in data generation, removing noise, enhancing signals and transform time-based sound data into spatial representations of the subsurface. This scaffolding of seismic data involves manual cleaning and preparing of the data:

> Ships never travel in a straight line. And we have to compensate for wave height. Not only do waves dynamically change the distance between hydrophones and seabed. Waves ripple through the hydrophone array over time, so different hydrophones are at different heights from the seabed as the different reflections reach the surface. This is more complex, and is usually done by signals geophysicists by hand. (Field interview, geophysicists)

Exploration projects rarely draw upon only a single seismic data set. Rather, they combine seismic data of the area under investigation with data from a wide array of different company internal as well as publicly available data sources. These may be old seismic data from the same area, from adjacent areas, or other data sources such as well logs (detailed measurements of geological formations along the trajectory of a well), old reports, or even existing models from previous efforts to find oil. Project data managers (PDMs) collect data from the various sources, preparing and importing them into project files explorationists can load onto the seismic interpretation software. This involves a lot of manual inspection, cleaning, and transforming of data files. A situation from our fieldwork, where we sat down with a PDM that walked us through the process of loading well data into an exploration project, exemplifies this. Loading well curve data into a project, she checked the calibration of the well data to determine if it was measured in calibush or mean sea level. "This matters, because if you do not get this calibration right, you skew the well path with 20–25 m, and that is unfortunate," she said laughing. She also made sure that the curves that were loaded for a well looked they way it was supposed to do. Each curve had a template for how they are to be displayed. For some curves, the values should be 0 or 1, true or false. For other curves the value should be between 0 and 100. Different min and max values that are actual for that curve. If there is a mismatch, it is typically because the curve has the wrong name, she explains. Different vendors name the curves differently, one company can have one name for a curve, and another company has the same name for a different curve. After loading the data, the PDM displayed the data and did a manual inspection verifying that the data seemed about right.

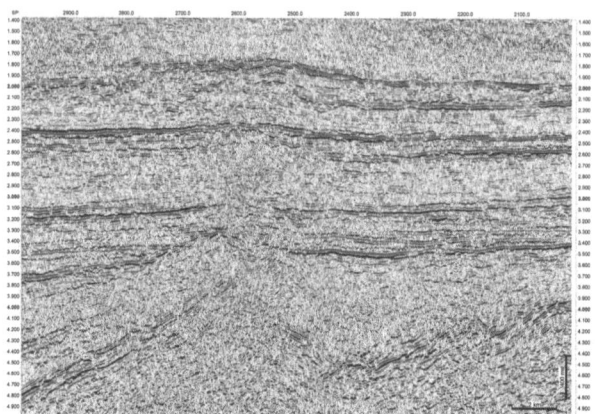

Fig. 1. Seismic cross-section. Continuous blue and red lines indicate geological layers in high-quality area of the picture. More pixelated areas of the picture are indicative of poor seismic. Source: DISKOS, national data repository for the Norwegian oil and gas industry. (Color figure online)

Over decades, oil companies have gone through a series of databases to archive exploration data. One PDM referred to herself as the octopus spreading her tentacles through legacy databases in order to draw together the disparate datasets. Before importing seismic data into a project, the PDM will quality check the data. This can be particularly challenging with old seismic surveys:

–I will first look through the raw data file. Having worked with this for so many years, I know exactly what the file should look like. If I see any errors, I will see if I can correct them. To do that, you basically have to know exactly the kind of equipment used in shooting the survey, down to the minutest details of particular hydrophone designs. I does help having been in the game a while to do that. (Interview, PDM)

4.2   Scaffolding Geological Interpretation

It is not possible to tell from a seismic cross-section whether or not there is an oil reservoir in an area. To do so, explorationists need to establish the presence of an active source rock (i.e. a layer of organic matter that pressure and temperature have transformed into hydrocarbons at some point in time), a geological formation that can trap the hydrocarbons to prevent them from seeping to the seabed and disappear, and a path within the subsurface leading the hydrocarbons from its place of origin to the trap. This cannot be told from cross-sections alone. Seismic data measures the boundary between different geological layers, but tell little about the geological composition of the layers: whether they are sandstone, shale, chalk, and so on cannot be determined from the data. Furthermore, seismics are well suited to measuring rock properties, but do not measure whether or not geological strata contain hydrocarbon deposits. Exploration companies address the shortcomings of seismic cross-section in many ways, but the most common approach in exploration projects is to hand the initial seismic interpretation (in form of cross-sections) over for geological interpretation.

We learned early on to have pen and paper ready when interviewing exploration geologists. They would quickly as 'Do you have a pen and some paper?' when starting to talk about geology. Thematising this with the corporate chief geologists, he affirmed: –*Geology is very pictorial* (Fig. 2). Geophysicists, on the other hand, showed little or no interest in drawing to explain their work. Indeed, when we pointed this out to more data-oriented geophysicists they would somewhat condescendingly refer to geologists as '*artists who like to draw*' or even as a '*dying breed*' implying that data-oriented quantitative approach to geo science is, as one geophysicist put it, '*explorationists for the digital age*'. Geologists would scoff or even bristle when confronted with such statements.

Bracketing these professional tensions, we view them as expressions of how geological interpretation scaffolds exploration data distinctly different than seismic interpretation. The exasperation of a geophysicist offers a point of entry into this:

–It is quite annoying, you know, when you have spent weeks calculating exact uncertainty ranges [for the seismic horizons], and the first thing the geologists do is to say "let's get rid of the uncertainties so we can start working'." (Field note excerpt, conversation with geophysicists)

Seismic interpretation scaffolds exploration data to represent the subsurface as it is today. Geological interpretation, on the other hand, is a theory-methods conglomerate oriented around understanding the structure of the subsurface in narrative terms; narratives of geological processes and events, their sequences and timing, how they unfold and transform the geology over millions of years. It approaches the layers of a seismic cross-section as indicators of geological processes and events.

–Geophysics is given too much emphasis in exploration. Their [the geophysicists'] interpretations need to be grounded in geological understanding. That is why so many exploration wells are dry. (Geologist working with a software vendor, field notes excerpt)

The geologist's reference to '*geological understanding*' illustrates how geological interpretation performs a more conceptual scaffolding. Rather than being neatly stacked, geological layers are usually jumbled and mixed, as geological processes and event cover traces of past geological processes and events in layer upon layer of sediments. All of this is evidence to be used actively in geological interpretation.

–If you have something like this, says the geoscientist trying to explain the limitations of seismic cross-sections in providing a proper picture of the subsurface. Drawing two triangular shapes on a piece of paper, she continues: –This shape can indicate two distinctly different processes. Either the slope here, she points to the bottom-most triangle, indicates erosion. Then the topmost structure is sedimentation on top of it. Or, the reason for this shape is that this (pointing at the shared diagonal between the two triangles) is a rift and the topmost layer has slipped under the other layer. In this case, we may have a migration path. Or the whole scenario may be because of sedimentation losing momentum and therefore creating a triangular shape that has been pushed up.

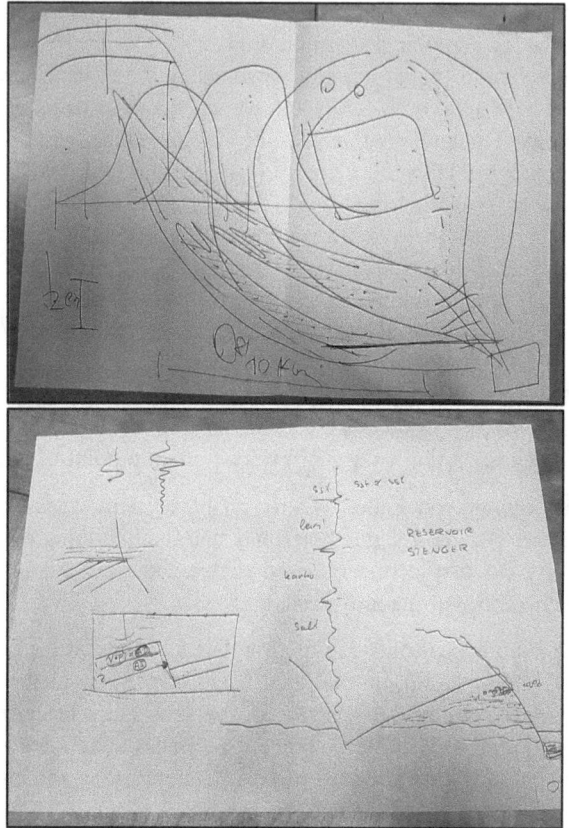

Fig. 2. Hand drawings made by exploration geologists during interviews. Top: the drawing was used to re-tell the creation and modification of different geological histories while making sense of a prospect. Bottom: the drawing supported the explanation of the subsurface stratigraphy and how porosity could be used to interpret a geological formation. Source: pictures by the authors.

Drawing upon a wide array of methods of knowing the "deep past" with scant and usually degraded evidence, geological interpretation seeks to establish a narrative of geological events and processes that could have led to the situation of today. In so doing, they seek to verify whether or not the area has an active source rock, a trap, a migration path, and that the timing of geological events is such that hydrocarbons migrating from the source rock have been caught by the trap. This is a process of cycling back and forth between seismic and geological interpretation. Seismic images are rarely so of such a quality that it is obvious to explorationists how the subsurface is today:

Using his pen to follow a clear red line in the pixelated seismic mage, the geologist explains: "This horizon is fairly clear. We can distinguish this as the border between two geological borders clearly. But here, you see, it is much harder to distinguish the horizon." At this stage he has reached what occurs as a sea of red and blue pixels in the seismic cross-section. "Here the signal is no longer any good, and we can hardly discern any boundaries." (Field interview with academic geologists teaching seismic interpretation)

5 The Performativity of Scaffolding

The central problem in oil exploration, starting from measured observations of geophysical properties of the geological formation as evident today, is to tie these to an inferred, narrative account of the rich, geological processes (erosion, sedimentation, tectonic plate movements, diagenetic processes, faults, etc.) that could have yielded the current situation. Making sense thus involves the entanglement of the quantitative (measurements, IoT generated data) with the qualitative (narrative of the geological processes). Data about the current geological situation come from measurements subsequently manipulated algorithmically (in the case of seismics, by several non-linear filters whereby only less than 1% of the original data is kept) that need a narrative hence qualitative contextualizing. The sensemaking amounts to working backwards, from the data, to a geological narrative capturing the processes whereby the current geophysical measurements could have resulted. There is no opposition between the quantitative and the qualitative. Rather, they recursively draw on and implicate each other. Drawing on Wylie's notion and post-humanist theorizing, the scaffolding of sensemaking in oil exploration is performative. With basis in this, we will now proceed to discuss a theorization of practical working quantification of qualitative sensemaking with the push for big data in oil and gas exploration.

First, *scaffolding is dynamic*. In her work on interpreting material data in archaeology, Wylie [8] describes in strikingly similar way this 'reverse engineering' of a narrative understanding from measured data observed at the archaeological site. "Archaeological facts", exactly like facts in oil exploration, grapple with the problem "that the tangible, surviving facts of the record so radically underdetermine any interesting claims archaeologists might want to make that archaeologically based 'facts of the past' are inescapably entangled with fictional narratives of contemporary sensemaking." [9, p. 301] This, as Wylie [9, pp. 308–309] (emphasis added) goes on to argue, "shows how detailed histories of the travel of these [data] collections, records and interpretations (…) can play a critical role in the process [of] (…) grounding the adjudication of their epistemic integrity as a basis for framing factual claims about the past (*narrative facts*)."

In oil exploration, we find a similar form of reverse engineering. For instance, Sect. 4.2 describes how geological interpretation builds and supplement early seismic cross-sections with a narrative understanding of the area's geological composition. Deposition environment models – idealised models of the processes through which geological layers have been deposited over time in a geological region, and the subsequent composition of each layer's masses – are one of several data sources used in understanding the composition and layering of geological strata in a seismic cross-section:

–The seismics only show me the border between geological layers. A drilled well tells me quite exactly the composition of the rocks in each layer, but only for the width of the well. If the depositional environment were a desert, I would know that there was a continuous sand layer [to contain hydrocarbons] here. But if the depositional environment were a delta, for instance, I would know that it does not have a continuous mass of sand throughout the entire width of the layer. Sediments deposited by the rivers [flowing through the delta and into the ocean] will be formed into shales cutting through the reservoir. (Exploration geologist, field note excerpt)

As such, geoscientists make sense of the subsurface through successive geological and geophysical approximations of the subsurface. Drawing upon Chang's [2] history of quantification of temperature, Chapman and Wylie [7, p. 5] describe 18th century chemists' use of 'successive approximations' in ways much similar to interaction between geophysical and geological interpretation: "chemists relied on assumptions and methods they knew to be faulty but that made it possible to refine their under-standing of the phenomenon of temperature to the point where they could eliminate some initial hypothesis and articulate new, more sharply specified questions, questions that would require the construction of new scaffolding". Fully aware that early seismic cross-sections are mere approximations of the subsurface, geoscientists still use them for geological interpretation. Through geological interpretation they seek approximate narrative understandings of the subsurface that can inform further geophysical pro-cessing in the seismic interpretation software. Resulting analyses from this processing and a possibly revised seismic cross-section in turn inform further refinement and exclusion of possible geological narratives.

This is particularly apparent in the way geophysical and geological interpretation scaffolds and constitutes much the same data differently through a dynamic back- and foregrounding of aspects of the scaffolding. Geophysical interpretation scaffolds the data as representations of the subsurface as is. Geological interpretation scaffolds the data as traces, that is "downstream consequences of past events" [15, p. 10]. That is "how the world *is* depends how the world *was*" [15, p. 67] (italics in original). By constituting the seismic image and other exploration data as trace data, geological interpretation dynamically enacts a scaffolding where technical aspects relating to seismic processing and analysis is back staged. When the geophysicist in Sect. 4.2 laments how geologists ignore his hard-won statistical uncertainty ranges, they back-ground these aspects of the scaffolding to constitute the data as traces. Yet, through such dynamically back- and foregrounding aspects of the scaffolding explorationists successively build an increasingly more refined understanding of the subsurface.

Second, *scaffolding is provisional*. In archaeology as in the geosciences, there is significant competence in moving (hermeneutically, [cf. 16, 17]) between close-up, measured data points and taking a step back to gain an appreciation of the broader, formative processes: "[archaeologists] have built up a repertoire of research strategies specifically designed to mobilise the evidence of human lives and events that survives in an enormous range of material evidence…In the process, they have decisively enlarged, challenged, and reconfigured what we know, putting material evidence to work in the investigation of a great many different aspects of the cultural past." [27, p. 5]

Provisionality is most prominent in the way geoscientists formulate, compare, and analyse multiple and simultaneous geological narratives of the same seismic cross-section during geological interpretation. This is expressed through sketching of different scenarios, either by hand on paper and napkins or in the many PowerPoint presentations littering exploration project's shared folders. The previous example where the geoscientist considers different depositional models for the same area, and similarly the way the geoscientists in Sect. 4.2 offers multiple interpretations of the same geometric shape, exemplifies such provisionality. A seasoned geoscientist stated during an interview:

> There is but one thing geologists like better than finding oil, and that is to drill a dry well. Dry wells are an opportunity to better understand the subsurface.

New, and in particular unexpected data such as a dry well, challenges geoscientists' assumptions about the subsurface, calling for a re-interpretation – a re-scaffolding – to integrate new data with existing understandings of the subsurface. The provisionality of scaffolding is here a matter of revisiting and challenging ideas and assumptions about the data and geological processes leading up to the existing situation in the subsurface.

Although dynamic and provisional, scaffolding exhibits a degree of path dependence. As described in Sect. 4.1, seismic data is generated (both generation of sound reflections and the processing) to bring out particular geological structures or phenomena expected to be present in the area. Seismic data is, as such, entangled with prior knowledge and assumptions of the subsurface. Similarly, often invisible in the final result, the painstaking work of setting up geophysical models illustrates the importance of the scaffolding in moving from pluralistic qualitative narratives supported by multiple sketches to a single geophysical model. Geophysical models are defined by a large set of metadata that codify the model's basic assumptions. The metadata shape practical model construction by constraining valid values for populating the model's three-dimensional grid with geophysical properties. As such, revisiting the model's basic assumptions based on new hypotheses (which emerged from the evolving scaffolding) after the modeller starts populating the grid requires significant rework of the entire model, and is rarely done in practice. This investment, however, comes with clear advantages in terms of comprehensiveness, thus complementing the qualitative narratives for specific purposes. Whereas geological narratives are purposefully pluralistic and non-constrained, the completeness of geophysical models imbues a sense of certainty of understanding. Quantification enables simulation and formal verification in ways not possible with qualitative narratives. An in-depth look into this shifting relation between qualitative narratives and quantified models is useful to understand how predefined structures (e.g., metadata) become part of the scaffolding of the explorationists through practice. Although such structures are simplified typologies that are often hard to debunk, they are an essential basis to their conceptual scaffolding, acting as "a medium of communication" and a "framework for systematizing" data management "precisely because they reduce complexity" [8, p. 213].

Even though scaffolding stabilises, and necessarily so, over the course of an exploration project, explorationists strip away existing scaffolding when revisiting exploration prospects they have previously investigated. Sometimes this is a matter of practicalities:

We don't know the thinking behind the old project's interpretation, so it is easier to start from scratch than to try to reconstruct it. (Explorationist, interview)

At other times, such as when re-processing old seismics, most of the scaffolding is stripped off as basic assumptions about the data or area under investigation are revisited. Seismic data is always collected and processes in order to bring out structures and phenomena expected to be present in the subsurface (see Sect. 4.1). Exploration companies have therefore increasingly turned their attention to pre-processed seismic data, subjecting the data to alternative processing techniques in hopes of bringing out previously unseen geological formations that can provide clues to the presence of new oil and gas resources.

Third, *scaffolding is decentred.* Contrary to an actor-centric understanding of sensemaking, we adopt a post-humanist perspective one. We thus analyse the decentred, distributed, sociomaterial practices that go into sensemaking. As Hultin and Mähring [11, p. 572] point out, "[a]s agency is not attributed to actors but continuously flows through material-discursive practices, the 'who', the assumed subject or being, is constituted by the 'how'". Chapman and Wylie [7, p. 55] alludes to the decentered nature of scaffolding in describing fieldwork as "a process that depends on the development of scaffolding in the form of technical expertise and community norms of practices which are internalized by individual practitioners as embodied skills and tacit knowledge, and externalized in the material and institutional conditions that make possible the exercise, and the transmission of these skill and this knowledge". Forefronting the performativity of scaffolding further expand upon this.

Scaffolding decentres geophysical interpretation from explorationists working in seismic interpretation software on their workstations to the spatially and temporally distributed processes of producing, processing, cleaning, and preparing data (Sect. 4.1). As such, seismic cross-sections (one of geophysical interpretation's key outcomes) are the effect of data circulating through networks of sociomaterial practices. These practices reside along the continuum from fully automated, black-boxed computerised processing to more manual practices of filtering, sorting, massaging of data (e.g. PDMs cleaning and preparing data for explorationists). One of the PDMs interviewed described this continuum when explaining how errors occur as well data flows through a sociomaterial network:

A typical error [in a well log] occurs in the file headers. Sometimes it happens that they copy and paste a file somewhere else, and one file is modified locally, then the error is left there, if no one remembers to update it.

While some of the processes of circulating data through this network are linear (as in repeated in stable patterns, such as sequence of generating seismic reflections followed by standard processing techniques to correct for common errors in data generation, removing noise, enhancing signals, transform time-based sound data into spatial representations of the subsurface), the network of sociomaterial practices is rhizomatic and non-linear in nature. Explorationists are very clear on exploration project's contingent nature:

It is difficult to give a clear sequence of activities [in an exploration project]; it all depends on the data, what we expect to find, what we actually are able to find, the work plan we are committed to, and so on. (Geologist, field note excerpt)

Pursuing the performativity of scaffolding through the distributed processes of geophysical and geological interpretation brings out how scaffolding unfolds within a loosely coupled sociomaterial network of fluid agency. Many geoscientists we have talked with talk of this non-linearity in terms of analogical reasoning:

You see this curved shape, and it reminds you of a river bend. So you look for current examples of such bends to see what kind of deposition environment that can be. You find the shape is typical of rivers flowing through jungles and mangroves, so then you can work on the assumption that the shape you see has been deposited in a jungle environment. (Chief geologists, field note excerpt)

6   Conclusion

As our historic outline indicates, the relationship between a qualitative phenomenon and its quantified rendering is contested and conflictual. The 'macro' picture of a gradual quantification of the qualitative downplays to the level of non-existence the 'micro' level set-backs (reverse salient) and opposition to efforts of quantification. Against this backdrop, the proclamations for a new 'era of empiricism' (hence quantification taken to the extreme) or data with 'no theory' come across as exactly that, proclamations.

The practices of sensemaking we analyse – constructing geological interpretations from patchy, faulty and indeterminate data – represent the heartland of qualitative ingredients of knowledge work: judgement, assessment, evaluation [3]. The trajectory of efforts of quantification in our analysis, however, is anything but smooth and uni-directional. Drawing on the performativity of scaffolding, we demonstrate a thorough entanglement – reciprocity – between the qualitative and the quantitative.

The inherent reciprocity between quantitative/qualitative should not be taken to suggest that their boundary and relationship remains stable. The precise role, location, extent and sequence of quantified renderings within the traditionally qualitative domain of geological interpretation are subject to ongoing challenges and changes, not the least from big data/data science methods. Selected pockets or tasks, once accomplished by qualitative judgements, are through new digital tools quantified and automated. For instance, the tracing of horizons in a seismic cross-section is now functionality in the current digital tool for seismic interpretations. Selected geological objects such as faults may be identified from the initially undifferentiated seismic image. Drawing the line for what qualitative phenomena and tasks are amendable (or not) for quantification from also big data hence shifts over time and needs to be empirically analysed [28].

References

1. Crosby, A.W.: The Measure of Reality: Quantification and Western Society. Cambridge University Press, Cambridge (1997)
2. Chang, H.: Inventing Temperature: Measurement and Scientific Progress. Oxford University Press, Oxford (2007)
3. Autor, D.H.: Why are there still so many jobs? The history and future of workplace automation. J. Econ. Perspect. **29**(3), 3–30 (2015)
4. Brynjolfsson, E., McAffee, A.: The Second Machine Age. W. W. Norton & Company Inc., New York (2014)
5. Leonelli, S., Rappert, B., Davies, G.: Data shadows: knowledge, openness, and absence. Sci. Technol. Hum. Values **42**(2), 191–202 (2017)
6. Kitchin, R.: Big data, new epistemologies and paradigm shifts. Big Data Soc. **1**(1), 1–12 (2014)
7. Chapman, R., Wylie, A.: Evidential Reasoning in Archaeology. Bloomsbury Academic, London (2016)
8. Wylie, A.: How archaeological data bites back: strategies for putting old data to work in new ways. Sci. Technol. Hum. Values **42**(2), 203–225 (2017)
9. Wylie, A., Chapman, R.: Material evidence: learning from archaeological practice. In: Chapman, R., Wylie, A. (eds.) Material Evidence: Learning from Archaeological Practice, pp. 1–20. Routledge, Oxon (2015)
10. Barad, K.: Meeting the Universe Halfway: Quantum Physics and the Entanglement of Matter and Meaning. Duke University Press, Durham (2007)
11. Hultin, L., Mähring, M.: How practice makes sense in healthcare operations: studying sensemaking as performative, material-discursive practice. Hum. Relat. **70**(5), 566–593 (2017)
12. Orlikowski, W.J., Scott, S.V.: Exploring material-discursive practices. J. Manag. Stud. **52**, 697–705 (2015)
13. McKinsey & Company. http://www.mckinsey.com/industries/oil-and-gas/our-insights/the-next-frontier-for-digital-technologies-in-oil-and-gas, Accessed 28 Aug 2018
14. Knorr Cetina, K.: Epistemic Cultures: How Sciences Make Knowledge. Harvard University Press, Cambridge (1999)
15. Currie, A.: Rock, Bone, and Ruin: An Optimist's Guide to the Historical Sciences. The MIT Press, Cambridge (2018)
16. Frodeman, R.: Geological reasoning: geology as an interpretive and historical science. GSA Bull. **107**(8), 960–968 (1995)
17. Frodeman, R.: Hermeneutics in the field: the philosophy of geology. In: Babich, B., Ginev, D. (eds.) The Multidimensionality of Hermeneutic Phenomenology. CP, vol. 70, pp. 69–79. Springer, Cham (2014). https://doi.org/10.1007/978-3-319-01707-5_5
18. Gitelman, L. (ed.): Raw Data is an Oxymoron. The MIT Press, Cambridge (2013)
19. Agarwal, R., Dhar, V.: Big Data, Data Science, and Analytics: The Opportunity and Challenge for IS Research. Inf. Syst. Res. **25**(3), 443–448 (2014)
20. Anderson, C.: The End of Theory: The Data Deluge that Makes the Scientific Method Obsolete. WIRED (2008)
21. Davenport, T.: Big Data at Work: Dispelling the Myths, Uncovering the Opportunities. Harvard Business Review Press, Boston (2014)
22. Ribes, D., Polk, J.B.: Organizing for ontological change: the kernel of an AIDS infrastructure. Soc. Stud. Sci. **45**(2), 214–241 (2015)

23. Edwards, P.N.: Global climate science, uncertainty and politics: data-laden models, model-filtered data. Sci. Cult. **8**(4), 437–472 (1999)
24. Power, M.: The Audit Society: Rituals of Verification. Oxford University Press, Oxford (1999)
25. Farjoun, M.: Beyond dualism: stability and change as a duality. Acad. Manag. Rev. **35**(2), 202–205 (2010)
26. Van de Ven, A.H.: Engaged Scholarship: A Guide for Organizational and Social Research. Oxford University Press, Oxford (2007)
27. Zuboff, S.: Big other: surveillance capitalism and prospects of an information civilization. J. Inf. Technol. **30**(1), 75–89 (2015)
28. Pearl, J., Mackenzie, D.: The Book of Why: The New Science of Cause and Effect. Basic Books, New York (2018)

Understanding the Impact of Transparency on Algorithmic Decision Making Legitimacy

David Goad$^{(\boxtimes)}$ and Uri Gal

Department of Business Information Systems,
University of Sydney Business School, Sydney, Australia
david.goad@sydney.edu.au

Abstract. In recent years the volume, velocity and variety of the Big Data being produced has presented several opportunities to improve all our lives. It has also generated several challenges not the least of which is humanities ability to analyze, process and take decisions on that data. Algorithmic Decision Making (ADM) represents a solution to these challenge. Whilst ADM has been around for many years, it has come under increased scrutiny in recent years because of concerns related to the increasing breadth of application and the inherent lack of Transparency in these algorithms, how they operate and how they are created. This has impacted the perceived Legitimacy of this technology which has led to government legislation to limit and regulate its use. This paper begins the process of understanding the impact of Transparency on ADM Legitimacy by breaking down Transparency in Algorithmic Decision Making into the components of Validation, Visibility and Variability and by using legitimacy theory to theorize the impact of transparency on ADM Legitimacy. A useful first step in the development of a framework is achieved by developing a series of testable propositions to be used in further proposed research regarding the impact of Transparency on ADM Legitimacy.

Keywords: ADM · Algorithmic Decision Making · Transparency Legitimacy

1 Introduction

Over the last decade, we have experienced an exponential increase in the volume of produced digital data. Current estimates are that 2.5 exabytes of data are being created each day and the number is doubling every 40 months [1]. It is projected that by 2025 we will be creating 163 zettabytes (i.e., one billion terabytes, or one trillion gigabytes) of data globally each year [2]. In many cases a whole new infrastructure has been built to handle the volumes of data being generated. For example, the new Square Kilometer Array in Western Australia, which will be the world's largest radio telescope, is building a vast storage, data and communications infrastructure to handle the data collection requirements [3].

The velocity or speed at which data is being created and updated is also increasing: geospatial data/locational data derived from the IoT, which often needs to be analysed real time to have any value, is currently ranked as the third largest data type undergoing analysis by commercial organizations [4].

© IFIP International Federation for Information Processing 2018
Published by Springer Nature Switzerland AG 2018. All Rights Reserved
U. Schultze et al. (Eds.): IS&O 2018, IFIP AICT 543, pp. 64–79, 2018.
https://doi.org/10.1007/978-3-030-04091-8_6

In addition to high volume and velocity, data is being collected from an increasing variety of sources, such as GPS devices, social media feeds, financial history, and wearable technologies. This broad scope of data allows data owners to construct comprehensive representations of relevant events, processes, and people.

This Big-Data, characterized by high volume, velocity and variety, is being used to facilitate algorithmic decision-making (ADM). We define ADM as the use of computer programming to automate the decision-making process. ADM utilizes complex statistical techniques and other tools such as neural networks and deep learning to support or replace human decision-making. It has been argued that human decision making is often suboptimal, as humans employ heuristics or mental shortcuts to make decisions [5] and will revert to reducing effort over achieving the most optimal decision [6].

Many believe that data-backed algorithms can be used to render the decision-making process less biased and more rational, increase the effectiveness of decisions made, and help decision makers infer future trends and human behavior with a high degree of accuracy. For instance, retailers have predicted the health conditions of their customers based on historical purchase patterns in an effort to determine what offers might be of most interest to them [7]. Similarly, some financial institutions rely on ADM to predict consumers' financial behavior and make loan decisions.

The use of ADM to make decisions has been increasing over the course of time. In larger part, this is due to advancements in Artificial Intelligence (AI) and Machine Learning (ML), which are key components of ADM but also due to an increase in the availability of the Big Data which feeds ADM. As the use of ADM increases, so too do the concerns about the accuracy of algorithmic processing, the inaccessibility of algorithms, and the ethical implications of their use. Some have directly called into question the legitimacy of ADM [8] whilst others have chosen to ascribe a nefarious nature to the use of ADM in business, describing them as tools that "undermine both economic growth and individual rights" [9]. Several authors have described ADM as inherently discriminatory [10] and as a set of tools that promotes security over privacy, increases societal control and also the dependence of humanity on technology [11]. In many ways then the Legitimacy of ADM, which is defined as the degree to which one's actions comply with social norms, values and beliefs [12], is being called into question.

In this paper, we posit that many of the critiques of ADM have less to do with the nature of the technology as such; rather, they stem from issues of transparency around the application of ADM. By addressing these issues, ADM can be used in a way that would alleviate the practical and ethical concerns typically associated with it. We acknowledge that increased transparency can have both positive and negative effects on ADM legitimacy. We view the relationship between transparency and ADM legitimacy as a complex one where various types of transparency can have several effects on different types of legitimacy.

We also emphasize that we take no view as to the efficacy of Transparency as a phenomena or its ability to actually achieve organizational accountability, increase organizational knowledge, or impact organizations in other ways. Rather we are strictly focusing our research on the impact of Transparency on the Legitimacy of ADM in organizations and note that Transparency can have an impact on Legitimacy without necessarily affecting organizations in other ways.

Accordingly, our approach to ADM legitimacy is a pragmatic one and focuses on articulating ideas that engender desirable outcomes [13]. We maintain that increasing ADM legitimacy is important because, in a very real sense, the application of algorithms to big-data is an unavoidable part of contemporary society. This technology relies on a vast ecosystem of enabling infrastructures, from data centers, to communication protocols, to computer languages, to business and consumer applications, all of which are geared towards deepening and expanding the use of ADM. Consequently, ADM plays a broad role in allowing decision-makers to cope with the mounting quantities of data at their disposal. We aim to increase ADM legitimacy by scrutinizing its potentially harmful elements that result from the effects of transparency that often characterizes its application.

In what follows we define the concept of ADM and outline the main concerns around its use. After reviewing the literature on transparency and legitimacy we propose several ways in which ADM transparency impacts the pragmatic, moral and cognitive elements of legitimacy. These propositions break down ADM transparency into issues of validation, visibility and variability, and present the potential to introduce processes for improving ADM legitimacy. We illustrate the theoretical concepts developed through an applied example.

2 Background

2.1 ADM Applications and Underlying Technology

ADM is not a new phenomenon. For years we have trusted algorithms to run our nuclear power plants and to fly our planes. It is estimated that 90% of commercial airline flight time is done on autopilot [14]. Automated production lines – from cars to integrated circuits – are controlled by algorithms. Similarly, supervisory control and data acquisition systems, which are used extensively in manufacturing, rely on complex process control algorithms to make the everyday products we use safely.

Algorithms are characterized as a combination of logic and control and defined as "a set of defined steps to produce particular outputs" [15]. We consider algorithms in a software programming context and define ADM as the use of computer programming to automate the decision-making process.

Broadly speaking, ADM can be applied in two ways [16]. The first is to facilitate the processing of data to allow analysis by humans. In this scenario, algorithms make provisional recommendations, but the final decision is made by a human being. An example is the algorithm that presents an Uber driver with a ride which he/she can choose to accept or reject. A second application of ADM is where the final decision is made by an algorithm and may or may not be subject to human judgement or evaluation. For example, algorithms used by banks to place a hold on credit cards when certain suspicious activity is identified.

ADM is commonly applied through Artificial Intelligence (AI) by utilizing software code that detects internal and external factors through various sensors and then takes action or interacts with its environment through some form of automation to achieve pre-specified goals. In this way, AI is designed to mimic the natural intelligence displayed by humans.

One of the underlying techniques AI relies on is machine learning (ML). ML refers to mathematical models based on historical information that are constructed to predict the impact a specific action the machine takes will have on its environment. ML encapsulates a large set of mathematical modelling techniques which includes amongst other techniques the deep learning used in neural networks. The term neural networks denotes that the mathematical models are designed to represent in a coarse sense the function of a neuron or brain cell. The term deep learning implies that the models created using neural networks are highly complex using a number of hidden layers to represent various aspects of a system.

These distinctions should be noted as some of the criticisms of ADM (e.g., bias in the learning data set and opacity of the decisions taken) are specific to one or a few of its underlying technologies but not necessarily to ADM as a whole.

2.2   The Concerns and Challenges of Deploying ADM

There are several reasons that can make the deployment of ADM concerning or challenging. The first involves the quality of data used by ADM applications. Often ADM is applied to understand human behavior and categorize it based on limited data. For instance, some banks use ADM to assess clients' loan applications by analyzing their social media profiles[1]. Similarly, several health insurers use data from wearable fitness devices to determine the coverage they offer to their customers[2]. In both instances, limited data is used as a proxy to subtle and complex human behaviors (people's credibility and general health). Such simplistic proxies are used because they are readily available, not because they present a comprehensive view of the behaviors they purport to model.

Another issue with ADM is the creation of self-fulfilling prophecies where decision-makers that act on predictions borne out of ADM, can create the conditions that realize those very predictions. For example, a company may use an algorithm to predict the performance of its recently-hired salespeople. Such an algorithm might draw on data from the salespeople's standardized tests, reviews from previous employers, and demographics. This analysis can then be used to rank new salespeople and justify the allocation of more training resources to those believed to have greater performance potential. However, this is likely to produce the very results that the initial analysis predicted. The higher-ranked recruits will perform better than those ranked lower on the list because they have been given superior training opportunities.

A further issue with the use of ADM is the complexity of the mathematical and statistical techniques that they are based on. Because they are designed using computational language that is only understood to specialized data scientists and computer programmers, their logic is black-boxed from most of the population and, in most cases, from the businesses, people, and communities whose lives are impacted by

---

[1] https://www.smh.com.au/business/banking-and-finance/how-your-social-media-account-could-help-you-get-a-loan-20171219-p4yxw0.html.

[2] https://www.usnews.com/news/national-news/articles/2017-02-17/could-fitbit-data-be-used-to-deny-health-insurance-coverage.

ADM. In some cases, the development of ADM unfolds over time, through multiple design iterations and the use of patched code by multiple programmers. In these cases, the algorithmic logic is hard to decipher even for those who were involved in its development. As a result, often even data scientists cannot explain how the ADM application that they have built makes a prediction or comes to a decision.

Another concern with ADM is the breadth and variety of the data that is used in the models to analyze and predict behavior. In an era of constant connectivity through computers, and mobile and wearable devices, we leave behind us a digital trace which can be used to determine our location, personality, behavior, financial status, work performance, and health. This data can be used in ADM for such activities as credit risk assessment, the calculation of insurance rates, and identification of preferences for product advertising. It is the use of data that is potentially sensitive and discriminatory which has induced the European Union to ban the use of ADM in certain scenarios and to require disclosure as to how a decision is made in others [10].

The challenges described above have led to increasing concerns around the deployment of ADM. These concerns have been particularly acute given the increasing visibility and pervasiveness of ADM in recent years. The visibility of ADM has increased as it has become part of the general discourse. For example, discussions around the role of ADM in transportation[3], health[4], and military[5] have received wide media attention. ADM has also become increasingly pervasive. Whereas initially used predominantly in computer science and specialized business settings, today ADM is applied across various domains, which impact us in multiple ways: from whether we receive a loan, to what news we read, to what people we date, to how quickly we board our flight, to whether we get hired, promoted or fired.

3   The Importance of Transparency to ADM Legitimacy

As argued at the outset of this paper, we maintain that many of the concerns surrounding ADM have to do less with its underlying technology and more to do with the transparency around its use. We posit that transparency impacts the various facets of the legitimacy of ADM in both positive and negative ways, that there are factors which moderate this impact, and that there is a complex interrelationship between the various types of transparency and legitimacy. To elaborate on this further, we next explore the concepts of transparency and legitimacy in the literature and build a nomological scaffold upon which to make several testable propositions about the relationship between transparency and legitimacy (Fig. 1).

---

[3] https://www.independent.co.uk/life-style/gadgets-and-tech/ethical-challenges-self-driving-cars-driverless-vehicles-tempe-arizona-crash-a8287776.html.

[4] https://www.engadget.com/2018/05/20/uk-promises-funding-for-ai-cancer-detection/?guccounter=1.

[5] https://www.techrepublic.com/article/googles-ai-pact-with-pentagon-sparks-resignations-highlighting-leadership-disconnect/.

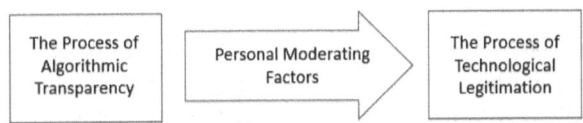

Fig. 1. Proposed high-level nomological structure between transparency and legitimacy

3.1 Transparency Theory as an Organizational Concept

There is a broad body of research on transparency, much of which examines transparency in the context of information provision and accuracy, and focuses on the social and communicative processes around it [17]. Transparency has variously been defined as "a matter of information disclosure... the conditions of transparency are directly linked to the quality and quantity of information, its transmission, and the resulting degree of observability" [17]. Transparency has also been described "as a social process constituted within a set of socio-material practices" [17].

The myth that is organizational transparency has been around for some time [18]. The idea that increased transparency improves insight and therefore accountability and thus organizational governance has pervaded common culture. And yet research has disputed this arguing that information does not necessarily equate to insight [19] and that transparency does not necessarily equate to information [18]. Further, it has been argued that increased information can lead to a distancing of individuals from their surroundings, making them less capable of comprehending the world in which they live [20]. Moreover, increased information can also lead to less trust in institutions that lose their revered status when there is increased transparency and understanding of how they actually operate [20]. All of this literature points to the potentially negative impacts of transparency and increased information on the organisation. But none of it draws a direct relationship between transparency and legitimacy specifically.

3.2 Transparency Theory as It Is Applied to ADM

Various authors have suggested that transparency is not necessarily positive in ADM and have argued against its benefits, specifically with regards to the goal of accountability in organizational governance [21]. These authors maintain that transparency in ADM can be harmful, that it can intentionally occlude by presenting non-relevant information, that it can create false binaries, that it does not infer increased understanding, and that it has technical and temporal limitations. The literature also argues that more transparency does not necessarily ensure more accountability in ADM based processes [22].

Considering the issue of transparency in ADM, Burrell [23] defines three types of opacity (the opposite of transparency) based on the cause of the opacity (intentional concealment, specialist knowledge, model complexity) and discusses the issue of opacity specifically as it relates to classification and discrimination. Transparency has also been categorized based on the level of human involvement, the data used, the model involved, the inferences made by the ADM and the algorithmic presence [22].

De Fine Licht [24] demonstrated that in Sweden greater transparency in allocation of public health care resources did not necessarily guarantee procedural acceptance or decision acceptance. This study points to several moderating factors which have an impact on the effectiveness of transparency such as the framing of the information provided through transparency. This concept of transparency moderating factors is explored in more detail later in this paper.

To sum, transparency has been examined from various perspectives and in different contexts for organizations in general and as it relates specifically to ADM. The desirability of transparency as an end state has been questioned as has its impact on organizational accountability. However, only one study has considered the relationship between transparency and legitimacy as a factor separate from accountability and this study only offered a crude conceptualization of legitimacy.

It is important for the subsequent discussion to emphasize that we take no view as to the efficacy of transparency as a phenomena or its ability to increase accountability. Rather we will strictly focus on the effect of transparency on legitimacy perception.

3.3   ADM Transparency as a Process

We define ADM Transparency as a process not as an end state in that we believe that complete transparency can never be achieved and to main a level of transparency requires ongoing organizational effort. In our analysis we add to the existing literature on transparency by defining Algorithmic Transparency as a process that involves Validation, Visibility and Variability. That process is moderated by the qualities of Experience, Volition and Value which impact the degree of transparency and its impact on the ADM process. We define each of these terms in this section, set out a basis of Legitimacy Theory in the next section and then in the subsequent section discuss the impacts of each form of ADM Transparency on ADM Legitimacy, using Legitimacy Theory [12, 25, 26] and Technological Legitimation as the basis.

To begin we define *Validation* as the degree to which the actual decisions made by algorithms are reviewed and approved by humans. We acknowledge that the nuclear power plant is run by a computer or that a plane is flown by an auto-pilot but we also ensure that there is a physical human being constantly reviewing the decisions made by these algorithms.

The Validation of these algorithms can be further subdivided based on a temporal view into forward validation and backward validation. Forward Validation involves a decision made by an algorithm which is validated by a human before it takes effect. Frequently, these decisions are presented as recommendations to people, whom then must determine whether or not to follow the algorithmic recommendation. Backward Validation is where actions taken by algorithms are reviewed by human after they have been carried out. Following the review, the algorithm can be adjusted to improve the performance of the decision. To be effective those conducting either forward or backward validation should be independent third parties with sufficient skill sets to perform the validation but motivations independent of those who have developed the algorithms.

Drawing on Johnson, Dowd [25] and Binz, Harris-Lovett [26], ADM Validation can also be characterized based on the scope of application. Validation regarding a specific application of ADM we call Local Validation whereas validation across a whole class of ADM application is known as General Validation.

We define *Visibility* as the degree to which there is an effective presentation layer which distils down the large volumes of data involved in algorithmic calculations to an understandable representation, which then allows us to consider how an algorithm has come to a decision. Visibility impacts the degree to which we can critique the decisions made by the algorithms we use to run our businesses and our lives. Often referred to as Business Intelligence this presentation layer is often the first step in the transition of either a business or process management system to an ADM supported process.

Variability is the degree to which decisions about people, processes or systems can vary based on the diversity of data sets provided. Does an Algorithm based on big data with a large variety of information actively reject a person's loan application because they live in a certain geography or does it simply flag the issue for the follow up and human supervision. Variability reflects the degree to which people are treated differently and the impact on those people of how an Algorithm is designed. Increased Variability present in the Algorithmic models increases the potential for accusations of bias and drives much of the concern presented in recent regulation used to limit the use of Algorithms and to increase the transparency of their use.

Even with the best tools to render and present the information under consideration, people reviewing that information must have the Experience to understand what is being presented. A lack of experience can contribute to a lack of transparency and represents a moderating factor in the relationship of transparency to legitimacy [16]. For example, a person who is not a trained pilot would likely find the outputs from algorithmic decisions made by the plane's auto pilot system as they are presented on the cockpit display screen to be opaque and ambiguous. The operators which run nuclear facilities often have years of training to before being allowed to supervise the algorithms running nuclear power plants.

We further define Volition as the degree to which an organisation willingly provides Visibility into their ADM practices to allow for Local and General Validation as another moderating factor. For example, some organizations such as Google and Uber restrict access to their algorithms as they regard them as a source of competitive advantage. This lack of volition therefore moderates the impact of Visibility and Validation on ADM Legitimacy.

Value is the level of importance assigned to the underlying system impacted by ADM and represents another moderating factor. For example, the ADM used in a chat bot to answer common call center queries regarding billing may be perceived to have less value than the ADM in a driverless car that is making regular decisions about a drivers physical safety. This factor provides a further moderator of the effect of transparency in ADM.

To examine the impact of transparency and legitimacy in further detail, we next elaborate on the concept of legitimacy as a multi-faceted phenomenon.

3.4 Organizational Legitimacy as a Concept

Legitimacy is commonly understood to be "a generalized perception or assumption that the actions of an entity are desirable, proper, or appropriate within some socially constructed system of norms, values, beliefs and definitions" [12]. Legitimacy Theory has been used in the context of corporate reporting around social and environmental issues [27]. Legitimacy Theory gives consideration to the expectations of various parts of society and the implicit social contract between an organisation, its actions within that social contract, and the society in which that organisation operates. As social norms change, so do societal expectations and organizations must adapt accordingly. As this adaptation process takes time, there will be a gap between organizational actions and practices and societal expectations. Organizations must seek to actively minimize this gap in order to be allowed to operate freely within society. Organizations can do this by changing their practices, influencing societal norms, values, and beliefs about those practices, or by the better communication and positioning of their practices within those societal norms, values and beliefs.

Organizations and individuals may choose not to work with other individuals or organizations due to a perceived lack of legitimacy associated with the organization as a whole, or with its practices, technologies, and products. Governments may undertake legislative action when the perceived gap between an organisation and societal expectations becomes too big and when organizational practices or technologies are perceived to be illegitimate. This was recently demonstrated when the European Union enacted legislation to reduce the use by organizations of ADM and give consumers a "right to explanation" to understand how the ADM in question has made a decision about them [10].

Legitimacy can take three broad forms: *Pragmatic Legitimacy,* which provides value to the organization's interested constituents (e.g., customers, shareholders and employees) and can be gained through organizational policy [28]; *Moral Legitimacy* which is developed from a positive normative evaluation of organizational practices by external stakeholders, and; *Cognitive Legitimacy* which is based on external stakeholders' understanding of organizational practices and which is neither self-interested nor evaluative in nature [29]. Cognitive Legitimacy occurs when an organisation pursues activities and goals which have become "taken for granted" by society.

To illustrate the three forms of legitimacy in the context of ADM, consider a bank which uses ADM for its home loan origination and approval process. *Pragmatic Legitimacy* might be achieved with a bank's shareholders when they see that the use of ADM in loan origination reduces administrative effort and operational costs, consequently improving profit and raising the stock price. *Moral Legitimacy* might be gained for the same loan origination process when it is clear to external stakeholders that the use of ADM does not unfairly disadvantage individuals from a specific background; for instance, that people's racial or religious backgrounds are not used to assess their eligibility for a loan. Finally, *Cognitive Legitimacy* may be achieved when stakeholders accept that the use of ADM in loan origination and approvals is common place with financial industry as a whole.

3.5   The Process of Technological Legitimation

Technological legitimation is the process of narrowing the legitimacy gap between an organization and its external stakeholders, specifically as it concerns technologies employed by the organization. Technological legitimation is described as a cumulative, non-linear process that moves through the stages of innovation, local validation, diffusion and general validation [25, 26].

In this process there is a technological innovation. Organisational actors attempt to link that new technology to existing organizational activities, hoping to passively validate that new technology and/or hoping that it does not get challenged [25]. Challenging of that technology may be on pragmatic, moral or cognitive grounds. If local validation is achieved then the new technology diffuses to other applications and contexts either within that organisation or to other organizations. Over the course of time as this diffusion of that technology continues it "increasingly interferes with more broadly shared normative, regulative and cognitive rules. The relevant audience is no longer restricted to an isolated project or community, but rather comprises the general public that assesses the legitimacy of both the technology and the 'industry' that emerges in the new field" [26]. In so doing the technology begins to go through a process of general societal legitimization. In order to continue to diffuse through organizations and eventually society the technology needs to have Moral Legitimacy before it is applied and it needs to achieve Pragmatic Legitimacy as part of each local validation process. As the technology diffuses it either is adapted to or adapts societal values through an ongoing process of normative re-evaluation. Once the application of the technology becomes broad based, society begins to take for granted the new innovation and Cognitive Legitimacy is achieved.

An useful illustration of the process of Technological Legitimation is found in the work of Binz, Harris-Lovett [26]. As a case study they analyze the practice of introducing purified wastewater into surface or underground drinking commonly known as Indirect Potable Reuse (IPR). Up until the year 2000 the practice of IPR was restricted due to public perceptions. Yet after 2010 many reports demonstrate a significant uptake of the technology [30]. What occurred in between was a series of activities to achieve IPR Legitimacy through increased diffusion, demonstrating that even highly undesirable technological practices of organizations can achieve Legitimacy.

3.6   The Complex Relationship Between Transparency and ADM Legitimacy

Summarizing the previous sections, we posit that ADM transparency impacts ADM legitimacy in a complex process that involves multiple components of both transparency and legitimacy, and that this process is moderated by several factors (Fig. 2):

Transparency is not the only factor which impacts legitimacy and transparency may or may not have impacts on other facets of an organisation (for example accountability). But for the purposes of this article, and due to space constraints, we focus on the interactions between transparency and legitimacy. We discuss these interactions in the subsequent section and make several propositions as to the nature of this relationship between ADM Transparency and ADM Legitimacy within this nomological structure.

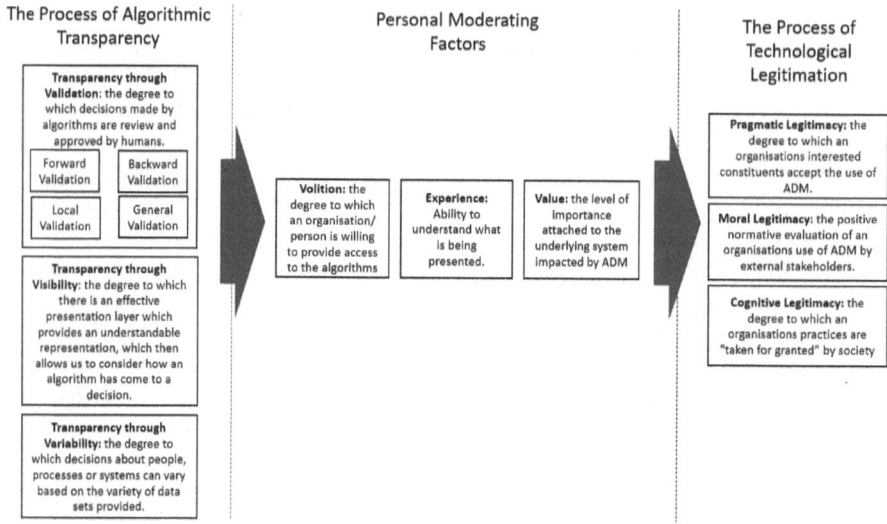

Fig. 2. Expanded nomological structure between transparency and legitimacy

4   Towards an Understanding of the Impact of ADM Transparency on ADM Legitimacy

After the previous discussions of ADM Transparency, Legitimacy, and Technological Legitimation we next make several propositions as to how ADM transparency affects the different forms of ADM legitimacy throughout the legitimation process. The purpose of these propositions is to lay the groundwork for further research into the impacts of ADM Transparency on ADM Legitimacy.

To begin, we look at the degree of ADM Validation. Reiterating that Validation has a temporal component (Forward Validation vs. Backward Validation) and scope of application component (Local Validation vs. General Validation) we consider the effects Validation may have on Pragmatic, Moral and Cognitive Legitimacy. As discussed in Binz, Harris-Lovett [26], organizational practice will gain local validation in a specific context. It will then diffuse to other similar contexts to eventually achieve general validation. In our view of ADM legitimization there is a temporal component to validation as well as the contextual component of validation already presented in the literature. We also see that the temporal and application aspects of validation can be combined together in various combinations. For example we further propose that...

Proposition 1: *An increase in the amount of Forward and Local Validation of an Algorithm will increase the Pragmatic Legitimacy of the algorithm.*

Referring back to the definition of Pragmatic Legitimacy as a phenomena involving an organizations immediate constituents, we perceive this form of legitimacy as a local phenomenon where validation will improve an ADMs perception of fitness for use but not necessarily its acceptance morally or cognitively. Further we propose that:

Proposition 2: *General Backward Validation of an application of ADM is required for Cognitive Legitimacy.*

… as the "taken for granted-ness" required for Cognitive Legitimacy requires actual application of the ADM in the specific context for Cognitive Legitimacy to attach. In line with the Technological Legitimization process described by Binz, Harris-Lovett [26] we view that…

Proposition 3: *Increased Local Validation of ADM in a greater variety of contexts will lead to increased General Validation of ADM across all forms of Legitimacy (Pragmatic, Moral and Cognitive).*

This leads to our next proposition regarding transparency in ADM and the impact of Visibility on Legitimacy:

Proposition 4: *An increase in Visibility will increase the Cognitive Legitimacy of the algorithm but not necessarily Moral Legitimacy or Pragmatic Legitimacy.*

We derive this view from the observation that greater visibility does not necessarily create moral acceptance and that the users of an expert system may lose trust in an expert system the more they understand it [20]. Further we present…

Proposition 5: *That the effect of Visibility on the Cognitive Legitimacy of ADM will be moderated by the degree of human experience with the system being modelled and managed algorithmically.*

… in that information does not bring understanding without a degree of expert knowledge [31].

In terms of the moderative effects of Volition and Value we view that…

Proposition 6: The Volition of an organisation to provide Transparency around ADM will be inversely proportional to the perceived Value assigned to the system the ADM is managing. Decreased Volition will decrease Visibility of the ADM which has an impact on all forms of legitimacy.

Clearly, even if an organisation is compelled by legislation to provide more transparency the way that transparency requirement is affected by the organisation moderate it's impact. Finally we present our last proposition which is that…

Proposition 7: *The degree of Variation present in an Algorithm will have an inverse effect on the Moral Legitimacy of the Algorithm.*

… in that the more significant the difference in how people are treated through the ADM process the higher the likelihood than Moral Legitimacy will be impacted.

As previously discussed, these seven propositions based on Transparency and Legitimacy Theory and the interplay between the two in an ADM context are intended to be used and tested in future research on ADM Legitimacy.

5 Affecting ADM Legitimacy Through Transparency: An Illustrative Example

As discussed in previous sections, we maintain that the issues with Algorithmic Decision Making relate not necessarily to the automation of the decision but rather to the degree to which the decision making process is *Transparent*. This *Transparency* has many characteristics including the degree to which the Algorithmic Decisions are *Validated* by Humans, the *Visibility* humans have of these decisions as they are made by these ADMs and the impact of the potential *Variation* in the decisions implemented by these algorithms which in turn impacts human perceptions of the Algorithms itself. By designing Algorithmic Decision Making Processes to address the issue of *Transparency* it is proposed that it may be possible to affect their perceived Legitimacy. We illustrate the use of the previously proposed framework with an example.

Recent concerns about how Uber's App algorithmically manages its drivers has received significant news coverage [32]. Concerns that have been expressed include how Uber sets the rates, performance targets and schedule. We apply the concepts of *Transparency* and *Legitimacy* in this case to illustrate the nomological structure we have constructed in this article.

First, the practices of rate setting and scheduling have already achieve *Cognitive Legitimacy* in that they are already take for granted in the ride-sharing industry. Other ride-sharing applications such as LYFT, GET, and JUNO use ADM in similar ways [33]. *Pragmatic Legitimacy* is demonstrated every time someone uses Uber accepts the quote for the ride sharing service. The ride sharing market was over $10 Billion USD in revenues in 2016 [34]. What is at question here is the *Moral Legitimacy* of the process. Is there a positive normative evaluation of Ubers practices by its drivers and by the general public that use Uber?

With regards to how Uber sets performance targets, those targets would likely be better received by its drivers if it was known that there was a level of *Validation* of the performance grading assigned to the drivers by human managers. Preferably this would be by *Foreword Validation* before the statistics were published, although *Backward Validation* would probably also have an impact. With regards to how Uber sets rates, it is reasonable to assume that perceived legitimacy would increase if the *Variation* in the rates and performance targets was reduced. With regards to the scheduling *Visibility* of both the surge pricing zones to the passengers as well as the drivers there would be less concerns about the process.

These Transparency processes are moderated by the *Experience* the Uber drivers and Uber ride users have with the Uber pricing and scheduling and would be impacted if the average *Value* for each ride remained small. In all cases the use of Algorithmic Decision Making is not precluded but the perceived Moral Legitimacy of the system on the part of its users is impacted. Overall Legitimacy and social acceptance of the ADM processes increases through transparency. Thus designing ADM processes with a view on transparency can have an impact on Legitimacy. As discussed previously, legitimacy theory tells us that organizations must always seek to minimize gap between an organizational actions and practices and societal expectations if for no other reason than to avoid government and market reaction. In this case it is clear the Uber needs to be more transparent with regards to its ADM practices in order to avoid further actions on the part of governments that are already actively seeking to address the disruption that Uber and other Ride Sharing applications have caused to the taxi industry.

6 Conclusions

Algorithmic Decision Making represents one path to increased benefits realization from Big Data and the Internet of Things. Algorithmic Decision Making can resolve many of the cognitive issues present in human decision making and takes advantage of the volume, velocity and variety of the Big Data presented by the IoT that human decision making cannot. But it has also been shown that a recent increase in the pervasiveness of Algorithmic Decision Making has led to several concerns which may limit its application. In some cases governments have already legislated against its use.

In reviewing the theory on Transparency and Legitimacy we build a series of propositions on how we believe Transparency impacts the different forms of Legitimacy in an ADM context. We posit that in some cases this effect will be to increase legitimacy but in other cases transparency may decrease legitimacy and that there are moderating factors which may affect this impact. We use an example to illustrate the interplay between transparency and algorithmic decision making and how business practices can be redesigned to improve ADM Legitimacy. We identify that ADM Transparency has many elements including the levels of Validation, Visibility and Variation. We reframe Transparency as a process as opposed to an end state. By unpacking the issues of transparency we create the foundations of a framework for understanding Algorithmic Technology Legitimization which can be used to analyze, redesign and thereby affect the acceptance and appropriation of ADM.

It is important to reiterate that the analysis presented is not intended to be a holistic or complete view of Algorithmic Decision Making Legitimacy. Rather it is intended to provide a key precursor for future research into this subject. The intention being to further refine and add to the theory through field research and the analysis of case studies where the level of transparency within an organisation has varied over time with corresponding changes in ADM appropriation due to improved levels of perceived ADM Legitimacy. In this way the described nomological structure for the impact of transparency on ADM Legitimacy could be further refined. This could then be further validated through empirical studies which track ADM adoption in specific industries, with specific use cases over time. Finally the interrelationship between legitimacy and technological acceptance could further be explored in subsequent works.

References

1. McAfee, A., Brynjolfsson, E., Davenport, T.H.: Big data: the management revolution. Harvard Bus. Rev. **90**(10), 60–68 (2012)
2. Reinsel, D., Gantz, J., Rydning, J.: Data Age 2025: The Evolution of Data to Life-Critical. IDC (2017)

3. Luchetti, D.: The Square Kilometer Arrary. Square Kilometer Array. http://www.ska.gov.au/Pages/default.aspx. Accessed 21 Dec 2017
4. Heudecker, N., Hare, J.: Survey Analysis: Big Data Investments Begin Tapering in 2016. Gartner Research (2016)
5. Tversky, A., Kahneman, D.: Judgment under uncertainty: heuristics and biases. Science **185** (4157), 1124–1131 (1974)
6. Todd, P., Benbasat, I.: The use of information in decision making: an experimental investigation of the impact of computer-based decision aids. Mis Q. **16**, 373–393 (1992)
7. Hill, K.: How target figured out a teen girl was pregnant before her father did. Forbes Mag. (2012). https://www.forbes.com/sites/kashmirhill/2012/02/16/how-target-figured-out-a-teen-girl-was-pregnant-before-her-father-did/#1999ad516668. Accessed 12 Dec 2017
8. O'Neil, C.: Weapons of Math Destruction: How Big Data Increases Inequality and Threatens Democracy. Broadway Books, New York (2017)
9. Pasquale, F.: The Black Box Society: The Secret Algorithms that Control Money and Information. Harvard University Press, Cambridge (2015)
10. Goodman, B., Flaxman, S.: European Union regulations on algorithmic decision-making and a "right to explanation". arXiv preprint arXiv:1606.08813 (2016)
11. Newell, S., Marabelli, M.: Strategic opportunities (and challenges) of algorithmic decision-making: a call for action on the long-term societal effects of 'datification'. J. Strateg. Inf. Syst. **24**(1), 3–14 (2015)
12. Suchman, M.C.: Managing legitimacy: strategic and institutional approaches. Acad. Manag. Rev. **20**(3), 571–610 (1995)
13. Goldkuhl, G.: Pragmatism vs interpretivism in qualitative information systems research. Eur. J. Inf. Syst. **21**(2), 135–146 (2012)
14. Cox, J. Ask the captain: how often is autopilot engaged? USA Today (2014). https://www.usatoday.com/story/travel/columnist/cox/2014/08/11/autopilot-control-takeoff-cruising-landing/13921511/. Accessed 28 Jan 2018
15. Kitchin, R.: Thinking critically about and researching algorithms. Inf. Commun. Soc. **20**(1), 14–29 (2017)
16. Barocas, S., Hood, S., Ziewitz, M.: Governing algorithms: a provocation piece (2013)
17. Albu, O.B., Flyverbom, M.: Organizational transparency: conceptualizations, conditions, and consequences. Bus. Soc. (2016). https://doi.org/10.1177/0007650316659851
18. Christensen, L.T., Cornelissen, J.: Organizational transparency as myth and metaphor. Eur. J. Soc. Theory **18**(2), 132–149 (2015)
19. Baudrillard, J.: Simulacra and simulations. In: Poster, M. (ed.) Jean Baudrillard: Selected Writings, pp. 166–184. Stanford University Press, Stanford (1988)
20. Tsoukas, H.: The tyranny of light: the temptations and the paradoxes of the information society. Futures **29**(9), 827–843 (1997)
21. Ananny, M., Crawford, K.: Seeing without knowing: limitations of the transparency ideal and its application to algorithmic accountability. New Media Soc. (2016). https://doi.org/10.1177/1461444816676645
22. Diakopoulos, N.: Accountability in algorithmic decision making. Commun. ACM **59**(2), 56–62 (2016)
23. Burrell, J.: How the machine 'thinks': understanding opacity in machine learning algorithms. Big Data Soc. **3**(1) (2016). https://doi.org/10.1177/2053951715622512
24. De Fine Licht, J.: Do we really want to know? The potentially negative effect of transparency in decision making on perceived legitimacy. Scand. Polit. Stud. **34**(3), 183–201 (2011)
25. Johnson, C., Dowd, T.J., Ridgeway, C.L.: Legitimacy as a social process. Annu. Rev. Sociol. **32**, 53–78 (2006)

26. Binz, C., et al.: The thorny road to technology legitimation—institutional work for potable water reuse in California. Technol. Forecast. Soc. Change **103**, 249 (2016)
27. Deegan, C.: Methodological Issues in Accounting Research: Theories, Methods and Issues (2006)
28. Dowling, J., Pfeffer, J.: Organizational legitimacy: social values and organizational behavior. Pac. Sociol. Rev. **18**(1), 122–136 (1975)
29. Aldrich, H.E., Fiol, C.M.: Fools rush in? The institutional context of industry creation. Acad. Manag. Rev. **19**(4), 645–670 (1994)
30. Schroeder, E., et al.: Direct potable reuse: benefits for public water supplies, agriculture, the environment and energy conservation. National Water Research Institute White Paper (2012)
31. Christensen, L.T., Cheney, G.: Peering into transparency: challenging ideals, proxies, and organizational practices. Commun. Theory **25**(1), 70–90 (2014)
32. Rosenblat, A.: The truth about how Uber's application manages drivers. Harvard Business Review (2016). https://hbr.org/2016/04/the-truth-about-how-ubers-app-manages-drivers. Accessed 21 Dec 2018
33. Coomes, K.: The Best Ridesharing Apps. Digital Trends (2018). https://www.digitaltrends.com/mobile/best-ride-sharing-apps/. Accessed 22 Aug 2018
34. Hensley, R., Padhi, A., Salazar, J.: Cracks in the ridesharing market and how to fill them. McKinsey Q. (2018). https://www.mckinsey.com/industries/automotive-and-assembly/our-insights/cracks-in-the-ridesharing-market-and-how-to-fill-them. Accessed 22 Aug 2018

Advancing to the Next Level: Caring for Evaluative Metrics Monsters in Academia and Healthcare

Iris Wallenburg[1] , Wolfgang Kaltenbrunner[2] ,
Björn Hammarfelt[3] , Sarah de Rijcke[2] , and Roland Bal[1(✉)]

[1] Erasmus School of Health Policy and Management,
Rotterdam, The Netherlands
{wallenburg, r.bal}@eshpm.eur.nl
[2] Centre for Science and Technology Studies, Leiden, The Netherlands
{w.kaltenbrunner, s.de.rijcke}@cwts.leidenuniv.nl
[3] Swedish School of Library and Information Science, Borås, Sweden
bjorn.hammarfelt@hb.se

Abstract. In this paper we use the notions of play and (finite and infinite) games to analyze performance management practices in professional work. Whilst evaluative metrics are often described as 'monsters' impacting on professional work, we illustrate how metrics can also become part of practices of caring for such work. Analyzing the use of evaluative metrics in law faculties and in hospitals, we show how finite games – games played to win – and infinite games – games played for the purpose of continuing to play – are intertwined and how this intertwinement affects academic and healthcare work.

Keywords: Gamification · Performance management · Universities
Health care

1 Introduction

Academic and healthcare life have increasingly metricized in the past two decades. Citation indexes, teaching quality assessment, research assessment, and league tables – and their underlying algorithms – have set a new scene for academic work and academic career development [1, 2]. Likewise, healthcare professionals face a myriad of different metrics, ranging from performance indicators for measuring and comparing quality of care, clinical registries to monitor patient outcomes and medical decision-making, and training quality evaluation, to instruments to measure patient values and establish cost effectiveness ratios for clinical treatment [3, 4].

A growing body of (STS) literature discusses how evaluative metrics transform professional work as they value certain worths over others, and shape what gets obscured, what gets highlighted and what is conceived of as good performance – thoroughly changing how organizations and individual practitioners shape their services and how they compete [5–9]. In academia, metrics like the h-index characterize and value the scientific output of the individual researcher, stressing the importance of

U. Schultze et al. (Eds.): IS&O 2018, IFIP AICT 543, pp. 80–95, 2018.
https://doi.org/10.1007/978-3-030-04091-8_7

individual excellence and drawing attention away from collective work [10]. Also, the focus on publishing in (highly rewarding) high-impact journals displaces the importance of books and edited volumes, particularly those in a non-English language [11]. Kelly and Burrows [1] have stated that "(…) the enactment of value and relative worth in academic work by formal processes of academic judgment, measurement and algorithmic resource allocation has become fundamental to survival" – indicating how performance metrics actively reshape academic fields and their (e)valuation infrastructures [e.g. 5, 12]. Such conclusions often reflect the (private) worries of scholars about the impact of performance metrics on both their beloved academic fields and their individual careers, especially concerning the epistemic changes that metrics make happen, valuing specific kinds of knowledge and specific types of research over others. Healthcare practitioners express similar concerns. They argue that the increasing emphasis on performance measurement and control [e.g. 3, 4, 13], causes paper work and 'red tape' [14] stealing away time from their real jobs – that is, curing and caring for patients. Hence, metrics change healthcare work through emphasizing measurable aspects of care over others.

Yet, professionals, scientists and physicians alike, are not just victims of performance management but have played an active part in their construction. Universities themselves have crafted the first university ranking and evaluative instruments to pin down academic performance, and they have continued to do so [e.g. 15]. Similarly, medical associations have played a crucial role in designing performance indicators and evaluative instruments for setting clinical norms for good care and comparing clinical outcomes. They closely collaborate with other stakeholders (e.g. healthcare authorities, third party payers, patient associations) in defining performance instruments and outcome measurements [16, 17]. Hence, while practitioners groan under evaluative pressures, they have similarly embraced evaluative metrics that (re)shape their work. In medicine, for instance, physicians actively adopt value-based healthcare instruments to design patient-centered treatment trajectories, simultaneously establishing new and ambitious research lines and hence prompting new career opportunities [18]. This seems to point at another direction than that usually taken by the literature on audit and accountability, and allows for a conceptualization of metrics in more open ways, considering how metrics are used and play out in unfolding professional worlds. Empirical findings suggest that evaluative metrics allow for more diverse and 'playful' ways of evaluating and assessing professionals [8, 19]. Online tools, for instance, may also liberate scholars as they can profile themselves and their research to a wider public (or, more strategically, to a specific public in case of for instance a grant application) through building an online research identity [20].

This double-sided view on evaluative metrics is the central concern of this paper: evaluative metrics are seen as monsters threatening the 'real work'. They would evoke practices of 'gaming' in which professionals seek to 'cheat' with numbers in order to cosmetically comply with them while actually continuing their own practices, as Bevan and Hood have strikingly pointed out as "hitting the target but missing the point" [21]. Yet, as we claim in this paper, evaluative metrics are also cared for, actively used and played with, prompting a more reflexive approach on performance – also among practitioners that can be quite cynical about them. So, what if we consider performance metrics as a matter of play, encompassing both matters of concern [22] and matters of care [23]?

In this paper, we apply an experimental and explorative view on evaluative metrics, asking: How do academic and healthcare professionals playfully employ evaluative metrics in constituting academic/care work and professional routines, as well as to the purpose of building a professional position? With what emerging consequences for professional identity construction?

2 Playing the Metrics Game

In *Homo Ludens*, Johan Huizinga portrays the human being as intrinsically playful, and positions 'play' as a serious and necessary form of social interaction and cultural development [24]. Play, Huizinga argues, is something common and contributes to human and cultural development through modulation of experience [25]. Playing is a medium where lived experience is organized as a structured situation. It is something outside 'normal' life; play is spatial-temporal as playing is bounded to a well-defined situation, comprising clear rules. Play, Huizinga contends, expands from early childhood to old age. It can be both fun and serious and may also encompass suffering. Huizinga situates play in children living their own phantasies at the playground, but also in religious (and sometimes cruel) rituals, in poetry, art, science, the law, and sports.

Although Huizinga demarcates play from ordinary life, at the same time he acknowledges that boundaries between playing and non-playing can be permeable. For example, people may play with one another over dinner slipping in and out of serious interaction throughout an entire evening [25]. Stressing the complexity of separating the two in contemporary times he states (written in 1938): "it [the civilization] plays false, so that it becomes increasingly difficult to tell where play ends, and non-play begins" (25: 206). The problem of distinguishing between play and non-play becomes evident when considering our ability to move in and out of a play and reflect upon it from the outside. The duality between being totally immersed in the game, while at the same time being able to reflect upon it from the outside ('it is just a game') is especially important when contemplating the ambiguity of describing activities as play [26].

Carse [27], in turn, distinguishes finite from infinite games. The finite game, like Huizinga's notion of play, is bounded and played for the purpose of winning. The infinite game, like life itself, is ongoing and is played for the purpose of continuing the play: "If the rules of the finite game are the contractual terms by which the players can agree who has won, the rules of the infinite game are the contractual terms by which the players agree to continue playing." (p.9) In the infinite game, playing is a way of interacting. Finite games are about the outcomes (training to win and obtaining prestigious titles), while infinite games are about surprises as these generate new possibilities to reconsider the world, revealing a new beginning "like the grammar of a living language" (p. 9). As Carse aptly states: "To be prepared against surprise (as in the finite game) is to be trained, to be prepared for surprise is to be educated." (p. 19) Whilst training regards the future to be finite (yielding a clear end result), "(e)ducation leads towards continuing self-discovery" (p. 19). In terms of our fields of concern, academia and healthcare, we are interested in how these finite and infinite games play a role in dealing with evaluative metrics: how evaluative metrics produce norms for 'good' academic and healthcare work and encourage scholars and practitioners (and their managers alike) to reach their goals by playing the finite game. The infinite game, then, would be about changing the grammar of academic and healthcare work; prompting new and embodied routines of doing research and providing care.

The separation of games from non-games, or Carse's distinction between finite games from infinite games, is crucial when discussing another aspect of our matters of play: gamification. In fact, the concept of gamification itself rests on this separation, with the application of game features in non-game contexts being a common trait [28]. Gamification aims to "transplant" some of the motivational qualities of games – especially points and scores, displaying performances and the desire to level up and win – into contexts that are not inherently leisure-focused or motivating in themselves [29, 30]. Raczkowski [29] discerns three features of games and gamification: (1) games as experimental techniques; (2) games as sources of flow; and (3) games as governed by points and high-scores. Games as experimental techniques refer to the more or less risk-free environment of a game in which certain tests but also training can be conducted in a less expensive way and without the fear of consequences beyond the game-world. Think for instance of a skills-lab in which a medical resident can practice a surgical procedure on a computer instead of a real patient [31]. Game as a source of flow addresses the ability of game features to transform daily routines in optimal (or optimizing) experiences by turning them into personal meaningful games. Lastly, games as governed by points and high-scores portrays the 'magical' aspect of gamification; the speaking to pleasure, convenience and personal entertainment [32]. Here, games simulate value through measurements that feed into circuits of reproduction, making performance visible and comparable, inserting an element of competition – typically through leaderboards. Pantzar and Shove [33] argue how such measurements feed into circuits of reproduction of everyday practice, linking micro-level performance to macro-level organization while simultaneously spanning past, present and future.

This quantified 'points and high-scores' feature of gamification is most elaborated on in the (STS) literature on gaming and the flourishing stream on personal analytics and self-tracking [20, 29, 34, 35]. Self-tracking has gained attention with the emergence of The Quantified Self movement [36]; people gathering quantitative data about themselves, using mobile apps and always-on gadgets, seeking to convert previously undetected bodily functions and behavioral clues (e.g. heartbeat, the number of steps taken) to traceable and perceptible information [34]. Self-tracking enables the making of "data doubles" [37]; ways of knowing and valuing the self in rather abstract and sliced ways, that can be reflected on and used for various purposes like self-optimization. Ruckenstein [38] points out how this theme of visibility – and, we like to add, 'invisibility', because by making some aspects visible, others are also (deliberately) ignored [38] – links personal analytics to modern notions of control and governmentality. With the aid of digital technology, optimization becomes not only possible but also desirable and an associated responsibility to act [39]. Through making unknown aspects of the body – or, in our case, professional performance – detectable and evaluable, we (or, for that matter, 'others') can gain more control over life or professional ways of doing and knowing, reconfiguring existing professional identities.

Gamification and self-quantification can also have liberating effects, revealing a more 'infinite' aspect of gamification. Digital platforms like ResearchGate allow scholars to constitute and 'better' their scholarly reputation [20], for example by putting a project on ResearchGate and downloading and liking papers of co-authors – who are then enticed to 'like' the other in return. Others have pointed out researchers' and particularly group leaders' abilities to renegotiate values attached to evaluative metrics, for instance through negotiating how a specific journal is valued in a certain academic field and how publication achievements count in career mobility decisions – showing how evaluative metrics themselves become renegotiated, worked around and used by professionals [19, 40] and are embedded in wider practices of valuation.

In public administration and sociology, 'gaming' has also come to notify the ways in which practitioners and organizations 'work around' performance evaluation. For example, Espeland and Sauder define gaming as "a more or less cynical effort to manipulate the ranking data without addressing the underlying condition that is the purpose of the measure. It's about managing appearances without really changing anything" [41]. Although we recognize that there might be cynical elements in playing evaluative games, we want to turn our attention to a type of play that is more generative in nature and is attuned to creating conditions for doing professional work. This is the reason why we link our notion of play to those of matters of concern (that is, the restaging of representative 'objects' as lively matters of interest that must be engaged with, [22]) and matters of care (the relating to objects or 'things' by affectively engaging with them and exploring their potential to affect others, [23]). That is, we see play as the serious matter of caring for and working with the things that are of concern through the use of numbering practices.

In this paper we use the notions of play, games and gamification – hence resembling in the notion 'matters of play'– as analytical lenses to study how evaluative metrics produce professional practices and how these practices of (e)valuation are reshaped in return through the playful actions of professionals. Matters of play, we will argue, are relational practices that encompass concerns for professional practice (i.e. academia and healthcare), and the caring work this implies. This involves the play of both finite and infinite games, revealing the dispersed work and distributed effects of valuation practices and how these affect professional identities.

3   Research Settings and Methods

This paper is part of an ongoing collaboration between two research groups, one situated in the field of academic evaluation and the other in healthcare, both intrigued by the politics of evaluative metrics and its influence on professional work [6, 35, 42]. We draw on separate research projects that we bring together for the purpose of our analytical questions. We do not so much compare clear or 'neat' results between both fields (i.e. their similarities and differences) but rather embrace the messiness and hence lack of clarity in both fields in their dealings with evaluative metrics, mobilizing insights from one field to elucidate and discuss findings in the other field, and the other way around [43].

In academia, we draw on a primarily interview-based research project in law faculties in the Netherlands, investigating how epistemic dynamics of scholarship are mediated through emerging evaluation schemes, in particular through the 'micropolitics' of indicator use [40]. In healthcare, we build on an ongoing research project in which we study how quantified evaluation practices (i.e. performance indicators, rankings) influence (the valuation of) medical and nursing work as well as healthcare organizations [4, 35].

4 Findings

4.1 Academia: Politics of Metrics and the Politics of a Discipline

In the past three decades, academic research has been increasingly governed through evaluative metrics; i.e. numbers of (international) publications and citations, position in university rankings, and obtained (international) research grants at the individual, group and institute level. Evaluative practices ('what counts?') impact the design of research programs, the establishment of endowed chairs, and the finance of research projects. Doing well in those aspects, as an institution or research group, but also as an individual scholar, is crucial to building a good academic reputation – and subsequently gaining more rewards. In this section we turn to legal scholarship in the Netherlands, scrutinizing how finite and infinite games are played in this particular academic field. Law is a salient example as substantial parts of legal scholarship are domestically oriented and projects often focus on policy or national legal issues that may not be immediately interesting for a wider academic audience. This tension is particularly prominent in the case of non-English speaking countries like the Netherlands, where it has given rise to a complex politics of valuing publications and other forms of 'output' in assessment contexts.

As part of a comprehensive national evaluation system across all fields of research, Dutch law departments are subjected to an assessment exercise in a regular interval of six years. While criteria of 'societal relevance' have recently been strengthened, evaluation modalities continue to place significant emphasis on the publication output of departments. This creates a particular challenge for the epistemic culture of law: English-language, journal-based publications are weighed against the tradition of writing books in the national language and having a more practical orientation. The mismatch between the value ascribed to international publications and a strong professional, domestic orientation of the field is often seen to require an explicit disciplinary strategy [44] – a need to react to evaluative expectations of funders and policy actors by making a particular "move" in a larger game, namely the competition for prestige and resources with other academic fields. However, we encountered very different opinions among legal scholars about what kind of move this should be. On the one hand, there are those who advocate a 'scientific turn' of legal scholarship, i.e. a research style that seeks to generate relevance not just by focusing on the national legal system, but through its methodologically and conceptually rigorous approach. Another position is to instead push for altering evaluative conventions in such a way as to confer greater appreciation for activities relevant to professional audiences – both on the level of the national evaluation exercise and the more implicit expectations of funding bodies towards publishing behavior.

These disciplinary arguments inter alia play out through a specific technical-administrative venue, namely diverging local practices of registering the collective departmental output that constitutes the basis for the regular evaluation exercises. In the course of the last years, all Dutch universities have adopted centralized digital information systems through which researchers are expected to register their publications and other activities. The different ways in which individual actors can access this information infrastructure affects their ability to enact professional routines as either finite or infinite games. To regular researchers, the need to register output often appears as an administrative chore that is squeezed into late working hours at the end of the month or semester. Seemingly mundane aspects such as user friendliness here directly affect the likelihood that certain activities are rendered visible. For example, when publications need to be manually entered rather than being automatically detected by the software – as is often the case for small-scale Dutch publication venues –, there is a chance that users simply forget to register them. Another aspect is that the use of a digital information system creates a certain barrier to what researchers consider 'worthy' of explicit registration in the first place. For many legal scholars, activities that would potentially qualify as societal engagement – such as public lectures, elective courses, consulting work for diverse public and private organizations – appear so naturally as part of their job profile that they often do not bother to register them in the first place.

On the other hand, a prominent role is reserved for the so-called program coordinators, i.e. scholars in group leader positions who are tasked with overseeing and signing off on the output data submitted by regular department members. Their administrative responsibility allows program coordinators to adopt a panoramic view on the totality of the activities of a research group. These collective activities here are much more easily perceived as a resource in an infinite, knowledge-political, game – should a group position itself as more societally relevant, as academically excellent, or in terms of some other specific institutional profile? A particular strategic opportunity for the program coordinators arises from the fuzzy distinction between academic and professional journals in the field of law. Often, it is unclear how to deal with particular publication genres (such as case annotations), and how to determine what audience(s) a journal is exactly catering to. Program coordinators promoting a 'scientific turn' tend to police the formal distinction between academic and professional journals particularly strictly, with the intention of 'disciplining' individual researchers to publish in rigorously reviewed, preferably international, outlets. The following quote describes a case where a program coordinator would reclassify publications submitted as 'academic output' by members of his department, but which in his opinion did not live up the criteria of rigorously peer-reviewed publications.

(...) when I joined this law faculty, legal scholarship here was more traditional than what I was used to [from working at another university]. ... lots of annotations, lots of professional publications, resistance against a real scientific turn in our field. And I really had a lot of discussions about this. Specifically, the cause of the conflict was – and this used to happen a lot more in 2008 and 2009 than now, because now the hygiene has improved in this respect – so the conflict played out like this: I took them out [i.e. removed publications of program members from the list of peer-reviewed output] only for them to go upstairs to the fourth floor, where the administration was, and to say 'no, this has to be reversed, I'm telling you, I want to see this reversed'. So things were reversed behind my back! But I always had the last laugh, because whenever the reports for the evaluation committee had to be prepared, I took them out again, even though I had to do double work. (Professor of administrative law, 21 April 2015).

Other program coordinators instead adopt the position that too strict a focus on purely academic audiences threatens to disrupt the current embedding of scholarly work carried out at university departments to the domestic legal system, thus undermining a key function of the field in Dutch society. They tend to see the very fuzziness of the boundary between professional and academic publications as a virtue, as something that enables academics to be useful to diverse stakeholders across academia and legal practice. This position is nicely illustrated in the following quote by one of the program coordinators we interviewed. When it comes to double-checking whether publications of his research group are correctly classified as either scholarly or professional, this researcher generally adopts a laissez-faire approach. His reasoning is that a strict enforcement of the distinction is problematic and undesirable, given the heterogeneity of different intellectual approaches in legal scholarship. The only respect in which he makes proactive use of his administrative power is the way program members register professional output. He actively encourages members of his research program to highlight as many of their nonacademic activities as possible, thereby attempting to alter the hierarchy of value ascribed to different types of output.

My problem with the Metis-lists [the online information system used for registering output] is that people do not register a lot of validation activities. They have always registered their publications, but not their contract work. Not the 20 times per year that they teach a course. They also don't register it when they present a paper in a congress or participate in an expert meeting. In my own case, 10 out of 100 items are publications. 90 are other things that can be registered through Metis and that should be in there, if you want to show the relevance of your work. (Professor of private law, 05 May 2015).

The above examples show how finite and infinite games are intertwined. On the one hand, the need to produce publications in particular types of outlets constitutes a finite game from the perspective of individual researchers, with implications for their career development in institutions and the competition for funding. Program coordinators leverage these finite games in diverse ways in their attempts to make a move in a larger, infinite game, namely the perpetual struggle between different intellectual positions in the disciplinary research culture of law. In turn, these higher-level moves have implications for the perception of the field by funders and policy-makers.

Counting as Caring for the Group

However, not all program coordinators use their specific administrative power with the intention of making a particular strategic move in the larger debate about the orientation of legal scholarship in the Netherlands. Instead, some of them simply opt to continue playing the evaluation game in its current form, but in such a way as to try and maximize their success in both evaluation and the acquisition of funds. For example, many law departments are particularly dependent on income from contract work, including public bodies such as national ministries and institutions of the European Union. Such work often puts significant strain on researchers to combine commercial activity necessary to maintain their institutional revenue streams with research proper. A particular complicating factor are contractual obligations that frequently prevent reusing empirical material generated for commissioned projects as a basis for publishing academic articles. One of the program leaders described a particular way of quantifying output that makes it easier for his researchers to reconcile the twin mission of conducting both 'excellent' academic research and contract work. More specifically, he is inclined to count particularly thorough pieces of contract work as scholarly output, even though they would formally have to be classified as professional:

> The reason why I reclassify more than others in this department within this university, or within this law school, is that the research groups like we are, have a much higher financial target, because we do less education (…). So, two thirds of the budget I need to earn outside (…). We do a lot of work also for the European Union. And that also is published in books or in articles, but sometimes in reports. And I think it's unfair if I say, this report is just as scholarly as this book, but I cannot calculate it because it has not been published in a book or because the Commission prohibits to publish again. Then I cannot give credits to something that is a research project of two years with the exactly the same work as if it was not externally funded. So, then I give credits for those outputs. (Professor of international law, 30 June 2015).

Classifying research output and subsequently counting their worth here is part of the caring craft work [45] that group leaders conduct to enable their research groups to flourish in the academic world. Group leaders like the professor quoted above seek to mold their research context and make it fit into the evaluative metrics system. This can be seen as a finite game: the game is strategically prepared and played in such a way as to make financially attractive yet unpublishable research count nevertheless. But while such practices are not meant as a stance in the broader debate about a 'scientific turn', they nevertheless have subtle implications for the disciplinary research of law. Through making it easier to reconcile principally different types of activity – contract work for legal stakeholders and academic research proper –, the 'grammar' of law research at particular departments is being shaped in the context of longer-term research and societal goals. Again, infinite games thus comprise finite ones – being relevant to societal actors in the Netherlands or an EU level entails stretching the rules of the finite game.

4.2   Healthcare: Finite and Infinite Games to Sparking Good Care and Clinical Reputations

Caring for Reputation

Also in healthcare, evaluative metrics have gained great importance in recent years. Performance indicators, like the number of pressure ulcers on a nursing ward, the percentage of readmissions after hip surgery and the measures on pain scores among oncology patients (to name a few), are increasingly considered important instruments to assess (and compare) quality of care. In the Netherlands, performance indicators are used among a wide variety of healthcare actors (insurers, regulatory authorities, patient organizations, professional associations) to define and improve quality of care. Health insurers, for example, use performance indicators to contract preferred providers – for instance those hospitals that meet the quality requirements of the breast cancer associations (amongst others, percentage of remaining cancer tissue after surgical treatment, presence of a specialized nurse, waiting time – also illustrating the diverse range of quality aspects that are assembled in the indicators). Furthermore, based on the scores on performance indicators, league tables are composed displaying the best hospitals. Such league tables are widely discussed, both in the media and among healthcare providers. And although practitioners and managers alike are highly ambivalent towards the hospital rankings – as one hospital manager exclaimed: "the one year you can be on top, and the next you may drop to a much lower level without actually changing your care policies" –, it has also enabled healthcare managers to come to grips with governing care provision, moving it out of the direct control of the medical profession [4]. The displaying of quality of care, and with that the hospital's reputation, has turned (measured) health care quality into a shared concern and strategy:

> Managers and doctors are hotly discussing whether lowering the age from 70 to 60 [for screening on delirium] makes sense, and whether screening for delirium is a useful indicator [with regard to investment and return for patient safety] after all. The executive ends the discussion and argues: "We have to put a stop to the discussion. We lose out in important points in the [ranking] due to the delirium case. This simply has to happen." (Observation, Hospital C management team, November 15, 2012).

This 'has to happen' argument has become more common in medical practice; evaluative metrics have changed the rules of the game, rendering healthcare managers, insurers and government authorities more central players [4]. Indicators enable hospitals to gain a good reputation (being seen as an 'outstanding hospital') and through that gain rewards, for instance by being appointed as a preferred provider. Furthermore, a good (quality) reputation has a liberating effect as having good scores and obtaining a high-ranking position provides confidence to regulatory authorities (i.e. the inspectorate, health insurers) that hospital executives and clinicians are in control of healthcare quality, leaving them with more room for maneuver – and thus less external control. Such hospitals are also inclined to attract high-qualified practitioners; being a preferred provider or obtaining a prestigious quality certificate or research license attracts ambitious physician and nurses. Hence, the finite game of obtaining a high ranked position yields infinite elements as well, as the use of evaluative metrics transforms the grammar of hospital governance; good quality becomes a shared game.

Bending Indicator Thinking

Hospitals have installed dashboards to monitor the scores on performance indicators and compare nursing wards on their achievements (e.g. to what extent they comply with the protocol to measure and jot down the score on fall risk among elderly patients three times a day). During our observations, we noticed hospitals executives carrying around print-outs of the dashboard scores when visiting clinical groups and nurse managers 'to insist on the importance of indicator use'. Furthermore, we observed a staff meeting of quality managers discussing how they could best visualize the scores on performance indicators (translating scores into diagrams and flow charts) in order to induce an element of competition between wards to encourage them to do (that is, score) better. As one of the informants explained:

> It is demotivating if wards remain in the red area [representing the lower scores] for longer periods of time. In the new reports, we don't make it all red and orange but focus on the green; how you can work towards the green zone. This is the first month we do it like this, and now we wonder: does this motivate them enough? Because now people may no longer notice they are actually in the red zone. So maybe we will add an orange area again. (Hospital quality staff, 19 September 2016).

This excerpt reveals the 'points and high-scores' feature of gamification; installing elements of competition in order to 'do better' (fulfilling the indicator requirements). It also shows the messy reality of indicators and the tinkering involved in making sense of indicator scores; for staff quality indicators have become strategic attempts to standardize professional work. Professionals, however, may ignore or work around these quality policies. One of the nursing ward managers was quite skeptical about indicator use. He demonstrated the dashboard of his ward on the computer screen to us, showing how he could 'real time' monitor whether the nurses conducted the measurements according to the protocol. Yet, to him it was only important that the nurses conducted those measurement that mattered to the clinical and social condition of the patient, and that they did not waste their time on what he thought were bureaucratic activities:

> I want them to use their clinical gaze; what are the risks their patients face? If a patient runs the risk of getting a delirium, I want them to measure their patients three times a day [using the delirium score list], no doubt. And if they don't do these measurement, I'll let them know. But if a patient walks around without showing any signs of pain, it's ridiculous to do the pain scores. I will fill them out for them. (Nurse ward manager, 15 November 2017).

This nurse ward manager played the indicator game by embracing the indicators that help to improve care ('signaling an emerging delirium in order to take preventive measures in time') while only cosmetically complying with those that he thought to be redundant as they do not contribute to the quality of caring work; the manager thought up (and registered) those scores himself in order to not fall behind in overall scores and end up low on the hospital's internal (and, in the end, national) ranking. Whilst the quality manager, expectantly, was quite cynical about this manager 'ignoring' important quality improvement work, an anesthesiologist involved in fabricating the national pain indicator reacted with a smile when sharing our anecdote: "They at least consider the possibility of pain, that is much more important than actually doing the score; you have to really think about it." (anesthesiologist, 5 October 2017)

Mobilizing Care Improvement

The micropolitics of indicator-use [40] further play out in mobilizing (new) care routines. Indicators actively produce care practices as they set the norm for 'good care'. The Dutch Healthcare Inspectorate plays a central role herein. It employs indicators as strategic instruments to evoke other ways of organizing care. A striking example is the norm of involving a geriatric physician in the treatment of patients suffering from hip fracture:

> It took us years to get this done...and we're still underway. Hip fracture was one of our first indicators and has changed over the years. We became increasingly aware that hip fracture primarily is a social problem. It is not so much about fixing a fracture, that's easy, but about the social problems frail elderly experience at home. This should be taken care of. So, we mobilized

the geriatric physicians. They were a bit hesitant to play a bigger role [in the treatment of hip fracture], but we managed to move them into a central position. Now they are part of the [indicator's] definition. [Interview inspector, 7 March 2018].

This excerpt demonstrates how the inspectorate has played a strategic game by moving the geriatric physician in a central caring role in case of hip fracture. Through rendering the geriatric physician part of the indicator definition, the involvement (and, in some cases, employment) of a geriatric physician was set as a norm for good hospital care. This example reveals the infinite game that is played to improving care. The old hip fracture indicator is reframed to adjust vested hospital practices to the increasing problem of a growing group of elderly patients admitted to the hospital because of urgent clinical problems that actually mirror troubled situations at home where elderly people suffer from loneliness and lack of care. Through adjusting the hip fracture indicator, positioning it as a finite game (hospitals compete on scoring levels for high scores on the Inspectorate's indicators) the inspectorate sought to mobilize social care for elderly patients in the hospital and, through that, at home. This playing hence comprises recognition and anticipation of the performative effects of the new practices that come with metrics – rendering them a matter of concern and care.

5 Discussion

Evaluative metrics have entered academia and healthcare as metering and disciplining techniques to improving and accounting for professional performance, entering a point in which they are increasingly considered 'necessary for survival' – turning into an evaluative monster that begs for attention and ever more data, scores, benchmarks and resources. As Latour [46] remarks, however, the monster of Frankenstein only became a monster after it was left on its own by its creator. In similar fashion, todays 'metric monsters' are not monstrous from birth, and subsequently their 'evil' is not in their design, but in how they come to be used and cared for – or not. In fact, many professionals in health care and academia do try to find a way of living with their monsters, and caring for them becomes an integral part of the daily work – also, or maybe particularly because, they can be beneficial to them. This form of care can consist in putting the metric monster to work when needed (when a patient is in risk of delirium), and playfully resisting (rather than ignoring) it when its services are unwarranted. As we know, monsters have great strength, and when used strategically – as with the example of the hip fracture indicator – metrics can, when cared for, be utilized to change established practices which would be hard to transform without the magical power of indicators and scoreboards.

The analytical distinction between finite and infinite games has allowed us to open up the ways evaluative metrics are enacted in daily professional practice, but also to understand how particular metrics are often leveraged in conflictual dynamics. A key point here is the reflexivity that underpins the use of metrics. Actors not only 'do' measurements but also reconsider and negotiate them, using metrics to reach particular goals but also playfully ignoring them when they are not considered useful. As a finite game, individuals will often see metrics as a force set in motion by remote superiors or a faceless policy apparatus – something that must be obeyed and can only be made beneficial by using it for one's own purposes (e.g. building up a scholarly CV according to metrics criteria). In finite games, professional practices in academia and healthcare become contests that have winners and losers, stimulate game players to live up to the rules of the game, and at the same time change epistemic and caring work by reframing them in the language of evaluative metrics uses. In the infinite game, however, evaluative metrics do not so much appear as an obtuse monolithic force, but rather are leveraged in a reflexive manner – think about the pain indicator forcing clinicians to at least consider the possibility of pain when treating a patient; or, turning to the academic context, categorizing scientific output in certain ways to allow for different relations between academic and practical work. Infinite games are played not to follow rules, but for continuing the game itself. In doing so, they create new possibilities and vocabularies for professional work. The very effects of such moves (e.g. a new practice of counting of publications) may in turn however be perceived as monstrous by others – elucidating how finite and infinite games in practice play together, as well as create tensions.

This leaves us with some compelling concerns, hopes, and desires for further research. For one, while playing together may at first sound peaceful, Huizinga actually reminds us that playing can involve cruel behavior and suffering as well. Tensions may arise not only when players compete with each other in well-defined finite games, but also when the more strategic, infinite, games restructure practices in unforeseen ways. Think for example of a situation where researchers embrace a form of evaluation that may be useful to themselves or their institution in the short run, but that also creates more undesirable longer-term consequences for their field as it heightens (publication, administration) expectations for all. A problem here is that the reflexivity that under-pins particular attempts to strategically leverage evaluation practices is always boun-ded. Individual actors may act in ways they believe are in the best interest of their professional group or field, but in reality, the effects of their moves may cause unpredictable reactions and counter-moves by other players.

A simultaneously analytical and political problem – to be pursued in further work – is that strategic agency in evaluation games is usually unequally distributed. Some actors thus are more capable of making moves in infinite games, whereas others are primarily stuck in reactive positions [8]. For example, nurses may experience more pressure to fulfill scoring requirements than doctors who are in a better (i.e. more powerful) position to legitimately question evaluative metrics or bend metric rules in ways that allow them to pursue their professional goals. Similarly, researchers in important administrative positions at universities are clearly more powerful to locally interpret evaluative practices than their colleagues. A comparable dynamic is likely to play out on an institutional level. Elite universities are more likely to shape evaluative conventions (either by proposing their own research practices as an evaluative model, or by refusing to follow the "latest trend" in research and evaluation), whereas less well-reputed universities are more dependent on short-term approval and funding by policy [47]. As Espeland and Saude [7: 188f] argue, powerful actors have greater possibility to make use of inherent ambiguities involved in evaluation and measure-ment, and thus 'change the rules of the game'.

We also have hopes, however, that tie into our research ideas. Play, games and gamification are useful concepts that point out the reflexivity and relational aspects of evaluative metrics. Metrics not only enforce particular forms of accountability, but also render visible new and experimental forms of performance governance. Recognition of those performative effects of metrics also turns them into matters of concern, care – and play.

References

1. Kelly, A., Burrows, R.: Measuring the value of sociology? Some notes on performative metricization in the contemporary academy. Sociol. Rev. **59**(2), 130–150 (2012)
2. Rushforth, A.D., de Rijcke, S.: Accounting for impact? The journal impact factor and the making of biomedical research in the Netherlands. Minerva **53**(2), 117–139 (2015)
3. Essén, A., Sauder, M.: The evolution of weak standards: the case of the Swedish rheumatology quality registry. Sociol. Health Illn. **39**(4), 513–531 (2016)
4. Wallenburg, I., Quartz, J., Bal, R.: Making hospitals governable: performativity and institutional work in ranking practices. Adm. Soc. (2016). https://doi.org/10.1177/0095399716680054
5. Burrows, R.: Living with the h-index? Metric assemblages in the contemporary academy. Sociol. Rev. **60**(2), 355–372 (2012)
6. de Rijcke, S., et al.: Comparing comparisons. On rankings and accounting in hospitals and universities. In: Press, M. (ed.) Practising Comparison: Logics, Relations, Collaborations, Mattering Press, Manchester, pp. 251–280 (2016)
7. Espeland, W.N., Sauder, M.: Rankings and reactivity: how public measures recreate social worlds. Am. J. Sociol. **113**(1), 1–40 (2007)
8. Fochler, M., de Rijcke, S.: Implicated in the indicator game? An experimental debate. Engag. Sci. Technol. Soc. **3**, 21–40 (2017)
9. Hazelkorn, E.: Rankings and the Reshaping of Higher Education: the Battle for World-Class Excellence. Palgrave Macmillan Publishers, Basingstoke (2011)
10. Fochler, M., Felt, U., Müller, R.: Unsustainable growth, hyper-competition, and worth in life science research: narrowing evaluative research repertoires in doctoral and postdoctoral scientists' work and lives. Minerva **54**, 175–200 (2016)
11. Hammarfelt, B., de Rijcke, S.: Accountability in context: effects of research evaluation systems on publication practices, disciplinary norms, and individual working routines in the faculty of Arts at Uppsala University. Research Evaluation, pp. 1–15 (2014)
12. Müller, R.: Crafting a career in STS: meaning making, assessment, and interdisciplinary engagement. Engag. Sci. Technol. Soc. **3**, 84–91 (2017)
13. Levay, C., Waks, C.: Professions and the pursuit of transparency in healthcare: two cases of soft autonomy. Organ. Stud. **30**(5), 509–527 (2009)
14. Bozeman, B., Anderson, D.M.: Public policy and the origins of bureaucratic red tape: implications of the Stanford yacht scandal. Adm. Soc. **48**(6), 736–759 (2016)
15. Hammarfelt, B., de Rijcke, S., Wouters, P.: From eminent men to excellent universities: university rankings as calculative devices. Minerva **45**, 391–411 (2017)
16. Wallenburg, I., et al.: Onderzoek naar risicoselectie met de basisset kwaliteitsindicatoren ziekenhuizen: op weg naar verantwoorde keuzes. Amsterdam Public Health, Amsterdam (2018)
17. Berg, M., et al.: Feasibility first: developing public performance indicators on patient safety and clinical effectiveness for Dutch hospitals. Health Policy **75**, 59–73 (2005)
18. Bonde, M., Bossen, C., Danholt, P.: Translating value-based healthcare: an experiment into healthcare governance and dialogical accountability. Sociol. Health Illn. **40**(7), 1111–1274 (2018)

19. Bal, R.: Playing the indicator game: reflections on strategies to position an STS group in a multi-disciplinary environment. Engag. Sci. Technol. Soc. **3**, 41–52 (2017)
20. Hammarfelt, B., Rushforth, A.D., de Rijcke, S.: Quantified academic selves. The gamification of research through social networking services. Res. Inf. **21**(2) (2016)
21. Bevan, G., Hood, C.: What's measured is what matters: targets and gaming in the English public health care system. Public Adm. **84**(3), 517–538 (2006)
22. Latour, B.: Why has critique run out of steam? From matters of fact to matters of concern. Crit. Inq. **30**(2), 225–248 (2004)
23. Puig de la Bellacasa, M.: Matters of care in technoscience: assembling neglected things. Soc. Stud. Sci. **41**(1), 85–106 (2011)
24. Huizinga, J.: Homo Ludens: A Study of the Play Element in Culture. Beacon Press, Boston (1955)
25. Rodriguez, H.: The playful and the serious: an approximation to Huizinga's Homo Ludens. Game Stud. 6(1) (2006)
26. Raessens, J.: Making points the point: towards a history of ideas of gamification. In: Fuchs, M., et al. (eds.) Rethinking Gamification. Meson Press, Lüneburg (2014)
27. Carse, J.P.: Finite and Infinite Games: a Vision of Life as Play and Possibility. The Free Press, New York (1986)
28. Raczkowski, F.: Making points the point: towards a history of ideas of gamification. In: Fuchs, M., et al. (eds.) Rethinking Gamification, pp. 141–160. Meson Press, Lüneburg (2014)
29. Ruckenstein, M., Pantzar, M.: Datafied life: techno-antropolgy as a site for exploration and experimentation. Techné: Res. Philos. Technol. **19**(2), 193–212 (2015)
30. Deterding, S., et al.: Designing gamification: creating gameful and playful experiences. In: CHI 2013: Changing Perspectives, Paris, France (2013)
31. Johnson, E.S.: Out of my viewfinder, yet in the picture: seeing the hospital in medical simulations. Sci. Technol. Hum. Values **33**, 53–76 (2008)
32. Whitson, J.: Gaming the quantified self. Surveill. Soc. **11**(1/2), 163–176 (2013)
33. Pantzar, M., Shove, E.: Metering everyday life. In: 17th Annual SASE Meeting, Budapest (2005)
34. Lupton, D.: The Quantified Self: A Sociology of Self-tracking. Polity, Cambridge (2016)
35. Wallenburg, I., Bal, R.: The gaming doctor/nurse: how practices of datafication and gamification 'redo' care. Health Inform. J. (2018). https://doi.org/10.1177/1460458218796608
36. Wolf, G.: The data-driven life. In: The New York Times Magazine (2010)
37. Ruckenstein, M.: Visualized and interacted life: personal analytics and engagements with data doubles. Societies 4(1), 68–84 (2014)
38. Pinto, M.F.: Tensions in the agnotology: normativity in the studies of commercially driven ignorance. Soc. Stud. Sci. **45**(2), 294–315 (2015)
39. Viseu, A., Suchman, L.: Wearable augmentations: imaginaries of the informed body. In: Technologized Images, Technologized Bodies: Anthropological Approaches to New Politics of Vision. Berghahn Books, Oxford, New York (2010)
40. Kaltenbrunner, W., de Rijcke, S.: Quantifying 'output' for evaluation: administrative knowledge politics and changing epistemic cultures in Dutch law faculties. Sci. Public Policy **44**(2), 284–293 (2016)
41. Espeland, W.M., Sauder, M.: Engines of Anxiety: Academic Rankings, Reputation, and Accountability. Russel Sage Foundation, New York (2016)
42. Hammarfelt, B., et al.: Advancing to the next level: the quantified self and the gamification of academic research through social networks (2017)

43. Deville, J., Guggenheim, M., Hrdličková, Z. (eds.): Practising Comparison: Logics, Relations, Collaborations. Mattering Press, Manchester (2016)
44. Stolker, C.: Legal journals: in pursuit of a more scientific approach. Eur. J. Legal Educ. **2**, 77–94 (2005)
45. Davies, S.R., Horst, M.: Crafting the group: care in research management. Soc. Stud. Sci. **45** (3), 371–393 (2015)
46. Latour, B.: Love your monsters: why we must care for our technologies as we do for our children. Breakthrough J. **2**, 21–28 (2012)
47. Paradeise, C., Thoenig, J.C.: Academic institutions in search of quality: local orders and global standards. Organ. Stud. **34**(2), 189–218 (2013)

Hotspots and Blind Spots

A Case of Predictive Policing in Practice

Lauren Waardenburg[(⊠)], Anastasia Sergeeva, and Marleen Huysman

School of Business and Economics, Vrije Universiteit Amsterdam,
Amsterdam, The Netherlands
{l.waardenburg, a.sergeeva, m.h.huysman}@vu.nl

Abstract. This paper reports on an ethnographic study of the use of analytics in police work. We find that the introduction of predictive policing was followed by the emergence of the new occupational role of "intelligence officer". While intelligence officers were initially intended to merely support police officers by making sense of algorithmic outputs, they became increasingly influential in steering police action based on their judgments. Paradoxically, despite the largely subjective nature of intelligence officers' recommendations, police officers started to increasingly believe in the superiority and objectivity of algorithmic decision-making. Our work contributes to the literature on occupational change and technology by highlighting how analytics can occasion the emergence of intermediary occupational roles. We argue that amidst critical debates on subjectivity of analytics, more attention should be paid to intermediaries – those who are in-between designers and users – who may exert the most consequential influence on analytics outcomes by further black-boxing the inherent inclusion of human expertise in analytics.

Keywords: Analytics · Algorithms · Predictive policing · Occupational change
Future of work · Data-driven work

1   Introduction

Many activities of individuals' everyday lives can now be captured, quantified, and processed into data. As a result, organizations increasingly engage with analytics technology – the combination of practices, skills, techniques, and technologies to develop actionable insights from data [12] – to make work more effective, efficient, and objective [18, 19].

In response to this so-called "data-revolution", a growing scholarship voices critical questions regarding the nature and consequences of analytics [11, 14, 17, 21, 25, 28, 29, 31]. These scholars point out that, due to the complex and inherently subjective nature, introducing analytics is likely to have a significant impact on work. Consequently, they call for scrutinizing the consequences of analytics for work, relations and occupations [15, 23]. Responding to these repeated calls, we provide an empirical case of how analytics occasions occupational transformation.

We report on an ongoing ethnographic study (currently spanning 23 months) at the Dutch Police, following how the police develops and uses predictive analytics. In the

U. Schultze et al. (Eds.): IS&O 2018, IFIP AICT 543, pp. 96–109, 2018.
https://doi.org/10.1007/978-3-030-04091-8_8

police, predictive analytics is referred to as "predictive policing" – the use of analytics to predict, for example, where and when crime is likely to occur [27]. It was introduced in the Dutch police in 2013 and is currently used across nearly all 168 police stations in the Netherlands. The general aim of using predictive policing is to facilitate a change in the nature of police work towards more data-driven and efficient policing and in such a way to prevent crime from happening.

The findings of our study indicate that the shift towards predictive policing was followed by the emergence of a novel occupational role – "intelligence officers". Initially, intelligence officers were intended to support police officers in the use of predictive policing technology, by helping them to make sense of algorithmic outputs. However, by investing a lot of expertise into interpreting and translating algorithms and the outputs, intelligence officers became increasingly influential and started to steer police action. As a consequence, the practices of intelligence officers came to paradoxically reinforce police officers' belief in the superiority of algorithmic decisions over human expertise. We conclude by reflecting on the implications of our findings for the literature on occupational change in the age of analytics and artificial intelligence.

2   Theoretical Background

2.1   Criticisms on the Nature of Analytics

In response to a so-called "data revolution" in organizations of all sorts, critical questions start to be raised about the problematic nature and consequences of analytics [9, 11, 14, 17, 21, 28, 31]. One recurrent critical argument is that the *input data* is subjective, because categorization is a product of human judgment [1, 6, 14, 22]. For example, Ribes and Jackson [29] propose that it is impossible to separate data from data-making practices that instill data with decisions, judgments, and values dictating what is taken into account and what is not. Pine and Liboiron [28] argue that data is not neutral but politically influenced. Similarly, Gitelman [17] cautions that: "The imagination of data is in some measure always an act of classification, of lumping and splitting, nesting and ranking" [15, p. 8].

A related argument is that the *output of analytics* is black-boxed [21, 25]. It is generally assumed that, due to the large amount of data, analytics is not about the "why" (causation) since indicating the "what" (correlation) is enough [18]. Newell and Marabelli [21] question the societal impacts of this kind of knowledge production and reflect on what it means when it is sufficient that an algorithm produces accurate predictions, even when little is known about what led to these predictions.

Moreover, *algorithmic logics* are considered often too complex to be fully understood by humans, thus triggering questions about the implications of such algorithmic complexity. For example, in a recent conceptualization of so-called "learning algorithms" Faraj et al. [15] reflect on the black-boxed nature of analytics technology itself (instead of merely its output). Although algorithms always include design choices – for example, the designer's values, beliefs and ethical standards – these often cannot be straightforwardly understood by human actors [13, 15]. While an algorithm can be constructed in such a way that it might have hidden political consequences, such as including and excluding certain groups of people, the danger is that design choices will likely remain hidden or can only be understood by a few, highly specialized professionals [15].

Managing this complex, black-boxed nature of analytics therefore requires human interpretation [14]. But scholars also highlight that the process of *interpretation* necessitates careful attention, as it is contingent on cultural and organizational conditions. For example, Schultze [30] demonstrates how interpretations of information made by three occupational groups (system administrators, intelligence analysts, and librarians) were shaped by their struggles over the legitimacy of their organizational position. Striving to show how the individual occupations added value to the collective process of knowledge production, the separate actors engaged in expressing, monitoring, and translating information. These three informing practices consequently showed that the interpretation of information is not independent and objective but can be driven by status struggles of individual occupational groups vis-a-vis each other and the organization.

Introducing such a complex and subjective technology is thus likely to prompt changes in work, relations, and occupations [15]. A relevant question that emerges is how the use of analytics influences occupational work.

2.2 Analytics and Occupational Change

Previous research on occupational change due to technology use generally identifies two possible scenarios for the transformation of work and occupational expertise. One scenario involves an occupation transforming the expertise that is key to its existence, thereby significantly reconfiguring its identity and nature of work [4, 10, 20, 24, 32]. An early account is provided by Zuboff [32], who described how the occupation of pulp workers, faced with the introduction of information technology into the factory, had to shift their skills from action-centered to "abstract" and "intellective". Pulp workers traditionally relied on direct sensing of materials, for example, defining the quality of pulp by its look and feel. In the new situation they had to learn how to judge the quality of materials from a distance, relying on computerized signs and symbols and using abstract thinking and procedural reasoning. Similarly, Nelson and Irwin [20] explain how the occupation of librarians, faced with the development of Internet search, had to completely redefine the core of their expertise and identity. Not only did librarians have to learn how to master the Internet search effectively, they also had to expand the repertoire of their work by becoming experts in new domains, such as learning how to interpret different Internet results, how to teach Internet search to clients, and how to connect disparate web-sources. Generally, the first scenario in current literature would thus predict that an occupation faced with new technology goes through a considerable reconfiguration of the nature of its work, letting go of old expertise and developing a range of new ways of working.

A second scenario concerns rising tensions or conflicts between occupations as a result of technology introduction [3, 5, 7, 8, 26]. For example, Barrett et al. [7] describe how the introduction of a pharmaceutical robot led to tensions in the relations between three occupational groups in pharmacy work: pharmacists, technicians, and assistants. While the robot allowed technicians and pharmacists to specialize in novel and exciting domains – such as fixing robots' mechanical failures and engaging in cutting-edge clinical research – it simultaneously produced strain in the relationships between technicians and assistants; i.e., while the technicians developed new expertise and gained authority, the robot took over many of the assistant's tasks which had a detrimental effect on their expertise and status. Similarly, Pachidi et al. [26] found that the introduction of analytics in telecommunications work led to a serious clash between two groups in the workplace: account managers and data scientists. The claim of data scientists that they could predict customer behavior through data sources without the need for any personal relations significantly threatened the whole raison-d'etre of account managers, who relied on cultivating personal relations with customers as an important source for their income. The fundamental disagreement between the two occupational groups resulted in account managers refusing to engage with analytics altogether, which escalated into a significant conflict between the two groups and ultimately led to layoffs of account managers.

In sum, available research thus far would lead us to expect that occupational groups engage in either redefining their core expertise or find themselves in conflictual relationships with other occupational groups. Our empirical study of the use of analytics in the police points to a different scenario: that of the emergence of a new occupational role that, in collaboration with other occupational groups, makes analytics meaningful for work. Less is known about how such a scenario plays out in practice. In what follows, we report on a study that identifies what happened when the police intentionally introduced a new occupational role to be in charge of analytics to support police officers in the shift to data-driven work.

3 Case Setting and Research Methodology

Our study focuses on the situated work practices of the Dutch Police, to which we gained access in October 2016. The data collection took place in a large city in the Netherlands in which four police stations are located, collectively housing over 700 full time employees. We examined the activities of the use of a Dutch predictive policing algorithm – the so-called "Criminal Anticipation System" (CAS). The algorithm was developed in-house by a data scientist (Dennis) who joined the police in 2012. After extensive work experience as a data-miner in the marketing industry, Dennis started to consider his work as "not very satisfying" and wanted to apply his data preparation and modelling skills to a more meaningful purpose. Inspired by the PredPol algorithm – which was first introduced by the Los Angeles Police Department in 2008 [27] – Dennis was excited about the opportunity to use his insights from the marketing industry to infer patterns in crime behavior and predict crime chances. Dennis remained the lead developer of CAS throughout the process of its roll-out across all Dutch police stations.

CAS runs on a logistic regression algorithm. Influenced by the limited amount and types of data made available to the data science department, Dennis included 50 different variables and divided them into two categories: location-specific characteristics and crime history. Location specific characteristics are based on statistical data that indicate, for example, the size of families, the family income, and the number of social securities. It also includes police data about, for example, the distance to the closest-known burglar or the number of suspects living in a specific area. Crime history is based on the number and spread of criminal incidents over the last three years in and surrounding a location.

Using these variables, Dennis developed the CAS algorithm that calculates crime chances in hot times (time blocks of four hours) and hotspots (area blocks of 125 by 125 m^2). The hot times and hotspots are made visible in a heat map (see Fig. 1) with the aim to answer two essential resource allocation questions for police management: where to deploy police officers and at which times to do that. CAS was introduced to the Dutch Police in 2013 in one police district. By the end of 2017 over 90 Dutch police stations were using it and CAS is currently deployed across all police stations in the Netherlands.

Fig. 1. An example of a CAS heat map.

Our ethnographic fieldwork consists of observations and interviews supplemented by archival documents such as job descriptions. All observations are conducted by the first author. The total of 410 h of observation includes daily work at the police station, 90 briefings and 22 team meetings.

In addition, we conducted 18 formal semi-structured interviews (ranging from 25 to 120 min), including 4 interviews with data scientists, 5 interviews with police management, 3 interviews with intelligence officers, and 6 interviews with police officers. During these interviews, participants were asked to describe the trajectory they went through in the police, their everyday activities, and their use of CAS. We also asked them about their view on the usefulness of such a technology for crime prevention. Most formal interviews were voice recorded, summarized, and transcribed. In case voice recording was not possible, detailed notes were taken during the interview and expanded afterwards into an interview summary.

4 Findings

The findings are divided into four sections. We first explain the background and aims of introducing predictive policing technology. Second, we describe how the introduction of predictive policing occasioned the establishment of a new occupational mandate for a group that became labelled as "intelligence officers". Third, we explain what expertise intelligence officers developed in practice. Fourth, we describe that while police officers increasingly depended on the human expertise of intelligence officers, their work paradoxically reinforced police officers' belief in the superior value of algorithmic decision making.

4.1 Intelligence Led Policing and Predictive Policing Technology

In 2013, the Dutch police introduced predictive policing through an internally created algorithm called the "Criminal Anticipation System" (CAS). The introduction of CAS was part of the "intelligence led policing" policy change, which had started in 2008. The overall aim of this strategy transformation was to increase the awareness and importance of working with data, including a differentiation between strategic and operational information, improving the reporting skills of police officers, making information available in real time, and establishing formal procedures for analyzing existing data which otherwise remained unutilized.

As part of this approach, introducing CAS promised to achieve three specific goals. First, knowing where to go at what time should give the police a possibility to more efficiently schedule their resources, for example, through reducing or increasing the number of police officers scheduled depending on predicted hot times. Second, due to the large amount of data included, policing decisions during fieldwork – e.g., about where to surveil to counter housebreaking – should become more objective by replacing "gut feeling" for data-based decisions. Finally, the overall aim of introducing CAS was to transform the traditionally reactive nature of police work into a more proactive stance towards preventing crimes such as housebreaking or young gangs creating nuisance. In essence, CAS should assist in preventing crime and safeguarding the lives of police officers while on the road; it should become just as important as every other police skills and tools. To illustrate this ambition, police manager Marga compared the importance of using analytics to police officers' personal gun; "they also don't leave their gun on the table", she explained, referring to analytics being just as indispensable.

To achieve these goals, CAS had to be adopted and used by police officers. Previous experiences with the introduction of new technologies had shown to police management that, as police manager Anna recalled, merely "throwing a new technology over the fence" and expecting police officers to start using it would likely result in a failure of technology adoption. According to data scientist Dennis, this was even more risky when introducing an algorithm such as CAS because of its complex and math-based nature. Dennis believed that police officers would be unwilling to engage deeply with deciphering and interpreting the output of CAS because of their occupational culture, referring to police officers as "people who are selected for being very eager to act and not very eager to think". In order to shift the police officers to a more data-driven way of working, Dennis argued that algorithmic outputs should be explained by "echoing what the police officers themselves say". To do this, Dennis argued that the "why, what and how", or as he put it "the qualitative stuff", had to be added to algorithmic outputs. However, adding context required interpretation and translation skills, which differed from data scientists' data preparation and modelling skills. This gap therefore had to be filled by people with a different kind of expertise. These people became so-called "intelligence officers".

4.2   The Intelligence Officer as a New Occupational Role

To fill the gap between data science and police skills, data scientists and police management wondered if they could introduce an intermediary who could support the work of police officers by making algorithmic output meaningful for police work. During the time of the introduction of CAS in 2013, there was a group within the police – referred to as "information officers" – that seemed most logical to take on this role since they were already working with information, albeit in a different way. Traditionally, the work of an information officer included supporting police management and criminal investigation by gathering various types of information. Former information officer Ben recalled what this role involved:

> I have assisted a lot in murder investigations. There you would get various work orders like 'map this', or 'figure that out', or 'how do the families relate'. These kinds of things. Or business relations. […] It was about delving into all different internal sources. You didn't really have access to Internet back then.

Due to their focus on information gathering, information officers had in-depth knowledge about where data – such as crime numbers, suspect data, or information about criminal networks – could be found in police databases. However, their work was regarded as relatively low-status, because information officers were not required to interpret the information they found. Instead, as data scientist Dennis explained, they would "collect all data, print it, put a staple in it and give it to their boss". Information officers were also sometimes described as "not very assertive", keen on "avoiding confrontations", used to "following orders" and doing "kind of boring work" (data scientist Dennis). Moreover, the information officer position was informally regarded as a back-office department for police officers who came to be unfit to continue working in the field. In essence, the information officers' position was considered as a "shelter for police officers with back problems or illnesses" (intelligence officer Ben).

Despite their relatively low status, the data scientists acknowledged the information officers' expertise with police databases and reasoned that this occupational group could be well-equipped to take on additional tasks that emerged with the introduction of predictive policing. Instead of just gathering information according to predefined requests, information officers were to take on novel responsibilities, such as interpreting algorithmic output, summarizing it for police officers and making suggestions of potential actions. This way, information officers were required to "add qualitative stuff" to algorithms and to provide back-office support to police officers for using algorithmic outputs. Using the example housebreaking, Dennis explained what that would involve:

> You could say: 'We have quite a drug problem over here [in this neighborhood]'. Then you could wonder: 'Maybe it [housebreaking prediction] is because of the junkies?' Well, junkies don't prepare much, so maybe it is just very easy to burgle there. Maybe the houses have bad locks so you can enter with a simple trick. That kind of information should be retrieved by the information officer. [...] Then we can think of what to do about it. As police, we are of course very inclined to just send a car there [for surveillance] but it could be that this is completely useless and that they should do something totally different.

Reflecting the shift in the nature of information officers' work, the new job title "intelligence officer" and a new job description were introduced in 2013. The novel job description was significantly longer and more focused on interpreting tasks, rather than the operational tasks that characterized the prior work of information officers. For example, the responsibilities now included so-called "data editing" requirements which involved making sense of the data and adding context to it. Intelligence officer Ben explains his perspective on the transformation:

> Back in the days, when we received a crime notification, we gathered all information and handed that package over [to police officers]. But I guess that when you gathered and read all that information, you can also interpret it, right? You can confirm or refute such a notification, or you can add some advice like: 'maybe this and that requires further investigation', you know. Information is more and more being interpreted.

As a result of the shifting nature of their work, intelligence officers started to gain in-depth expertise about interpreting and working with algorithmic output. This expertise centered around meaning-making practices, on which we elaborate below.

4.3   Intelligence Work in Practice

Although intelligence officers were initially intended to merely provide back-office support to police officers for using algorithmic outputs, they quickly discovered that working with CAS required more than simply "adding qualitative stuff", as was imagined by the data scientists. In practice, the algorithmic output was highly complex; for example, selecting hotspots and hot times required comparing between different graphs and maps. It was also voluminous, for example, the heatmap regularly showed entire districts covered in hotspots. The outputs often seemed nonsensical, for example, predictions of car burglary were shown in areas where cars were not allowed. And finally, the algorithm remained black-boxed, so the intelligence officers often complained that they did not understand the output because there was no transparency about which variables were most important for predicting hotspots or hot times. In order to make algorithmic outputs legible and meaningful for police work, the intelligence officers had to go beyond just "adding qualitative stuff" and slowly started to learn how to unpack the specific features of the algorithm.

Besides unpacking, intelligence officers also had to make sure that police officers would be able to accept the algorithmic outputs and were actively considering how to best integrate CAS outputs into police work. They reasoned that it was important not to overload the police officers with too many tasks for covering hotspots and hot times, because a large part of police work still consisted of responding to unexpected crimes not included in CAS, such as car accidents. Indeed, as commander Rudy emphasized, police officers had limited resources available: "Look, we [police] cannot handle everything [all crimes], but let's at least make a choice and set a priority like 'we will certainly handle this [type of crime], because we think it is now important".

Moreover, intelligence officers also anticipated that in their recommendations to police officers they should vary the hotspots and types of crime they introduced, so that the predictions would not look too repetitive and would keep the police officers interested in using them. For example, during one of the shifts, intelligence officer Louisa was trying to decide which hotspots to recommend for sending police officers to surveil against housebreaking. The algorithm had produced two hotspots that otherwise never showed up, and two "regular" hotspots that were common crime spots in the district. Louisa was not sure which hotspots to select: the new or the common ones? She asked Ben and together they decided to select the new ones. They reasoned that the police officers would get bored if the hotspots stayed the same and would be more excited to go into a new neighborhood. According to Ben, variety increases the chance that "police officers take hotspots seriously" (observation notes, 13-11-2017).

Finally, to make algorithmic outputs "echo what police officers themselves say", intelligence officers figured that it was important to make outputs appear closer to the context of police work. They figured this would be possible by including additional background information, such as suspects or information about surrounding neighborhoods. As police commander Rudy explained this viewpoint from the police officers' perspective:

> If you keep the goals [of the algorithmic output] too broad, then police officers will let it go too fast. If you dare to add possible suspects, then they will quickly start searching. Then they'll better scan the surroundings, like: 'Hey, we see someone strolling over there'. I think the concreter you are, the more feeling police officers will have for it [the output].

With the aim to make algorithmic outputs meaningful for police work, intelligence officers thus went beyond simply "supporting" police work. Instead, their decisions started to steer the work of police officers. Specifically, because working with algorithmic output required reducing the number of hotspots and hot times presented to police officers, it meant that intelligence officers in fact prioritized certain types of crimes according to their own judgement. Moreover, because they had to combine the results of their interpretation into a single succinct PowerPoint slide to be shown to police officers, this significantly simplified algorithmic outputs by compressing a messy picture into a seemingly clean and objective result. Finally, because intelligence officers also included information from other databases, such as possible suspects, this effectively gave the impression that contextual information was also part of the algorithmic output.

In sum, while intelligence officers' work was intended to merely support police officers in using algorithmic outputs, in practice they shifted into exerting a much bigger influence on how police work should be organized and where priorities should fall. Intelligence officers started to recognize this growing importance as well: "Most of the time, at least for us, police officers do not know what they need. And then I think 'well, I know what you need to do because I see a big problem in this neighborhood, so you should go there'. So then I tell them what they should do" (intelligence officer Wendy).

4.4 Police Officers' Perspective

Over time, the influence of intelligence officers became acknowledged by police officers and their activities were increasingly incorporated into police routines. For example, at the end of the first year of our observations, a new practice was established that required the police commander to meet with an intelligence officer each morning before the briefing. During this meeting the intelligence officer instructed the commander about the crime types, hotspots, and hot times, including background information, that they deemed most important to communicate and emphasize to the team. As intelligence officer Ben explains:

> We give an interpretation [to the algorithmic output] so that police officers can do something with it. In other words: 'It is this for these reasons'. You can also give them advice, like: 'I would focus on that or that person' or 'I wouldn't do anything about that [crime] because it's way too unpredictable and you can't do anything about it'.

Over the course of the two years of our fieldwork, intelligence officers acquired even more influence over police work. For example, they became the most important source for formulating strategically-focused work assignments – "to-do" lists for police action which are used for weekly guidance of police fieldwork. Previously, compiling a "to-do list" for police work was performed by local police officers, responsible for specific neighborhoods. With the use of predictive policing and CAS, the local police officers' to-do lists started to be viewed as too idiosyncratic; a messy and random list of activities. Gradually, the responsibility for making more strategically-focused work assignments was placed in the hands of police management, who embraced predictive policing and made intelligence officers their central source of input. Consequently, police actions became de facto driven by the intelligence officers' judgments and interpretations of CAS.

Furthermore, police officers often accepted suggestions of intelligence officers without questioning their reasoning. An example of a recent briefing discussion illustrates this. For one of the shifts, the CAS prediction indicated a high level of nuisance. Considering this as an important prediction, intelligence officer Louisa found a linkable suspect in the police databases and had manually added him to the slide to be shown during the briefing. Upon seeing the slide, a discussion arose about the suitability of that suspect. A couple of police officers claimed that this specific suspect was a much "tougher guy" and said that it was ridiculous to keep an eye on him "merely as a suspect of nuisance". The commander overruled the discussion by saying that this information came from the intelligence department, so there would "surely be a reasonable link". The other police officers acknowledged that and did not further question the suspect's suitability. The briefing ended without further ado (observation notes, June 2018).

One of the reasons for this ready acceptance was that police officers seemed impressed by the complexity of algorithms. "What I've seen and what I heard from [intelligence officer] Eva is that CAS includes so many variables, that machine must really be a monster!" said police officer Michael. As a consequence, police officers believed that they might not be "smart" enough to question such complex algorithms and assumed that it was better if they just accepted the output. As police officer Harry explained:

> "[W]hen I really think about crime predictions, then I wonder: is a burglar really influenced by something that can make us predict where burglary will happen? Or is it just his target area? But I shouldn't think too much about that, because I don't have the answer. I'm quite a follower in that sense. I trust that the people who really understand this thought about these things."

Even though it did not always make sense to them, police officers started to increasingly accept that crimes can be systematically explained through the use of data and algorithms, which they assumed transcended their level of understanding. Police officer Jay explained his trust in the expertise invested into the technology, without exploring the embedded assumptions or doubting the legitimacy: "I would say that it must come from somewhere. It won't be implemented just out of the blue."

Corresponding with their belief in the usefulness of algorithms, police officers started to regard their work as having higher value when they followed the advice generated by the predictions:

> I feel useless when I'm just driving around without seeing anything. […] If something [CAS] tells me that the chances are high that a burglary will happen over there, well that's what we want! Catching thieves or at least prevent crime. So I will go for it! (Police officer Harry).

Police officer Jimmy showed a similar perspective: "With the right information I can make the right decisions" he said, "and making the right decisions gives me a purpose." Moreover, mainly driven by the growing respect for the algorithmic recommendations the intelligence officers provided them, police officers also started to deem the insights and expertise associated with algorithms as superior to their own judgment, viewing the latter as "subjective" and "blind". Police officer Harry compared the recommendations of a local police officer with the ones generated based on data:

> I think a local police officer is also somehow subjective and has his own agenda. He may think that some type of crime is particularly important, but perhaps this is not at all what the data shows. […] Maybe the data points at something completely different [some other type of crime in another part of town]. I don't think we should blindly trust the local police officer's perspective.

In sum, police officers gradually embraced the growing influence intelligence officers came to exert over their work through the use of predictive policing. Even though intelligence officers were initially introduced to provide relatively simple back-office support to police officers, their work in practice came to include many interpretations and judgments to make algorithmic outputs meaningful for police work. Because police officers believed in an incomprehensible complexity of algorithms, they argued that they were not smart enough to understand algorithms, viewed their own tacit expertise as inferior to data-based recommendations, and eventually accepted the algorithmic outputs presented to them without questioning its reasoning. As a result, the new occupational role paradoxically reinforced the police officers' belief in the superiority of algorithmic decisions.

5   Concluding Remarks

This study aimed at understanding what happens to occupational work upon the introduction of analytics. Our findings offer three contributions to existing literature on occupational change due to technology use and the critical debate on nature of analytics. First, we show that analytics occasions the emergence of an intermediary occupational role that takes charge of analytics and unpacks specific algorithmic features. Prior literature on occupational change either focuses on the skill transformation of separate occupations [20, 32], or on the resulting tensions and conflicts when multiple occupational groups are involved [7, 26]. We extend prior literature by showing the possibility of the rise of an intermediary occupational role in-between analytics designers and users. Thereby, we respond to calls for a relational perspective on occupations [2].

Second, our study shows that analytics is not only constructed by the design choices of its creators, but is also iteratively shaped by the expert work of intermediary occupations who take on the task of unpacking the features of algorithms to make them usable. We thereby respond to calls for disentangling analytics technology [14, 15, 23]. We extend the current critical debate regarding the nature of analytics [6, 11, 17, 21, 22, 25, 26, 28, 29] by giving a detailed explanation of analytics in action by highlighting how different occupational groups perform work with analytics.

Third, our findings indicate that engaging in such "unpacking" practices is consequential for the relations between occupational groups. As such, identifying the role of intermediaries in analytics at work has important implications for the distribution of power between occupations. While prior literature acknowledged the growing power of data scientists as the designers of analytics who can determine what counts as knowledge and what not [15, 16, 26], we highlight that the growing power and steering influence of intermediaries also warrants attention. Growing legitimacy and use of algorithms is making this changing power distribution even more salient.

To conclude, we have shown how the introduction of a new occupational role intended to add interpretations to algorithmic outputs to support existing work also has a counterintuitive consequence. While on the one hand, unpacking the features and making algorithmic outputs meaningful for work by adding interpretations and human judgment encouraged the use of analytics, it also paradoxically reinforced police officers' belief in the superiority of algorithmic decisions over human expertise. In the long run, the danger of creating a new occupational role that interprets and unpacks analytics to make it readily available for its users is that specifically these practices might even further black-box the inherent inclusion of human expertise.

References

1. Ambrose, M.L.: Lessons from the avalanche of numbers: big data in historical perspective. I/S: J. Law Policy Inf. Soc. **11**(2), 201–277 (2015)
2. Anteby, M., Chan, C.K., DiBenigno, J.: Three lessons on occupations and professions in organizations: becoming, doing, and relating. Acad. Manag. Ann. **10**(1), 183–244 (2016)
3. Bailey, D.E., Leonardi, P.M., Barley, S.R.: The lure of the virtual. Organ. Sci. **22**(1), 262–285 (2012)
4. Barley, S.R.: Why the internet makes buying a car less loathsome: how technologies change role relations. Acad. Manag. Discov. **1**(1), 5–35 (2015)
5. Barley, S.R.: Technology as an occasion for structuring evidence from observations of CT scanners and the social order of radiology departments. Adm. Sci. Q. **31**(1), 78–108 (1986)
6. Barocas, S., Selbst, A.D.: Big data's disparate impact. Calif. Law Rev. **104**, 671–732 (2016)
7. Barrett, M., Oborn, E., Orlikowski, W.J., Yates, J.: Reconfiguring boundary relations: robotic innovations in pharmacy work. Organ. Sci. **23**(5), 1448–1466 (2012)
8. Bechky, B.A.: Object lessons: workplace artifacts as representations of occupational jurisdiction. Am. J. Sociol. **109**(3), 720–752 (2003)
9. Boyd, D., Crawford, K.: Critical questions for big data. Inf. Commun. Soc. **15**(5), 662–670 (2012)
10. Braverman, H.: Labor and Monopoly Capital: The Degradation of Work in the Twentieth Century. Monthly Review Press, New York (1974)
11. Crawford, K., Schultz, J.: Big data and due process: toward a framework to redress predictive privacy harms. Boston Coll. Law Rev. **55**, 93–128 (2014)
12. Davenport, T.H., Harris, J.G., Morison, R.: Analytics at Work: Smarter Decisions, Better Results. Harvard Business Press, Boston (2010)
13. Dourish, P.: Algorithms and their others: algorithmic culture in context. Big Data Soc. **3**(2), 1–11 (2016)
14. Elish, M.C., Boyd, D.: Situating methods in the magic of big data and AI. Commun. Monogr. **85**(1), 57–80 (2018)
15. Faraj, S., Pachidi, S., Sayegh, K.: Working and organizing in the age of the learning algorithm. Inf. Organ. **28**(1), 62–70 (2018)
16. Forsythe, D.E.: Engineering knowledge: the construction of knowledge in artificial intelligence. Soc. Stud. Sci. **23**, 445–477 (1993)
17. Gitelman, L.: Raw Data is an Oxymoron. MIT Press, Cambridge (2013)
18. Mayer-Schonberger, V., Cukier, K.: Big Data: A Revolution that Will Transform How We Live, Work, and Think. John Murray, London (2013)
19. McAfee, A., Brynjolfsson, E.: Big data: the management revolution. Harvard Bus. Rev. **90**(10), 60–68 (2012)
20. Nelson, A.J., Irwin, J.: Defining what we do – all over again: occupational identity, technological change, and the librarian/internet-search relationship. Acad. Manag. J. **57**(3), 892–928 (2014)
21. Newell, S., Marabelli, M.: Strategic opportunities (and challenges) of algorithmic decision-making: a call for action on the long-term societal effects of "Datification". J. Strateg. Inf. Syst. **24**(1), 3–14 (2015)
22. O'Neil, C.: Weapons of Math Destruction: How Big Data Increases Inequality and Threatens Democracy. Crown, New York (2016)
23. Orlikowski, W.J., Scott, S.V.: Digital work: a research agenda. In: Czarniawska, B.E. (ed.) A Research Agenda for Management and Organization Studies. Edward Elgar, Cheltenham (2016)

24. Orlikowski, W.J., Scott, S.V.: What happens when evaluation goes online? Exploring apparatuses of valuation in the travel sector. Organ. Sci. **25**(3), 868–891 (2014)
25. Pachidi, S., Huysman, M.H.: Organizational intelligence in the digital age: analytics and the cycle of choice. In: Galliers, R.D., Stein, M.K. (eds.) Routledge Companions in Business, Management, and Accounting. Routledge, London, New York (2016)
26. Pachidi, S., Berends, H., Faraj, S., Huysman, M.H., van de Weerd, I.: What happens when analytics lands in the organization? Studying epistemologies in clash. Acad. Manag. Proc. **4** (1), 15590 (2014)
27. Perry, W.L., McInnis, C.C., Price, S., Smith, S., Hollywood, J.S.: Predictive Policing: The Role of Crime Forecasting in Law Enforcement Operations. RAND Corporation (2013)
28. Pine, K.H., Liboiron, M.: The politics of measurement and action. In: Proceedings of the 33rd Annual ACM Conference on Human Factors in Computing Systems, pp. 3147–3156. ACM, New York (2015)
29. Ribes, D., Jackson, S.J.: Data bite man: the work of sustaining a long-term study. In: Gitelman, L. (ed.) Raw Data is an Oxymoron, pp. 147–166. MIT Press, Cambridge (2013)
30. Schultze, U.: A confessional account of an ethnography about knowledge work. MIS Q. **24** (1), 3–41 (2000)
31. Zarsky, T.: The trouble with algorithmic decisions: an analytic road map to examine efficiency and fairness in automated and opaque decision making. Sci. Technol. Human Values **41**(1), 118–132 (2016)
32. Zuboff, S.: In the Age of the Smart Machine: The Future of Work and Power. Basic Books, New York (1988)

Objects, Metrics and Practices: An Inquiry into the Programmatic Advertising Ecosystem

Cristina Alaimo[1]([✉]) and Jannis Kallinikos[2]

[1] Surrey Business School, University of Surrey, Guildford, UK
c.alaimo@surrey.ac.uk
[2] LSE, London School of Economics, London, UK

Abstract. Programmatic advertising is a large scale, real-time bidding process, whereby ads are automatically assigned to available spaces across types of media and geographic regions upon an individual user's browser request. The large-scale automation of programmatic advertising requires the establishment of standards and the development of technologies to govern the behavior of market participants (sellers, buyers, intermediaries). We present evidence on the rules of programmatic exchange and on the role played by a specific class of digital objects. We focus in particular on the metrics to which these objects are linked and how they define what is exchanged and the parameters of these exchanges. We furthermore demonstrate that the metrics and the technological complexes associated with them are constituted by the institutional field of digital advertising and its complex technological infrastructure. Rather than being simply means to monitor a pre-existing reality 'out there' (such as user or audience behavior) these metrics and techniques bring forward their own reality and heavily impact upon and shape the objects and processes of digital advertising.

Keywords: Automation · Digital advertising · Performativity
Digital objects · Information infrastructures

1 Introduction

Over the last two decades, the field of advertising has been undergoing dramatic transformations that are reshaping the very process of advertising and remaking the fundamental objects and actors involved in that process. This is forcefully evidenced by the recent diffusion of what is referred to as programmatic advertising, whereby ads are displayed to viewers or readers through a real time auction in a process of dizzying computational and organizational complexity. We view advertising as a social field or practice and we aim, accordingly, to document shifts in that practice that result from the introduction of new objects and metrics, exchanges between actors and systems, and, ultimately, economic and power relations. The intersection of economic pursuits with technology and their links to online media make the field of programmatic advertising a particularly germane object of study that links to central concerns of the conference call.

Advertisement - the process of calling user's attention to a product or service by way of paid announcements - has always been contingent on the assignment of advert

U. Schultze et al. (Eds.): IS&O 2018, IFIP AICT 543, pp. 110–123, 2018.
https://doi.org/10.1007/978-3-030-04091-8_9

content to individuals. This process has traditionally occurred via the construct of the audience, an anonymous and rather sizeable cohort of readers, viewers or listeners that are supposed to share a few fundamental attributes to which an advert seeks to appeal [29, 31]. The debate on the facticity of audiences has a long history in sociology and media studies [see i.e. 4–6, 30]. Ettema and Whitney speak of "institutionally effective audiences" [13, p. 5], a concept recently expanded by Napoli to signify audiences that are "constructed and defined to reflect the economic and strategic imperatives of media organizations" and that "can be effectively integrated into the economics of media industries" [24, p. 3]. Yet, IS scholarship is surprisingly lacking in debating the facticity of concepts such as "user attention" or "audiences", a fact that becomes particularly regretful in light of the recent technological advancements and the proliferation of metrics and tracking devices that are linked to the automation of advertising exchanges. The knowledge gap on the functioning of digital media buying and exchange and their connected technologies is even more striking if one considers the history and evolution of digital advertising and its profound interdependence with the history of the web and the importance advertising-based business models have had for the majority of content, information and entertainment providers.

In what follows we present preliminary evidence from an ongoing study of the process through which programmatic advertising operates. To grasp and better appreciate the current transformations, we retrace the recent evolution of the digital advertising industry and the user measurement and profiling they rely upon. The reliance of publishers to advertising-funded business models and the skepticism with which marketers originally met the new medium fueled a rush to develop a range of data tracking devices, better tools for measuring, and the consequent mushrooming of data analytics companies which help publishers find convincing ways to demonstrate marketers' return on investments (ROIs). Recently, the plunge toward more effective ways of buying and selling ads online led to the rise of programmatic advertising and the implementation of massive centralized virtual marketplaces called ad exchanges that offer in real-time individual user profiles to bid on (Google owns one of the biggest ad exchange platforms). Programmatic advertising is rapidly diffusing as a faster, cheaper, and scalable alternative to previous methods of ad exchanges such as ad networks and direct exchanges.

In its essence, programmatic advertising is a huge, real-time bidding process, whereby ads are automatically assigned to media spaces across types of media and geographic regions upon an individual user's browser request. This means that the entire ecosystem's exchange with its hundreds of platforms operates "on-demand", every time a user's browser opens a publisher website and triggers a real-time request for an ad. The whole exchange is usually completed under 100 ms and remains entirely invisible to the user who may experience a small lag in loading the publisher page. Dubbed as the "holy grail of targeting" [see 29, p. 79], the automated and real-time nature of ad exchanges characteristic of programmatic advertising requires the establishment of standards and the development of technologies to govern the behavior of market participants (sellers, buyers, intermediaries). Requests for real time bidding on available ad slots have to enter the ecosystem in appropriate data formats and be exchanged using data objects, standardized conventions and IT-based solutions that allow real-time computation to occur in an unprecedented, almost dizzying, scale.

The diffusion of automated exchanges and the move toward selling user attention on demand opens yet another chapter in the evolution of digital advertising and, consequently, of the web. Key in the developments we point to is the diffusion of complex and distributed automated marketplaces which is itself contingent on the introduction of a particular class of digital objects. In what follows, we recount their operations and the measures they black-box. We frame our empirical study against the background of tracking technologies linked to online marketing and we further draw on theories of information infrastructures [7, 10, 16, 33] and other contributions across the social sciences [11, 12, 21, 22] to reflect and theorize on our empirical findings. The evidence we present indicates that the specific class of digital objects that underlie programmatic advertising is closely linked to several metrics that define both what is exchanged and the parameters of these exchanges. We show the path dependence of such metrics and demonstrate that the metrics and the technological complexes associated with them are constituted by the institutional matrix of digital advertising and its complex technological infrastructure. Rather than being simply means to monitor a pre-existing reality 'out there' (such as user or audience behavior) these metrics and techniques bring forward their own reality and heavily impact upon and shape the objects of digital advertising.

The paper is organized as follows: in the next section we trace the history of digital advertising through the evolution of its digital objects. After having presented our research design, we describe the findings of our empirical study focusing on the protocol, measures and digital objects that constitute the programmatic exchange. Following it, we discuss and reflect on the facticity of these data objects and link our reflections to broader concerns on the performative role they have at the industry level.

2   The Evolution of the Field of Digital Advertising

Since the beginning of the web, online publishers (the majority of content producers such as newspapers and blogs and later also content distributors such as social media) understood that a paid subscription model was not a tenable business option and decided to rely on advertising-based business models. From that point on (early 1990s), the development of the web content has been inherently linked to the development of the digital advertising industry, its dynamics and technological evolution. Publishers found themselves competing in an ever-increasing fragmented space to convince marketers of the effectiveness of online advertising spending on their own websites [see 29]. This in turn, quickly brought the mushrooming of data tracking devices, measuring tools and data analytics companies.

In the mid-1990s, in fact, a systematic measurement of internet audiences did not exist. The newly born digital advertising industry rushed to assemble a toolkit of standards, measures and a lexicon borrowed from traditional commercial media and adjusted to the web. Some of the old measures and standards persisted such as the case, for instance, with the one used for the price setting. CPM or cost per mil (thousand) has been the traditional standard price model for newspapers and other mass media. In the CPM model, the price of a single ad is determined by the cost of reaching one thousand individuals. The newly instituted sector maintained also and relied on the concept of the ad impression used by traditional commercial media. The concept has always been contested, yet its adoption online added more ambiguity with respect to what constitutes an online impression. The basic definition of impression as [an] "advertisement that was sent to an individual who had clicked on a site's page" [29] does not specify if the ad is delivered on the site's page or to what extent an individual may effectively view the ad. As we show further ahead in the empirical section, these are fundamental aspects upon which the measurability of programmatic exchange and the cost of what is exchanged are constantly negotiated.

Other traditional methods of audience measurement crumbled under the changes imposed by the new digital medium. The fragmentation of offering in the online medium and the consequent dispersion of audiences across a number of sites rendered questionable the relevance of traditional panel-based models of audience measurement (like the Nielsen model) [see 6, 24, 25]. The difficulties in measuring audiences and the skepticism of marketers and big clients toward the digital medium pushed publishers and tech entrepreneurs to finding new ways to assess the presence of users and their activities online. One such way was indeed to track the user "click". Clicks not only gave advertiser evidence of the presence of users but it produced as well the detailed trace of their online activities. Publishers were quick in understanding that the measurability of "clicks" was one of the absolute novelties of the new medium. For the first time, marketers could have evidence of the effectiveness of their spending in advertising campaigns. It comes as no surprise that since roughly 1993 until today the digital advertising industry has grown spiraling around the central assumption that success in the business was a matter of finding more and more accurate ways of measuring audience and to eventually prove ROIs. Napoli defines the new concept of "audience" brought about by the proliferation of digital measuring and tracking technologies as "audience information systems" [24]. The term aptly signifies the major shift in the conception of audience caused by the use of data analytics [1, 2, 5, 6, 28]. To us, it also clearly points to the broader changes such shifts caused in the dynamics and organization of the digital advertising domain.

The complex relationship between publishers (or sellers) and marketers (or buyers) essentially developed on issues of measurability up to such extent that the entire evolution of the sector can be narrated in terms of measures and its associated devices. The evolution of the digital advertising industry has been driven by (i) crucial technological developments such as the development of the web browser, tracking technologies and automation; (ii) existing advertising industry dynamics, such as the concentration and increasing power of media-buying and -planning and their consequent push to audience measurability; and (iii) the overreliance of web content producers (from big publishers to individual blogs) on versions of an advertising-based business model. Within this paradigm, crucial technological developments coinciding with the implementation of a class of digital objects such as the cookies, the web beacons, the pixel and other tracking and measuring devices, together with what they measure and how, stand out as key to understanding the evolution of the field of digital advertising and the influence the rationalization and measurement of audiences exert on the development of the web.

Galloway aptly defines the web browser as a "hiding machine," given that its main filtering and translating function actually hides the web [14]. The browser uses a set of instructions (HTML) to filter, organize and display content. The browser allows hyperlinking and marks a difference with the preceding text-only based web. For the digital advertising industry, the browser allows the development of more sophisticated forms of graphic advertising, linking and the hiding of tracking devices. Cookies were invented by Lou Montulli in 1994 working for Netscape Communication to solve a shopping problem [9, 29]. In the original HTTP protocol, each request made by a user's computer to a web browser would be treated as new. Shopping carts back then had no way of linking different items to the same user. Machines read different items as different choices of different users. To solve this issue Montulli created a small text file that a website could place in a user computer with an identification code for the user and its activities (clicks), effectively solving the problem of user identification within and across sessions. Something invented as a solution to a relatively small problem led to the development of an entire industry of tracking which still constitutes the backbone of web advertising. Cookies gave computers a memory and user browsers the authorization of storing user histories by design without consent or knowledge from users [9]. The use of cookies quickly proliferated. Netscape installed cookie-capabilities into Navigator in 1994, followed by Microsoft's Internet Explorer in 1995.

The reaction of the industry was immediate and brought the development of a set of related industry practices and new service-related companies. The fact that cookies were implemented with a "same origin policy" – meaning that only the originator of the cookie could read the information stored in it, led to the emergence of ad networks. These alliances of publisher websites often led by an intermediary emerged to implement cross-sites tracking of users (with the so called "third-party" cookies) and, in so doing, they offered better audience analytics and measurement to advertisers [26, 29].

The activity of ad networks became fundamental to the field of digital advertising for a number of reasons. Ad networks offered a solution to the problem caused by the increasing fragmentation of content – what has been called the "long tail" [3] and the fact that audiences, differently from traditional commercial media, were spread across a number of different small websites. Ad networks aggregated publishers (called affiliates) and exchanged the possibility of installing and reading cookies across websites for a share of the revenue they made by selling the possibility to reach a certain kind of audience. They grew from accounting for 5% of ad impressions sold in 2006 to 30% of ad impressions sold in 2007 [IAB in 24, p. 71]. One of the reasons of this success was that ad networks capitalized on the oversupply of publisher inventory; that is, the available ad slots in a publisher's online space. This remnant inventory was thus aggregated and auctioned by ad networks to media buyers at a discounted price. Although ad networks helped publishers sell their remnant inventory (which on average accounted for the 80% of the total inventory) the long-term effect of their operations was to move the attention of media buyers and planners from contexts (i.e. the publisher site or its reputation) to users [29]. The ad network auction system let marketers bid for impressions but did not reveal the websites where the impression was being delivered. Effectively what was on offer was the trackability of users rather than an ad space on a reputable publisher outlet.

One of the most important ad networks was DoubleClick. Founded in 1995, the company has been at the center of the media attention several times, most notably for having merged with Abacus Direct, an offline database of consumers amidst fear of privacy breach, for having been investigated by The Federal Trade Commission and for having been bought by Google in 2007. DoubleClick also implemented the first automated version of ad serving technology with its DART (Dynamic Advertising Reporting & Targeting) a software which automated the ad buying process for advertisers and minimized unsold inventory for publishers. Ad serving technology is an important building block of today's media buying and planning. The basic functionalities of ad serving technology gradually evolved to respond to the need of publishers that wanted to sell the same ad slot to more than one marketer. At the beginning, ad serving was made of pieces of codes that rotated different creatives (the content of an ad) into a single ad slot on a publisher's site. This was followed by the development of a set of metrics to optimize the ad delivery. A ranking system called waterfall rotated the different creatives on the basis of a number of pre-set goals and performance metrics that related to user click, post-click and post-impression activities and interactions. The data from these basic functionalities were gradually incorporated into more sophisticated versions of serving technology like the DART system that was able to support decision making in an increasingly automated way. The system was eventually integrated with Google DoubleClick ad exchange, the centralized marketplace of programmatic advertising ecosystem.

3 Research Design and Methodology

The research is based on case study research design that combines the investigation of the field of programmatic advertising (the case) with a field-embedded case study of Smartology an independent, demand-side platform and trading desk [32].

The field-embedded study has been conducted over a period of 24 months in the company headquarters in London, UK and entailed two periods of 5 and 7 months respectively, with a year of follow-up communications and industry research in between. The first period covered the work of the company in the direct (traditional) digital advertising ecosystem. The second extended into the migration of the company to the programmatic advertising and its integration with the most important ad exchange platforms: Google Ad Exchange and Index Ad Exchange. Data were collected through semi structured ethnographic interviews (20), direct observations, company's internal documents (50) including reports, system screenshots, console screenshots, live logs examples and demonstrations. Additional data on the field of programmatic advertising have been collected with industry expert interviews (Google AdSense, Pangaea Alliance, Xaxis) but also a large range of industry documents, including Interactive Advertising Bureau (IAB) publicly available documents (35), other external documents (55), US patent applications (12) and other secondary resources such as industry reports, news articles and whitepapers.

Data were collected and analyzed following Yin's [32] procedure of constructing a case study database and case study protocol to maintain a coherent narrative and chain of events. Shifting between the two levels (filed and company) has been essential to acquiring a more complete and nuance view of the complexity of programmatic advertising.

4   The Programmatic Ecosystem: Facts and Processes

The drive toward effective ways of buying and selling ads online has led to the establishment of massive centralized virtual marketplaces called ad exchanges. Such marketplaces essentially overcome the fragmentation of online media and advertisers through massive, real time auction processes that evolve around the browsing behaviors (ad impressions) of huge user crowds. These centralized and automated buying systems hosted by ad exchange are rapidly diffusing as a more efficient alternative to the methods of ad exchanges reviewed in the previous section hosted by ad networks. In what follows, we paint the work of ad exchanges in large brush strokes.

The automated method of buying and selling ads in large scale, distributed ecosystems happens between platforms that act on behalf of traditional actors such as online publishers and marketers (buyers, sellers) and novel actors such as various data brokers and intermediaries. Demand Side Platforms (DSP that act on behalf of marketers), Supply Side Platforms (SSP that act on behalf of publishers) and many Data Management Platforms (DMP) exchange massive flows of data in real time as they seek to buy individual user attention. As indicated, the entire ecosystem's exchange, with its hundreds of platforms, operates "on-demand", every time a user's browser opens a publisher's website and triggers a real-time request for an ad. The massive, automated and real-time nature of ad exchanges occurring in the programmatic advertising ecosystem requires the establishment of standards and technologies to govern the behavior of market participants (DSP, SSP and SMP) and deal successfully with the protean data tasks their exchanges requires.

The Real-Time Bidding (RTB) protocol is the rule-book of the auctioning process in the field. The RTB Protocol derives from a concerted work undertaken by a group of demand-side and supply-side platforms in 2010. Under the supervision of the IAB, these platforms started to lay down the standards for the programmatic exchange. Following the adoption success, OpenRTB was introduced as an IAB standard in January 2012. JSON (JavaScript Object Notation) is the suggested format for bid request and bid response data payloads but not the only one adopted. Google AdX, for instance, offers three protocol options; (1) Ad Exchange protobuf, (2) Open RTB protobuf and (3) Open RTB JSON. Meanwhile, Index Exchange, an independent Toronto-based ad exchange, only supports Open RTB JSON [15].

Figure 1 illustrates the Open RTB exchange ecosystem, although it depicts the flow as unidirectional exchanges, most of what happens in the ecosystem is interactive and runs in both directions.

The automated process is made possible by the work of the protocol and the set of digital objects that the protocol requires. The bid request and bid response objects talk to each other via a set of embedded objects and pre-set parameters that allow the exchange to happen. One of the most important objects of the RTB protocol is the ad impression object. Ad impressions are digital objects that have been set up to represent the likelihood of a single user to view an ad. An ad impression is defined as "the moment (a window of opportunity) between the fetching of an ad from its source as the result of the user's browser activity and the delivery of the ad" [19]. Ad impression objects are encapsulated in the bid request object (Fig. 1: 1) that needs to contain at

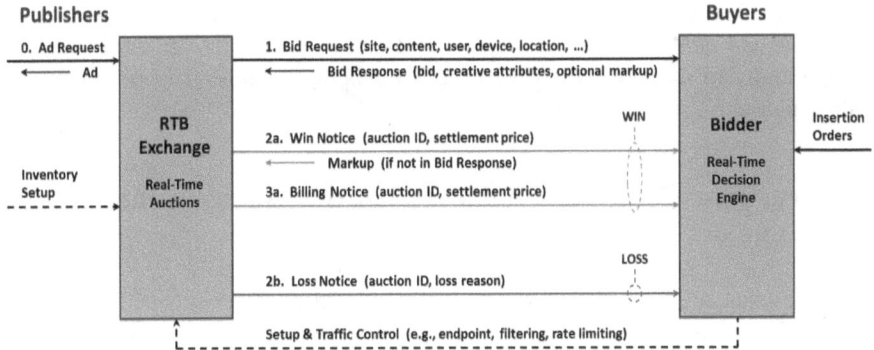

Fig. 1. Schematic representation of RTB exchange [18]. [From the top left] 0. A user browses online and opens a newspaper article (or any other content-based website). In so doing, the user's browser produces an ad impression. The article's ad inventory has been listed by the newspaper in a Supply Side Platform (SSP) (for instance, DoubleClick for publishers). 1. The ad exchange platform issues a "bid request" for the given impression of an ad slot. The different "bidders" or Demand Side Platforms (DSP) connected to the Google ad exchange platform will receive a "bid request" object, with details of the impression being sold, sometimes including minimum CPM (cost per mille impression), and other attributes or parameters. The DSP bidders respond with a "bid response" object, if the bid request they receive is of interest to them, they will respond with details about the ad and a bid offer in CPM. If not, a null bid response object will be sent. 2a. 2b. The ad exchange processes all the bid responses for the given bid request and declares the winner: the highest bid that fits all the requested parameters. The winning ad will be delivered and shown on the newspaper's article page within 100 ms from the moment the use's browser accessed that page. Data about user behavior and post-click activity are usually collected by different systems for assessing campaigns and retargeting users.

least one ad impression object to trigger the exchange. The ad impression object is at the same time the good being exchanged and the rules of the exchange (its attributes or parameters). It contains different attributes that refer to: type of ad (banner, video, native) subordinated to the impression object, size, price such as bid floor, if any, modality of exchange, such as for instance if the object is exchanged through private marketplace (PMP), the expected time lag between bid winning and effective ad delivery (exp) and an array of metrics.

AdX, in particular, supplies three metrics of the ad impression object: viewability, click-through rate and video completion rate. Viewability is an estimate of the likelihood that the ad slot will be viewable by the end user, based on a range of indicators. It is expressed as percentage and calculated by taking into account historical data on user behavior and ad slot attribute data such as certain pixel and exposure thresholds, usually counting a minimum of 50% of the ad's pixel exposure for 1 or 2 continuous seconds [23, p. 7], although this may vary across exchanges. Viewability refers to the likelihood or "opportunity to see". It does not therefore signify or stand for an actual viewing of the ad by the end user. It rather counts surrounding or environment factors of the ad slot such as visibility (if the ad is above or below the fold), a threshold exposure and a set of behavioral data on user (if available). These attributes can also be used as a selection and filtering criteria to find impressions and ad slots worth responding and bidding on. In this respect, viewability – an estimate of the likelihood or opportunity to see – becomes the criterion shaping a decision to bid in the pre-bidding phase.

5 Discussion: Conjectural Objects and the Management of Time

The automation of real time bidding in the programmatic domain depends on a very complex IT infrastructure which is quickly growing both in scale and scope. The complexity arising from the automation of the core exchanges in an over-fragmented landscape of actors, business contexts, media and technologies is partially dealt with the establishment of a range of new objects. These include ad impressions, bid requests, action requirements and templates and, crucially as our study suggests, a range of metrics that lend facticity to these objects and monitor their movements along the virtual space of programmatic advertising [10, 17, 20].

It is worth pointing out that these metrics act as soft industry or market standards. By this we mean that measures such as viewability in essence work as acceptable representations of the function and facticity of the entities or objects of programmatic advertising that – despite the structuring they are subject to by the real-time bidding protocol (RTB) – remain evasive. A good example that we have repeatedly touched upon is the fundamental entity of ad impression. What is an ad impression in fact? Ad impression has an institutional history yet it does not have a physical reality outside the advertising ecosystem.

As we have shown in the literature review section, ad impression has been the object of conflicts and highly contested definitions. A common definition of ad impression such as the "advertisement that [was] sent to an individual who had clicked on a site's page" [29] brought conflicts on issues of what is exactly delivered and whether this is actually viewed by the user. This is of particular relevance given that ad impressions are the building blocks of the CPM price structure, what marketers pay for. The advent of programmatic signaled yet another change to the definition of ad impressions that still remain highly contested. Ad impressions are now defined as the time lapse between a user's browser fetching a webpage with available ad slots and the effective display on the webpage of ads. This definition would suggest that every time a single browser fetches a webpage with at least one available ad slot a single ad impression is produced and exchanged. It is crucial to make clear that this change is of far reaching significance. Traditionally, impressions were quantified by *ex post* audience measurements, i.e. newspaper readership or television audience share constricted by panel measurements. Now, by contrast, they are sold *ex ante*, ahead of being effectively produced (i.e. the time lapse before ads are displayed) and therefore prior to user's attention being captured and measured.

Effectively, marketers bid on the likelihood that users see their ads. The metric of viewability is a way of fixing the unstable nature of ad impressions. Yet, these metrics are just industry conventions, the outcome of the negotiation of field participants with respect to how to manage the ambiguous nature of ad impressions and the intangible character of exchanges between actors and machines that on most essential respects are no more than data exchanges of future events. Viewability and click-through rates are the metrics intended to lend facticity to ad impressions. As it is often the case with metrics, because of the possibility of counting, viewability of impression appears as a fact rather than an object whose embedment in reality is variously problematic. These metrics are themselves hard to grasp. They are usually hidden away within complex multi-layered digital objects (viewability is an attribute of an ad impression object encapsulated in a bid-request object). They are estimates or likelihoods subjected to the limits, conventions and affordances of data tracking, recording and computing systems. They are often the result of complex industry negotiations [7] and they are ill-tolerated standards which have lost both their link with reality and their credibility within the industry.

Drawing on Elena Esposito, we call the entities constructed by these metrics conjectural objects [11, 12]. The term indicates that such objects do not exist as independent givens but only as relational constructs involved in the representation of yet-to-be objects. They are relational to the degree that they exist in a matrix of connections to other objects and actions and forward looking in the sense of seeking to regulate future occurrences. Conjectural entities are registered in other domains. They can be interest-rate shaping objects such as the LIBOR [13, 21, 22], ratios, indexes and soft standards such as measures that help structure actors' expectations by consolidating a practice that develops around their exchanges. In the case of financial-derivatives, for instance, such objects were developed to solve "the most pressing issue which was standardizing the underlying asset to an extent sufficient for claims on it to be tradable without reference to any specific physical entities" [22, p. 368].

A similar issue, we suggest, is present in the programmatic advertising domain, where the exchange is based on non-physical, yet-to-be objects such as ad impressions whose future realization is contingent on the interplay with other objects. As of today, one of the industry leading bodies, the IAB (Interactive Advertising Bureau) is pushing for the adoption of the "viewable impression" object. Viewable impressions are ad impressions that match "certain pixel and time exposure thresholds (minimum 50% of the ad's pixel for 1 or 2 continuous seconds for display and video respectively)" [23, p. 7]. As the Media Rating Council (MRC) digital audience-based measurement standards document continues: "viewable impressions are now the minimum required unit for digital audience-based measurement including digital and cross-media reach, frequency and GRP [Gross Rating Point]" [23, p. 7].

The excerpt is important because it attests to the shift in modes of measuring attention (and audiences) which now relies, rather heavily, on the affordances of the automated exchange. Standards such as viewability and pixels cannot measure user (actual) response. They can only count the time an ad can be visible on a page and the position the ad has on the screen (machine-to-machine). These metrics can be coupled with click measurement and other data as they are acquired from Data Management Platforms to calculate the likelihood of an ad being viewed. Audience measurement (reach, frequency and GRP) thus becomes the aggregation and computation of viewable impressions – while the ad impression measurability lends facticity to user attention.

It is worth to point out that there is no human agency involved here as these measurements and standards develop in highly automated exchanges, whereby machines talk to other machines in quick and massive interactions of data flows. Humans are of course the initiators of the process both in the form of end users whose clicking behavior triggers the web browser's request of an ad and, certainly, through the many actions and decisions of key industry actors that have been essential in setting up this hyper-complex ecosystem. However, the programmatic exchange of data, objects and measures which make today's digital advertising ecosystem – including the "user-audience" concept – is designed to operate without any further involvement of human-agents (on either side). As we have just seen, viewability is designed to measure the involvement of human users by substituting it with machine-readable metrics such as time and exposure of an ad on screen, plus history of clicks or profiles compiled and sold by third-party, data analytics, and platforms.

Conjectural objects arise out of the mutual expectations of the actors involved in the exchange and the infrastructure underlying the exchange, and act as reliable terms of reference for the actors involved. They are conjectural because they are involved in lending facticity to a promise that has yet to happen. It is crucial to clarify that the programmatic is neither involved in selling ads nor ad impressions (what would these be anyway?) The ecosystem rather trades the computable likelihood of an ad to be seen by a user, or as the industry calls it an "opportunity to see". This, we believe, makes them a different kind of objects that seem particularly germane to study, given their performative role in producing what is measured and exchanged, and how it is exchanged in the field of programmatic advertising. Effectively, here performativity assumes another dimension as it signifies the involvement of machines in the objects being measured which in the case of advertisement are audience and user attention. Even though IS as a field has only intermittently and indirectly dealt with these issues [1, 27], the debate on the facticity of concepts such as "audience" and "attention" has a long history in sociology and media studies, as pointed out in the introduction. Yet, the current developments that coincide with the diffusion of programmatic advertising aggravate the difficulties of establishing a field whose commercial relations are contingent on estimates and likelihoods of future occurrences realized out of the interactions of networks of intangible objects. As our empirical study illustrates, these difficulties are addressed not with a turn to reality but with a further leap into the conjectures of a probable world whose articulation (and calculation) requires the further separation of the entire ecosystem from real life events and the capabilities of human actors.

The advent of a data-driven rationalization paradigm in audience and attention measurement and the rush toward measurability has over time changed the objects observed. Traditional audience and attention mapping techniques measured content consumption with panels and adopted metrics and ranks on publisher outlets and reputations, audience habits and so forth. In the new paradigm we have presented here, publishers and their outlets have lost ground and power because marketers understood that the "click" was giving them the possibility of following user across contexts independently from publishers. The passage shifted the attention from the publisher to the user, making content outlets (webpages) less important. The machinery of ad networks relegated web publishers further into the background as on ad networks' auctions marketers actually bid on impression (user attention) without seeing where their ads will go. Ad networks made publishers literally invisible, contributing to their loss of power in the industry.

The advent of ad exchanges, we contend, has brought yet another important shift as it changed the modality in which audience measurement takes place and thus the object measured (audience). As seen, within the programmatic domain human-users loose importance as actors and as observable objects. In fact, their role is marginal for the effective completion of the exchange process. To work effectively on such a large scale, programmatic needs to replace human involvement with machines: software, platforms, and objects. In a sense, viewable impressions are purposely designed to replace other indicators to measure audience response with machine-readable ones. The unintended consequence of setting up such a complex data exchange and communication ecosystem that replaces human-machines assemblages with nearly closed circuits of machines-to-machine communication is the rise of what we conceive as path-dependent megastructures, massive automated infrastructures where each layer generates integral accidents that are solved by adding other layers [8, 10].

6 Final Remarks

Our empirical study suggests that the field of programmatic advertising carries the standard problems of attention capture and audience measurement into an entirely new stage by setting up a hyper-complex machinery of data tracking tools, semi-automated platforms, bidding algorithms and protocols. This technological complex and the practices and interests to which it is related establish a new institutional context in which attention is defined and tracked in new ways that further technicalize the perception and measurement of it and considerably automate the ways it is being traded and monetized. The changes we document have key attributes of a self-referential, or path-dependent, process whereby each step taken draws on, reinforces, and develops what is already in place [7, 16]. The outcome of this process is the creation of larger enclaves of automated sequences that considerably tweak and replace older practices with machine-to-machine data exchanges and which, in the case of conjectural objects, trade the future for the present [11].

By linking audience measurement to the technological affordances of automated exchange in massive platform ecosystems we contribute to the study of automation and of its consequences. Our findings clearly indicate a drifting away of measurement techniques from user behavior data to contextual data, something that allows for a faster and smoother exchange as it mostly relies on the mutual programming of digital objects. Furthermore, what we observe in the field of digital advertising has parallels to other industries which are becoming increasingly dominated by the reciprocal programming of conjectural objects such as finance and, increasingly, the digital travel industry sector. Programmatic advertising is then part and parcel of broader changes in which human exchanges are increasingly infiltrated and structured by the technological dynamics and the economic interests they serve.

References

1. Aaltonen, A., Tempini, N.: Everything counts in large amounts: a critical realist case study on data-based production. J. Inf. Technol. **29**(1), 97–110 (2014)
2. Alaimo, C., Kallinikos, J.: Computing the everyday: social media as data platforms. Inf. Soc. **33**(4), 175–191 (2017)
3. Anderson, C.: The Long Tail: How Endless Choice is Creating Unlimited Demand. Random House, New York (2007)
4. Ang, I.: Desperately Seeking the Audience. Routledge, London (2006)
5. Bermejo, F.: The Internet Audience: Constitution and Measurement. Lang, New York (2007)
6. Bermejo, F.: Audience manufacture in historical perspective: from broadcasting to Google. New Media Soc. **11**(1), 133–154 (2009)
7. Bowker, G.C., Star, S.L.: Sorting Things Out: Classification and Its Consequences. MIT press, Cambridge (1999)
8. Bratton, B.H.: The Stack: On Software and Sovereignty. MIT press, Cambridge (2016)
9. Carmi, E.: Regulating behaviours on the European Union internet, the case of spam versus cookies. Int. Rev. Law, Comput. Technol. **31**, 289–307 (2017)
10. Ciborra, C.: Imbrication of representations: risk and digital technologies. J. Manag. Stud. **43**(6), 1339–1356 (2006)
11. Esposito, E.: Probabilità improbabili. La realtà della finzione nella società moderna. Meltemi Editore, Roma (2008)
12. Esposito, E.: The structures of uncertainty: performativity and unpredictability in economic operations. Econ. Soc. **42**(1), 102–129 (2013)
13. Ettema, J.S., Whitney, D.C.: Audiencemaking: How the Media Create the Audience. Sage, London (1994)
14. Galloway, A.R.: Protocol: How Control Exists After Decentralization. MIT Press, Cambridge (2004)
15. Google for Developers: Real-Time Bidding Protocol (2018). https://developers.google.com/ad-exchange/rtb/openrtb-guide
16. Hanseth, O.: The economics of standards. In: Ciborra, C. (ed.) From Control to Drift: The Dynamics of Corporate Information Infrastructures, pp. 56–70. Oxford University Press, Oxford (2000)
17. Hanseth, O., Lyyttinen, K.: Design theory for dynamic complexity in information infrastructures: the case of building internet. J. Inf. Technol. **25**(1), 1–19 (2010)
18. IAB (Interactive Advertising Bureau): Open RTB Protocol Specification (API specification v2.5, 2016): S7 (2016). http://www.iab.com/wp-content/uploads/2016/03/OpenRTB-API-Specification-Version-2-5-FINAL.pdf
19. IAB (Interactive Advertising Bureau): Interactive Audience Measurement and Advertising Campaign Reporting and Audit Guidelines (2004). https://www.iab.com/wp-content/uploads/2014/10/Ad-Impression-Measurement-guideline-Global.pdf
20. Kallinikos, J.: The order of technology: complexity and control in a connected world. Inf. Organ. **15**, 185–202 (2005)
21. MacKenzie, D.: An Engine, Not a Camera. How Financial Models Shape Markets. MIT Press, Cambridge (2006)
22. MacKenzie, D.: The material production of virtuality: innovation, cultural geography and facticity in derivatives markets. Econ. Soc. **36**(3), 355–376 (2007)

23. MRC (Media Rating Council), IAB (Interactive Advertising Bureau): Digital Audience-Based Measurement Standards v5.1 Public Comment Draft (2017). http://mediaratingcouncil.org/MRC%20Digital%20Audience-Based%20Public%20Comment%20Draft.pdf

24. Napoli, P.M.: Audience Evolution: New Technologies and the Transformation of Media Audiences. Columbia University Press, New York (2011)

25. Napoli, P.M.: Audience Economics: Media Institutions and the Audience Marketplace. Columbia University Press, New York (2012)

26. Schwartz, J.: Giving Web a Memory Cost Its Users Privacy. The New York Times, 4 September 2001. https://www.nytimes.com/2001/09/04/business/giving-web-a-memory-cost-its-users-privacy.html

27. Scott, S.V., Orlikowski, W.J.: Entanglements in practice: performing anonymity through social media. MIS Q. 38(3), 873–893 (2014)

28. Taneja, H., Mamoria, U.: Measuring media use across platforms: evolving audience information systems. Int. J. Media Manag. 14(2), 121–140 (2012)

29. Turow, J.: The daily you: how the new advertising industry is defining your identity and your worth. Yale University Press, New Haven (2011)

30. Webster, J.G.: The Marketplace of Attention: How Audiences Take Shape in a Digital Age. MIT Press, Cambridge (2014)

31. Wu, T.: The Attention Merchants: The Epic Scramble to Get Inside Our Heads. Vintage, New York (2017)

32. Yin, R.: Case Study Research Design: Design and Methods. Sage, London (2013)

33. Yoo, Y., Henfridsson, O., Lyytinen, K.: Research commentary–the new organizing logic of digital innovation: an agenda for information systems research. Inf. Syst. Res. 21(4), 724–735 (2010)

Hybrid Agency and the Performativity of Technology

Re-figuring Gilbert the Drone

Mads Bødker[1]([⊠]), Stefan Olavi Olofsson[2], and Torkil Clemmensen[1]

[1] Copenhagen Business School, 2000 Frederiksberg, Denmark
`mb.digi@cbs.dk`
[2] Frederiksberg, Denmark

Abstract. In the paper we offer a story of *re-figuring* a consumer drone as a way of "living with monsters". If drones are "monstrous", what potentials might lie in re-framing them as more benign, civic, or even perhaps enchanted? Based on a field study of work at a makerspace, we present re-figuring as a process of reflecting, interacting and imagining the function of a drone, using gradually developing intuitions as well as an emergent *felt* 'sense' of the drone in practice. Using an analytic trajectory broadly based on philosophies of affect, we suggest how felt relations to technology can potentially become further involved in a critical move towards re-figuring "monstrous" technologies.

Keywords: Drones · Re-figuring · Design

1 Introduction

This paper explores the case of working with a drone as a companion technology in ways that deliberately attempt to *re-figure* the drone as a technology. The rate of privately owned drones is predicted to increase extensively over the coming years. An estimate from the US Federal Aviation Agency estimates that the number of privately owned hobbyist drones will exceed 3.5 million in 2021 [1]. Drones are here to stay, but what form will they take physically as well as discursively, affectively? How will we talk about them, what roles will they play, and how will we live with them? These are some of the broader questions that this paper pursues.

Drones may invoke images of war and violence, as well as connotations of privacy invasion and surveillance. Drones, as a phenomenon, have become at least partially anchored in representations that accentuate the more menacing properties of the technology [2]. Some analysts emphasize how drones are involved in a larger 'surveillant assemblage' [3] and how "the figure of the drone is useful because it offers a highly visible and controversial example of the deployment of networked surveillance and quasi-automated response and suggests the ways in which the implementation of drone logic across disparate spheres of social practice partakes of the military-inflected rationalization of everyday life" [4: 21]. According to e.g. [5], when users are confronted with actual drones, negative figurations seem to prevail. Long-standing concerns over privacy are compounded with "evidence of negative perceptions around drones such as fear of damage or injury and unwillingness to disclose personal information under drone surveillance" [5: 6765].

U. Schultze et al. (Eds.): IS&O 2018, IFIP AICT 543, pp. 127–139, 2018.
https://doi.org/10.1007/978-3-030-04091-8_10

The figure of drones is not only constituted discursively and in terms of "meaning", i.e. in terms of the narratives or signification, but also *affectively* within a particular historical present. *Droning* is an invisibly-menacing technological modus that is discursively constructed in language, but at the same time an incarnate, felt and affective ubiquitous presence: we cannot necessarily see the drones, but they are there, they may hover! It can create knots in our stomach when we think about the eye-in-the-sky, we may flinch involuntarily at the idea of small, autonomously flying vehicles.

We argue that drones are 'monstrous', but not necessarily violently so. Monsters emerge as hybrid assemblages of humans and technology in technologically affluent societies. Monsters can be felt as threatening but also invoke reveries, potentials and promises. They inhabit the liminal spaces between humans and things; a space where convenient and conventional classifications into essential categories such as "the human" and "technology" seem to collapse. Drones can be aggressive and violent in one figuration, invoking images and feelings of terror, surveillance and so on. They can also be benign, helpful, yet still somewhat "foreign bodies", mysterious and somewhat speculative. They fly, they travel, bafflingly, through the air, nimble floating creatures as well as rather mundane and grey plasticky things when they run out of battery. They are transgressive objects that have not yet become normalized within specific discursive boundaries. They have yet to become stable technological *objects* with circumscribed, discrete connotations. Perhaps because they were originally intimately linked to military applications, it is difficult to appreciate fully those (possible) benign figures as they are currently too unstable, explorative, and emergent.

As a response to the question of "living with monsters", our paper details the early parts of a process of working with a drone in a maker lab. In the paper, we employ ideas from affect theory (e.g. [6]) and the notions of enchantment and evocative objects (e.g. [7–9] as ways of conceptualizing the processes of re-figuring a drone.

2 Theories

Our paper relies on an overall orientation towards concepts from the so-called *affective turn* in the humanities and the social sciences [6]. We use these theoretical approaches to emphasize how a technology is *experienced* or felt as e.g. a threat or a promise, not only as semiotics, an icon, index or a symbol of "something else", but also *something* that 'flies below the radar' of signification: a mood, a felt sense of things, something in *excess* of meaning. In affect theories, sense and sensation seem to unfold in an embodied and sociomaterially entangled organism [10] before conventional notions of decoding or 'cognition' kicks in. This is a complex collection of literatures that we will not in any way present in much detail, but they tend to share a concern for what goes on "*beyond, below* and *past* discourse" [11: 350], shunning conventional language and conventional meaning. It reverses the concepts of "standard modernist blueprints" that "suggest the existence of a self-governing, psychological subject – a subject essentially assumed to be autonomous and informationally closed to the outside world – affect theories suggest instead that humans can be understood as intimately (and messily, unpredictably) entangled in continuous vital and felt exchanges with the world" [12: 179].

Affect as a form of excess beyond conventional meaning allow us to talk about the *felt* and embodied relations to technology [13]. It suggests potentials for research that explores the felt, messy, and ephemeral/fleeting senses of things that might appear in interacting with them. Affect theory also points to somewhat neglected aspects of sociomaterial theorizing. Affect is not posited as something internal to the subject. Unlike the idea of emotions, which provides us with a clear structure of an inside (the feeling) and an outside (the expression), as well as with a form of causality, affects are neither fully 'inside' the subject, nor fully outside in the environment or the objects [6]. In that way, affects are perhaps an expression of what we might term the "socioma-teriality of feeling". Material things are entangled in how we *feel* as well as in what we do. As Bødker & Jensen suggest; "the socio-materiality of practices can usefully be complemented by a notion of affective entanglements; i.e., the embodied materiality of *feeling*. In this way, moods, feelings, and felt embodiment (similarly to practices) are relational performances of people and machines" [14: 3005]. In particular, we find that Jane Bennett's notions of enchantment and vibrant materiality [7, 8] provide us with new ways of thinking about affective relations to things. Below, we suggest how these perspectives might play a role in design.

2.1 Design and Affect

The "generative valence" of affect has been noted by [15]. They suggest that affect is "the pre-conscious, pre-intentional, pre-verbal processes that occur between bodies" [15: 82] and they indicate how affective properties and materialities within a design practice are "a found (and an always reconstituting) force, one that stands out as a little-utilised, yet always pervasive, generative agent" [15: 90]. *Things* exert a force and afford an intensity, they attract and collect words, feelings or agendas. Places, situations, events and shared 'structures of feeling' [16 128 ff.] or 'atmospheres' [17] (en)force or modulate behaviors, ideas or moods. However, these qualities of a tend to go unnoticed by conventional social science vocabularies and more readily acceptable notions such as structure or agency, hierarchies, management, or process adherence.

With these initial concerns about the process and object of design, our approach trails a number of critical and speculative design approaches. Most notably Dunne and Raby's notion of Critical Design [18–21] that has been described as "a form of research aimed at leveraging designs to make consumers more critical about their everyday lives, and in particular how their lives are mediated by assumptions, values, ideologies, and behavioral norms inscribed in designs" [22: 3298]. Critical design "holds the design profession to account for its complicity with capitalist ideology and alienation. It names some design values of global capitalism - conformity, obedience, easy pleasure, and corporate identity, among others. It challenges designers and consumers alike to envision - and to demand - design products that reflect *a more challenging view of human needs and experience*" [22: 3298].

We understand the drone as a *figure* that has not yet been exhausted, where a number of potential figures lie beyond the image of drones as tools for policing or violence and towards even more benign and likable accomplices in everyday life. What happens if a drone is conceptualized as a companion technology or as a benign escort, maybe not unlike countless "science fiction" versions of autonomous machines, robots or drones that have personalities, alliances, histories, feelings, and expressive dispositions?

Such figures, we argue, can be explored affectively, as "[it] is through attention to these affective materialities that we can design for affect" [15: 90]. The affective dynamics of a design process can be a part of the fabric that engenders critical design and speculation based on affective and indeed fleeting imaginations or gut feelings can be a designerly means to engage critically with the inherent openness of objects and the unpredictability and hence malleability of material- and social futures. We propose that feelings and affective dispositions matter in (speculative) design processes and we propose some opportunities and motivations for extending the affect philosophical lines of inquiry in design- and information systems research.

3   Method

As the initial inspiration for our observations and subsequent reflections we relied on Pink, Akama & Sumartojo's argument that "uncertainty [can be] re-figured as a *methodological device* rather than as just an object of study [...] uncertainty can be understood as a generative technology" [23: 43, emphasis in original]. In our case, one of the authors happened to work in a collective of people with an interest in building, trying out and hacking things, in an effort to re-think and re-know "drones" as an idea and as a thing.

The design process with the drone was not initiated or contextualized as a purposeful generation of a specific solution, but was driven along by what initially felt like a curiosity and an intense shared interest in the design group. The primary data collection by the second author was followed up by discussion and subsequent data collection and explorations by the 1st and 3rd author, who collaborated on the framing of the paper.

The intention in the paper is not to attempt a final interpretation of our data, but rather to begin training a theoretical lens on our fieldwork. What is presented are shorter stories and situations that influenced the direction and ongoing reconceptualization of the drone and the way it emerged as a particular object to us as researchers. The narratives below are created collaboratively by all three authors around the details provided by the second author. Primary data has been collected over the course of approximately 4 months, in the fall of 2016, primarily in a maker lab in Malmö, Sweden. The writeup here takes the form of a series of vignettes [24] that account for some of the processes and events during the stay. The material for writing up the vignettes is primarily notes and reconstructions at later stages of the 2nd author's work in the maker lab as well as emails, digital communications, and shared reflections between all three authors. Also, field trials and structured observations of drones and drone flying provided all authors a sense of what flying a drone feels like, and how people feel about being in the vicinity of a 'live' drone.

In late 2016, the first author began working in a local community maker lab in Malmö in Southern Sweden. It included visiting the space located at a defunct factory site multiple times per week, at different times of day. The researcher spent time with a small group of community members as well as guests in the space and other people who became enrolled in the various networks and projects around the facility. Over some time, the people in the space became informants for research, even if the site was originally not intentionally chosen as a research site, nor were the colleagues intended as informants. As colleague-informants, the designers in the maker lab were continuously commenting, sharing knowledge, adding suggestions and ideas in daily 'water cooler' conversations as well as in more structured reflections and idea generation processes. The 1st and 3rd author further provided structured observations and reflections on drone use, design, flying and the sense of operating a drone remotely. These observations and the sense of what drones are, how they are experienced, figured and felt are interspersed within the overall narrative of the drone that came to be known as Gilbert.

4 Life of a Drone

4.1 Arrival

So, a drone had been procured for our maker lab in order to complement the collection of hack-able gadgets and devices available to the maker community. Initially, the intention of my work at the maker space was simple: figure out what to do with the drone. It was all a bit confusing – here's an expensive drone, what can we do with it? I had no idea.

> "On one evening when I brought the drone home with me (pics attached) my wife was visiting Sweden. We began discussing drones, and we talked about how DJI is a Chinese company, and that DJI Phantom has a different name in China. In China, the DJI Phantom drone is called DJI 'elf/fairy', in Chinese specifically jīnglíng 精灵 and based on a Chinese version of Wikipedia on Baidu the drone was meant to help non-tech savvy people by being easy to use and to do things for you as a helpful elf/fairy would. [...] I remembered this when looking for research documents yesterday and spotting an old email about a drone meetup event called "Phantoms in the Forest" (see http://url.ie/12bze) (Notes on September, 2016)

The primary focus of my observations was slowly turned towards seeing and trying to understand what was going on in some of those not very articulate and sometimes surprising moves in how we (the group) and I (as the observer) talked about, understood or conceptualized the drone. This included many discussions with community members in the maker lab, often taking outset in popular culture references. Taking the drone home, I began fantasizing about the drone as an elf, a helpful spirit that lingers in the periphery of your attention, but when I met with the others, they had some slightly less poetic stories to tell. Maybe an elf with its own Snapchat channel?

> When talking about the drone and how we could re-think it in a positive way, one of the community members shared a Parks and Recreation clip of the character Ron having shot down a drone for delivering a gift to his house. The company behind the drone had looked up his address, and the character is known for highly valuing privacy. Thus the scene shows him knocking on the main character's door (Leslie Knope) in the rain at night, holding up a mangled drone that he has shot down [...] (https://www.youtube.com/watch?v=Uw60ZLZUlDc). On a funny note, well more so a strange note, before conveying that we wanted to showcase drones in a positive way the community member had mentioned attaching a knife to a drone to knock down icicles in the winter. (Notes on October, 2016).

It feels as if the drone is a magnet of words, thoughts, feelings, and ideas. At the same time as it is fun and evocative, it's also a nuisance, a pest, sneaky, dangerous, unreliable, almost invisible, an eye in the sky, something you'd wanna throw a rock at. Or not. The clip has Ron holding the mangled drone in his hands, like a wounded animal, like a piece of game, helpless and quite useless.

> Our work is influenced by other products circulating in tech media [...], specifically Lily Robotics' Lily Drone (which turned out to be a scam) EHang's Ghostdrone as well as the extremely viral Snapbot by Snap (formerly Snapchat) which has just debuted in California. Lily and Snapbot both have anthropomorphic features including eyes and a mouth, and a description for Ghostdrone on TechCrunch's article states "Drone seeks companionship. Likes long walks in the mountains and the movie Airplane!" Furthermore, the founder of Lily Robotics refers to the Lily drone with the phrase "It flies itself," as a key selling point referring to a supposedly autonomous capability that does not really exist. (Notes on October, 2016).

Drones without a human operator? The buzz is there, it's all over the recommender engines when you're online. Drones are immensely practical and there are scores of business models and value propositions being pursued around the technology. But there was an emerging feeling in the community group that the drone had potential beyond the relatively low hanging fruits of other benign drone use: damage inspection, agricultural surveillance, aerial photography duties and so on. In our discussions, as we were toying around with it in the workshop and in my own private musings, our drone gradually became a thing that embodied many different future applications and purposes.

4.2   The Naming

We gave our drone a name. What is in a name? Well, quite a lot, it turns out. Naming the drone was a not a ceremony as such – it was indeed rather un-ceremonial. The group and I had discussed how (and *if*) we wanted to disrupt and distance the drone from being considered a tool or just another functional product with a neatly circumscribed and predictable business model, and giving the machine a name seemed a good starting point. In the spirit of our initial ethos of being explorative rather than closing the business case (whatever that meant), we toyed around with different ideas meant to contrast the recent tech naming conventions of personal assistants such as Alexa, Cortana, and Siri, all of which we perceived to be a bit high-tech or just about *exactly* what you'd call a robot. You can somehow feel what a person named Cortana would be like. The drone was eventually named Gilbert. Perhaps somewhat reminiscent of Dilbert, the cartoon character and perhaps a name that has a slightly old fashioned, cozy ring to it, a butler?

> Before the project switched names due to voting, we were looking to create a logo for the project and were initially focusing on a logo involving Gilbert. Some examples of this included having a drone by some blocks representing a skyline with the text "Gilbert learns to fly". However, before this we had conducted a search online for sources of inspiration specifically around robots and mustaches. After talking about Lyft giving drivers pink mustaches for their cars, we joked about how Gilbert as a name somehow sounded like a person who would have a mustache. This led to me searching for images of robots with mustaches to use as points of inspiration for our own logo. (Notes on October, 2016).

Gilbert was shaping up, getting somewhere. A version of the drone had struck a chord. "Are you with Gilbert" became a way of asking other members or the community whether you were using the drone, and it seemed the name meant something to people – at least for some period of time. From meeting with different community members, word had gotten around that a few individuals were looking into re-thinking how Gilbert could become something.

> We attributed positive character attributes to Gilbert. Gilbert was friendly, he was a member of the community, someone who could be helpful in some way. We had started creating an identity for Gilbert, and once Gilbert's personality became more concrete, we were less receptive to alternative applications for the drone that did not match his perceived character. (Notes on November, 2016).

One idea that emerged, based on a sense of Gilberts personality ("what would a Gilbert do?"), was for the drone to film locations to raise awareness of accessibility issues. After speaking online and meeting with the entrepreneur, he stated that there were several locations within the city that were dangerous for bicyclists. It emerged that Gilbert could perhaps be beneficial for civic engagement [25] by documenting dangerous areas and creating more tangible points of discussion with the public and local government. Gilbert would be a gentle public caretaker, a drone that was looking for opportunities and challenges in public spaces.

We began test filming with Gilbert, with the first run outside of the maker lab. This sparked new concerns and new challenges arose.

4.3   The Sociomateriality of Flying

The idea of drone is often kind of limited. What does it do other than fly. Or rather, it has this fantastic ability to actually *fly*. It's obviously not magic, but (just) a collection of wires, servos, propellers, protocols, algorithms, radio waves. It feels like it is challenging gravity, nimble, leaf-like in the wind. Maybe it will one day just fly along (silently), break the reins and connections to its human supervisors.

You learn a lot about drones by flying and doing test rounds with them. It's one thing to see the drone on a table, and another to touch it, fly it, and listen to it. It's noisy, feels a bit dangerous (until you get to know it a bit), and through flying it, a new sense of space emerges. Rather than merely looking at it in the maker lab, talking, brainstorming with a coffee and a laptop, flying Gilbert around included developing a new sensitivity to various weather conditions such as temperature, wind and humidity. You become gradually aware of the challenges of vertical and distance navigation, as well as obstacles in the form of buildings or other things that might obstruct line of sight or safety, both for people on the ground and for Gilbert. Flying outside highlights the materiality of the drone, as winter weather in Sweden quickly drains battery life. It also heightens the sense of the airspace being regulated in various ways and by various agencies. Of course, Gilbert cannot be flown near the airport, heavily trafficked public spaces and so on. But the announced yet still somewhat surprising presence of the Pope in our mid-sized Swedish city created a larger no-fly zone, practically grounding the drone for a period.

You develop a sense of a drone and the space it operates in, and concurrently you acquire a sense of the sociomaterial formation of the drone, the way conventions, ideas, discourse, rules, regulations, images, metaphors give shape to your sense of the airspace. Imagine: the drone cut loose from all this, free to roam around the city, free to go wherever it wants. Instead, what you typically get is a hash of concerns, of decisions and histories that govern the present, patrolling the airspace with regulations and all the 'social stuff', the infrastructural stuff. You can also feel it as a kind of inappropriateness; for example, if you are flying close to people you become very careful not to intimidate them, not to impart on them the kind of menacing presence that the drone can sometimes radiate.

> We flew Gilbert in the fall, often when the ground was wet from after a rain, and thus we had to wipe any mud and debris from the landing gear. During these times we would notice light scratches on the landing gear, normal wear from use. The type of scratches you wouldn't normally pay attention to. But you could feel them when picking Gilbert up and putting him back into the carrying case. [There was] a growing sense of attachment for an important thing that we were becoming more associated with, there was a bit of unease. (Notes on November, 2016).

The drone also feels vulnerable, brittle somehow. Its rigid plastic casing and light weight is not something that inspires a lot of confidence in its ability to survive a fall from, say, 10 meters. Also, it's clearly not waterproof, not particularly aerodynamic, light and overall just a bit delicate. The wind carries it along when you fly, so you have to adjust continuously as you dodge obstacles. You run into a lot of situations where keeping the drone flying and in presentable shape is a bit of an effort. And so, we cared for Gilbert, for a while, taking care to keep the (his?) innards and surfaces in good shape. We didn't want him to mess up or to be messed up.

5   Analysis and Discussion

In our case, the process of designing and 'making' was led along initially by a growing fascination of the drone as a malleable thing. When the drone entered the maker lab, a central figuration of the drone in the minds of the community leaned on the functional but also somewhat hostile assemblages of associations and figures described by [4]. The analysis shows how the process of re-figuration was not just a process of re-thinking, but also included a feeling of the drone as 'lively', alive in its capacity to enchant.

Scene 1 begins with the researcher struggling to figure out what to do with the drone. Taking the drone home and discussing its cultural associations led to a new sense of the technology, and facilitated new, emergent figures of the drone. Could such feelings of a magic creature emerge in relation to a plastic consumer drone? Back in the maker lab, the reflections were used to critically assess the conventional understandings of the drone, and activities were gradually devoted to destabilize those. A figure of the drone as a benign, helpful, considerate and inherently non-threatening thing arose. A significant event here was the un-ceremonial naming of Gilbert. It was unceremonial, but also offered the drone a form of autonomy, bestowing upon it some power to shape or inspire the community, to collaborate, behave, inspire. The drone was animated and anthropomorphized. The drone was decorated (and re-decorated), moustaches were considered, phrases and other embellishments were used to address the network around the drone, making Gilbert into a lively thing. Torres et al. have suggested that there are a lot of possibilities to extend technological artefacts with "unique expressive personalities" that "go beyond neutral, atomic, functional, and obedient "things". A name can help in creating a felt intimacy with devices leading to better experiences through increased "pleasure, social inclusion, and personal value in devices" [26]. The act of changing the point of reference, from 'are you using the drone?' to 'are you with Gilbert?' acknowledges the Gilbert project and the drone's appropriateness for entering into new relationships. The name and associated character perhaps also provided a more articulated presence of the drone as a member of the maker lab community.

The naming and the figure created by the name seemed to carry on through in the process, working as a way of anchoring the question "what would Gilbert do?". As Turkle puts it, things (or materials, assemblages) can be *evocative objects* rather than lifeless things. She suggests that "[w]e are on less familiar ground when we consider objects as companions to our emotional lives or as provocations to thought. The notion of evocative objects brings together these two less familiar ideas, underscoring the inseparability of thought and feeling in our relationship to things" [9: 5]. Evocative objects are also things that mean more than we can tell. They entail (somewhere in their constitution) something *in excess* of conventional meanings or essences. Such objects can feel subtly strange, unfinished or malleable. The researcher (the 2nd author) started the engagement with the drone by associating 'spiritual' characteristics with it, suggesting that it could be magic and enchanted. When flying with it, it felt brittle and potentially dangerous, but also enchanted and slightly magical.

Drawing on key ideas from the affective turn, political philosopher Jane Bennett [8] describes how things can be considered enchanted and how materials involve an element of vibrancy and vitality – things are, if we discard the strict separation of the organic and the inorganic so important to modernist scientific ontologies, *vibrant* with the possibilities of life, agency, and wonder. Bennett references Franz Kafka's story "The Cares of a Family Man", in which the narrator reflects on the creature *Odradek*, a simple spool of thread that is (curiously) alive, and shows how Kafka cultivates a "state of wonder" in a disturbingly mundane depiction of a strange and enchanted object. The Gilbert project and the project of re-figuring the drone enrolled a similar form of enchantment and curiosity. The naming did not just bestow upon the drone some human-like form of personality. Perhaps it also oriented the researcher and the community towards an appreciation of the wonder of drones and the relatively unexplored potentials of seeing the drone as a more benign and caring agent.

To Bennett, cultivating a sense of enchantment is not just a kind of fanciful, magical thinking. It has consequences for political and moral reasoning and action, since it calls into doubt the modernist project of "disenchantment" and the ultimate knowability of an object, to focus on new possible connections, attachments and hybrids. Enchantment, a form of awe that is not a "fall on your knees" awe, part of an ethics of caring, a story that "suggests that you have to love life before you can care about anything" [7: 4]. Enchantment, writes Bennett, "involves, in the first instance, a *surprising encounter,* a meeting with something you did not expect and are not fully prepared to engage" [7: 5, emphasis added]. Discussing the DJI drone in the context of Chinese meanings and connotations, the project unfolded from the unexpected proposition that the drone could be a slightly magical creature, an elf, a helpful spirit or a fairy in the woods. The drone was not just an inert object waiting to be elaborated through a design process. As a thing, it was articulated within a dispersed mood amongst the community in the maker lab that emphasized the drone as animated, alive and ultimately "cared for": When Ron, in the video clip, shoots down the drone, we feel sorry for the little deformed metal creature, like a dead animal in his hand.

Gilbert was a challenge to fly. He was caught up and entangled within material, social, political/regulatory and even religious concerns. Being part of the team, Gilbert was subjected to many of the same kinds of legislations and structures – being grounded, being immobilized or locked away. Flying a drone, with all the complications, can better articulate the felt, embodied relations that we can have with enchanted objects, as well as the more readily recognizable categories we invoke when we talk about technologies as sociomaterially entangled with 'the social'. When flying, a drone is revealed as both threatening and fragile, menacing and a little unpredictable, but with a brittle, defenseless side too. It is noisy and perhaps nosy, it is cute but will cut your fingers or peep down your backyard if you're not careful. If it becomes too threatening, we can readily imagine the response: shoot it out of the sky with a shotgun! But the engagement with the drone gradually became a caring one, one of relishing in an interaction with Gilbert, keeping him safe from harm.

Is 're-figuration' (or indeed design) a fundamentally human-led activity? Design has a connotation of "intentional" shaping (the designer shapes an object, leads the pencil, cuts the material), but we suggest that there might be other, "more-than-human" energies at play in design. The engagement with the drone was at least in part driven along by the shared feeling of the drone as an enchanted object, a thing that is lively and agential. The emergent sense of the drone as somehow alive guided the process towards exploring new experiential trajectories for the drone as a felt object, making the typical associations with violence and intrusion less of a gut reaction.

Re-figuring through design includes furthering a kind of fuzzy undecidability and the probing (sometimes chaotic, fumbling) frame shifting, and allows such processes to be seen not as noise, but as an indication of possibilities. It involves an explorative process where the progression is searching, reflective, and reckless. Gilbert, for example, might at times embody a particular mood or aura. These were based on popular depictions or vague metaphors and ideas, but also on a rather incidental grounding due to a papal visit and a budding sense of care toward the brittle plastic gadget.

We find that design and critical exploration of (monstrous) technology can be usefully extended with affective and materialist perspectives suggested in this paper. Understanding how affective modulations, gut feelings and enchantments might shape the design process is also learning what affect *does*. Asking "what or how do things enchant me" or "how do I feel about this technology", widens the possibilities for re-figuration. We suggest that there are many opportunities for further research in the intersection of critical design practices and the process of *re-figuring* and re-enchanting technology. Bennett suggests that 'enchantment' as a quality of objects or technology goes against the dominant enlightenment discourses [7]. These would suggest that things are essentially inert and that only human actors are agential. To accept the affective shaping of a design process, the way feelings, senses, atmospheres or moods are entangled in processes and indeed 'thinking' and doing, might allow for different enchanted figures to emerge, figures that resist the dominance of functional properties or pragmatic application. In our case, Gilbert emerged from the growing sense of attachments and care. The moods, the felt attachments and care cultivated in the project created a sense of Gilbert as a companion or an enchanted object, and resisted military-, surveillance-, or similar applications.

Thus, what unites the opportunities that this paper suggests, is the increased orientation away from a 'modern constitution' [27] towards recognizing hybridity, connections, and crossings between the human and the non-human. In this paper, we have suggested more specifically on how feelings and affective engagements might be at play in a design project, suggesting that people can hold extensive relations with technology that go beyond the pragmatic and the identifiably purposeful. We see an opportunity to extend these studies in ways that are attentive to how objects *become* 'evocative' (or stirring, awe-some, or indeed enchanted) in practice, and what this might entail for a critical engagement with things in design. Being open to the wonder or enchantment of technologies, to let oneself be guided by vaguely felt atmospheric conditions or moods of a 'project' is a way to further destabilize dominant associations and affective states related to a technological figure.

6 Concluding Remarks

Our case involved joining and participating in a local maker space where we had access to a shared public artifact in the form of a drone. Through the case, we sought to reconceptualize the concept of drones by exploring alternative, and potential futures while engaged with the maker space community. Over the course of a few months, through interactions with community members and participating within the space in daily activities and special events, new understandings and crucially a new 'sense' of the drone emerged. Along these lines, our analysis of the emergence of various affective and *felt* work that allowed the drone to materialize as a vital, enchanted object. We suggest that concepts drawn from literatures affect, 'enchantment' and evocative objects and the assumption from most theories on sociomateriality that mind and matter is entangled, are useful for forming a fuller understanding of what living with technology can be.

Suggesting the possibility for what she calls a "vibrant matter" [8], we indicate that the body and the experiential are not merely 'containers' or environments for politics, values or figures of technology. Moral and ethical thought is, following Bennett, tied up with the ability to become enchanted by things in the world. Cultivating this form of enchantment is a road to more ethical and sustainable relations to things and to the world at large.

Crucially, following the ethos of critical design, cultivating affective and enchanted relations to technology may allow us to consider more broadly what human-technology relations *can be* like – they may lead us to futures that are less menacing and more attuned to favorable and "live-able" assemblages and entanglements of the human and the non-human. This is perhaps particularly required for creating new approaches and understandings of digital, ubiquitous, and interconnected technologies that come loaded with potentially quite literate monstrous, confrontational or forbidding connotations.

References

1. Shepardson, D.: U.S. commercial drone use to expand tenfold by 2021: government agency. Reuters (2016). https://www.reuters.com/article/us-usa-drones/u-s-commercial-drone-use-to-expand-tenfold-by-2021-government-agency-idUSKBN16S2NM. Accessed 14 May 2018
2. Manjikian, M.: Becoming unmanned. Int. Feminist. J. Polit. **16**(1), 48–65 (2013). https://doi.org/10.1080/14616742.2012.746429
3. Haggerty, K.D., Ericson, R.V.: The surveillant assemblage. Br. J. Sociol. **51**(4), 605–622 (2000)
4. Andrejevic, M.: Theorizing drones and droning theory. In: Završnik, A. (ed.) Drones and Unmanned Aerial Systems, pp. 21–43. Springer, Cham (2016). https://doi.org/10.1007/978-3-319-23760-2_2
5. Chang, V., Chundury, P., Chetty, M.: Spiders in the sky: user perceptions of drones, privacy, and security. In: Proceedings of the 2017 CHI Conference on Human Factors in Computing Systems (CHI 2017), Boulder, Colorado, 6–11 May, pp. 6765–6776. ACM, New York (2017). https://doi.org/10.1145/3025453.3025632
6. Clough, P.: The affective turn: political economy, bio-media and bodies. Theory Cult. Soc. **25**(1), 1–22 (2008)
7. Bennett, J.: The Enchantment of Modern Life: Attachments, Crossings, and Ethics. Princeton. Princeton University Press, New Jersey (2001)
8. Bennett, J.: Vibrant Matter: A Political Ecology of Things. Durham. Duke University Press, North Carolina (2010)
9. Turkle, S. (ed.): Evocative Objects – Things We Think With. MIT University Press, Cambridge (2007)
10. Hodder, I.: Entangled: An Archaeology of the Relationships between Humans and Things. Wiley-Blackwell, Malden (2012)
11. Wetherell, M.: Affect and discourse – What's the problem? From affect as excess to affective/discursive practice. Subjectivity **6**, 349 (2013)
12. Bødker, M., Chamberlain, A.: Affect theory and autoethnography in ordinary information systems. In: Twenty-Fourth European Conference on Information Systems (ECIS), Istanbul, Turkey (2016)
13. McCarthy, J., Wright, P.: Technology as Experience. MIT Press, Cambridge (2004)
14. Bødker, M., Jensen, T.B.: Sounding out IS? Moods and affective entanglements in experiential computing. In: Twenty-Fifth European Conference on Information Systems (ECIS), Guimarães, Portugal (2017)
15. Kidd, A., Smitheram, J.: Designing for affect through affective matter. Interstices, vol. 15 (2014). http://interstices.aut.ac.nz/ijara/index.php/ijara/issue/view/1/showToc
16. Williams, R.: Marxism and Literature. Oxford University Press, Oxford (1977)
17. Böhme, G.: (Translated by A.-Chr. Engels-Schwarzpaul). The theory of atmospheres and its applications, Interstices, vol. 15 (2014). http://interstices.aut.ac.nz/ijara/index.php/ijara/article/view/201
18. Dunne, A.: Hertzian Tales: Electronic Products, Aesthetic Experience and Critical Design. Royal College of Art, London (1999)

19. Dunne, A., Raby, F.: Critical Design FAQ (2007). http://www.dunneandraby.co.uk/content/bydandr/13/0. Accessed 12 May 2018
20. Dunne, A., Raby, F.: Speculative Everything – Design, Fiction, and Social Dreaming. MIT Press, Cambridge (2013)
21. Dunne, A., Raby, F.: Design Noir: The Secret Life of Electronic Objects. Birkhäuser, Basel (2001)
22. Bardzell, J Bardzell, S.: What is "Critical" about Critical Design? CHI '13. In: Proceedings of the SIGCHI Conference on Human Factors in Computing Systems, pp. 3297–3306 (2013)
23. Pink, S., Akama, Y., Sumartojo, S.: Uncertainty and Possibility: New Approaches to Future Making in Design Anthropology. Bloomsbury Publishing, London (2018)
24. Orr, J.: Images of work. Sci. Technol. Hum. Values 23(4), 439–455 (1996)
25. Graeff, E., Matias, J.N.: Making drones civic. Values and design principles for civic technology. In: International Studies Association's 56th Annual Convention, New Orleans, LA (2015)
26. Torres, C., O'leary, J., Paulos, E.: LiveObjects: leveraging theatricality for an expressive internet of things. In: Proceedings of the 2016 ACM Conference on Designing Interactive Systems - DIS 2016 Companion (2016). https://doi.org/10.1145/2908805.2908807
27. Latour, B.: We Have Never Been Modern (Transl. Catherine Porter). Harvard University Press, Cambridge (1993)

Making a Difference in ICT Research: Feminist Theorization of Sociomateriality and the Diffraction Methodology

Amany Elbanna[✉]

Royal Holloway University of London, Egham, Surrey TW20 0EX, UK
amany.elbanna@rhul.ac.uk

Abstract. Over the last decade, sociomateriality appeared as a theme in IS research that has been interrogated with a variety of theoretical lenses. However, researchers have since raised methodological concerns regarding its application. This paper argues that a research methodology cannot be separated from either the theoretical lens that the research adopts or from its overarching purpose. Considering the broad range of theoretical lenses through which sociomateriality could be examined, this paper focuses on Barad's theory of agential realism [25]. The paper provides a brief history of agential realism to shed light on the reasons behind IS researchers methodological difficulty and offers a diffraction methodology as a possible methodological guide to IS research adopting this lens. Implication for research is discussed.

Keywords: Sociomateriality · Agential realism · IS research methodology
Diffraction methodology

1 Introduction

The term sociomateriality has been in circulation in the IS field for a decade. It was initially introduced as an umbrella term [1] that advocates and emphasizes the role of the material aspects in everyday organizing and social life [2]. It has been studied through different theoretical lenses including the sociotechnical approach [3–7], pragmatism [8], Gibson's concept of affordances [9], the practice lens [10], Actor Network Theory [11–14], and agential realism [15–17]. It has also received healthy (and sometimes heated) debates regarding its philosophical premises and alternative theoretical lenses to examine it. However, IS scholars largely agree that it broadens the definition of the technical and draws attention to the material aspects of social activities [18, p. 34 and 42, 19, p. 810].

Information systems' (IS) researchers have reported difficulty in designing research, collecting data, analyzing data and reporting on the non-human when adopting the Sociomateriality theme and in particular its agential realism theoretical lens [19, p. 813, 20]. They question "…where does one start, methodologically and analytically" [21, p. 219] and find it generally challenging to collect data [17, 22], analyze data [23, 24] and report on findings [10]. Indeed, the different lenses used to examine sociomateriality could have "very practical consequences" on the research process from the focus of the

U. Schultze et al. (Eds.): IS&O 2018, IFIP AICT 543, pp. 140–155, 2018.
https://doi.org/10.1007/978-3-030-04091-8_11

research and research questions up to the research contribution [18, p. 60]. Hence understanding the root of the methodological problems IS researchers face when applying agential realism requires an examination of the roots and orientation of this lens.

This paper aims to provide theoretical and methodological clarity within the sociomateriality research that adopts the lens of agential realism [25]. Agential realism is a useful lens for IS research that could provide fresh perspective on complex digital phenomenon that are significantly distributed and appear unbounded but produce observable effect [26]. It provides a theoretical grounding for the IS research to cross its traditional organisational boundaries to account for contemporary digital phenomenon such as having rating systems or health network systems based on thousands and millions of globally distributed members producing effect of evaluating or providing medical research. Hence, it could help us unpack and understand the complex relations of people, databases, algorithms, organisational strategy and profit opportunities that produce significant outcomes for society.

The paper traces the origin of agential realism in order to understand its methodological implications and the roots to the methodological problems IS researchers face. It introduces diffraction as a possible methodology for research adopting this lens and discusses how it could be adopted throughout the research process including literature review, data collection and data analysis. In doing so, the paper contributes to facilitating the adoption of the lens of agential realism in IS research, advancing its methodology and expanding the sociomateriality thinking.

The paper is divided into six sections. The following section presents a brief history of agential realism and its roots. Section Three discusses its adoption in IS and analyses the sources of methodological difficulty faced by researchers in its application. Following this, Section Four presents the concept of diffraction while Section Five discusses its application throughout the research processes including literature reviews, data collection, data analyses and in the formulation of research findings and purposes. The final section then provides a discussion and conclusion to the paper.

2 Agential Realism and Contemporary Feminist Theorization

Agential realism is undeniably part of a long history and trajectory of contemporary feminist theorization and "owes .... much to a thick legacy of feminist theorizing" [27, p. 168]. It aims to move beyond the traditional dichotomy of realism and social construction to provide "a more robust understanding of materiality …that enables feminists and other liberatory theorists to take account of the ways in which "matter comes to matter"" [28, p. 98].

Feminist theorisation has passed through stages of development from having a fanatic focus on women to attempting to find explanation to the different sexual orientations and hence developing the concept of gender. Contemporary feminist theorists argue that the development of the concept of gender, while ground-breaking in feminist theorisation, is still founded on a binary distinction between biological sex and sexual orientation (sexuality) or between nature and culture [29, 30]. Contemporary feminist theorists sought ways to avoid feminist research confinement in yet another power-producing binary. They propose an understanding of gender/sex as an entangled cultural-natural phenomenon and argue that material reality and the body are discursively constituted [31, 32]. Contemporary feminist theorist Judith Butler's work on "recasting the matter of bodies" and the re-thinking of materiality and power has been influential in this regard [33, p. xii]. Butler's revolutionary conceptualization of the notion of 'matter' has served as a milestone in contemporary feminist theorization and provided inspiration for many contemporary feminist theorists. She proposes a process view of matter "… not as a site or surface, but as a process of materialization that stabilizes over time to produce the effect of boundary, fixity, and surface we call matter." [33, p. xviii] [emphasis as in original].

Another milestone in contemporary feminist theorization has been established by Haraway's development of the notion of the hybrid or cyborg [34] and her positioning of 'material-semiotics' as an epistemological presupposition [35]. For Haraway, the hybrid or cyborg is an effect of complex interaction among the person, material and entity. Through this work, Haraway has encouraged researchers to explore the co-constitution of sociocultural and bodily material aspects in ways that avoid both traps of biological and material determinism or cultural essentialism [31, 36]. Researchers have since adopted this view to examine not only the production of the body, gender, and sexuality but have also extended it to study other intersecting power differentials such as race, ethnicity, class, disability and human rights [31, 32].

Likewise, Barad also demands a contemporary feminist theorization in which "[n] either discursive practices nor material phenomena are ontologically or epistemologically prior. Neither can be explained in terms of the other. Neither is reducible to the other. Neither has privileged status in determining the other. Neither is articulated or articulable in the absence of the other; matter and meaning are mutually articulated" [25, p. 152]. However, she finds "Butler's conception of materiality is limited by its exclusive focus on human bodies and social factors, which works against her efforts to understand the relationship between materiality and discursivity in their indissociability" [25, p. 34]. Hence, Barad offers a more radical theoretical reworking of binary that conceptualizes matter as "a sedimented intra-acting, an open field" that does not entail closure and rather finds the formation of mountain ranges in their multiplicity and liveliness to be attesting to "this fact" [27, p. 168]. Influenced by the context of her research on Physics, she crafted the concept of intra-activity; an originally physicist terminology. However, Barad develops the concept of intra-action to reflect the relationships between any organism and matter, human or non-human, emphasizing that "all matter can be understood as having agency in a relationship in which they mutually will change and alter in their on-going intra-actions" [37, p. 4]. In this sense, all matter are "understood not to have definite and inherent boundaries, but are always in a state of intra-activity of higher or lesser intensity or speed" [38, p. 530]

Barad proposes the notion of discursive practices as an ongoing material reconfiguration of the world [39]. In doing so, she advances contemporary feminist theorization through fundamentally rethinking ontology and epistemology as intermingled in what she terms 'onto-epistemology' and provides deconstruction based on this view[1]

---

[1] For more details on how Barad's research builds on the thick legacy of feminist theorization, see [27].

in the context of physics and the production of scientific practices [28, 40, 41]. Aiming to disrupt binary divisions and find a way to conceptualize differences in a new way, she developed an agential realist view of the world. Her agential realism theorization extends both Butler's work on materialization and the relationship between the material and the discursive [28, p. 89] and Haraway's development of the epistemological metaphor of 'diffraction' [35, 42]. In doing so, Barad's work aims to sharpen the theoretical tool of feminism and bring new insight to examine differences and their production [27, 39].

While contemporary feminist theorisation has departed from feminist theorisation in recognising and attempting ways to resolve binary thinking, it shares with its predecessor a concern for critique and transformation. However, contemporary feminist theorisation has widens this mission to include critique of all types of differences. Hence, it is considered a powerful theoretical lens to deconstruct preconceived notions and binary divisions such as those between object/subject and human/non-human [43–45]. It is not limited to feminism or the studying of women, gender or sexuality as it went well beyond this to explore differences and how they come into being [46, p. 18]. It has been adopted in a wide range of disciplines including economics [47, 48], politics [49], art [50], geography [51, 52] and health [53, 54] to fundamentally examine phenomenon as diverse, for instance, as globalization, mental health, human rights, poverty, disability and medical care.

3   Contemporary Feminist Theorization in IS and Its Methodological Difficulties

Contemporary feminist theorization including agential realism has been embraced in the IS field mainly through its adoption by the Sociology of Science and Technology Studies' (STS). STS's adoption of contemporary feminist theorizing, including Mol and Suchman's work, has been frequently cited in IS as the roots for 'sociomateriality'. This is despite, Mol's [54] recognition of her effort to develop a contemporary feminist theorization of science, technology and medicine. Through adopting contemporary feminist theorisation, Mol navigates the way between subject/object ontologies by stressing the multiplicity of ontologies for the human body. She argues for the performativity of ontologies and that "... *ontologies* are brought into being, sustained, or allowed to wither away in common, day-to-day, sociomaterial practices" [54, p. 6]. Her work consistently adopts contemporary feminist thinking to show the multiplicity of reality and the enactment of multiple ontologies and multiple logics of care, disease, diagnosis and medical discovery [54–57].

Lucy Suchman has also benefited from contemporary feminist theorization in her examination of technology design and use [58–60]. She argues that contemporary feminist theorization could "add[s] crucial sensibilities to the reconception of agency" [58, p. 6]. In particular, Suchman finds the work of Barad's agential realism to be providing 'materialist constructivism' that is radical in understanding that material phenomenon is inseparable from the apparatuses of bodily production and that it emerges out of the ongoing reconfiguration of subject/object boundaries [58].

The IS field's adoption of agential realism has focused mainly on its material and practice side and the view that it "puts capacity for action and entanglement in practice on our agenda" [17, p. 213]. As a result, the IS field has largely focused on materiality, inseparability, relationality and performativity [19, 61] and which and how many of these aspects must be featured in a study [61]. This understanding has contributed to the methodological difficulties that IS researchers face when applying this lens. Besides depicting agential realism's research as having fixed necessary components, it overlooks the fundamental views of intra-activity, ontological primacy to phenomenon and difference-making that this theoretical lens holds. Indeed, contemporary feminist theorization advocates a new mode of science that attends to complexity, indeterminate encounters, fluid ontology and intra-action. It accepts and account for multiplicity and stands firmly against having a universal truth. In this regard and considering its strong theoretical standpoint, it is not possible to adopt agential realism and associated contemporary feminist theorization while continuing the quest for objectivity with approaches rooted in chronology, order and fixed agencies. This gulf between the theoretical lens and its premises on one hand and the research methodology on the other hand creates methodological tension. It uncouples the link between the epistemology (knowledge of the phenomenon) and research methodology (scientific knowledge production). Hence allows researchers to pursue two different – and rather contradictory - logics in one piece of research. Since agential realism holds radical views on ontology and epistemology, its theoretical lens on phenomenon cannot be separated from the scientific knowledge production throughout the research process.

Contemporary feminist theorization contests the knowledge production mode of traditional science. The agential realism notion of intra-action applies to the research process as much as it applies to the phenomenon under examination. Indeed, it provide an alternative view beyond realism and relativism that have dominated the traditional production of scientific knowledge [62]. In doing so, Barad joins Haraway in moving beyond the notion of reflexivity advocated by relativism arguing that it has strong mirroring orientation where something is reflected from a stable entity [25, 28, 35, 42]. Contemporary feminist theorists argue that reflexivity consistently treats one side as fixed in order to measure against and reflect on and, in the process produces and emphasises sameness. The researchers' reflection on phenomenon assumes that researchers are outside the phenomenon, separated from it and looking at it [35]. In contrast, contemporary feminist theorization argues that researchers are irrevocably part of the phenomenon and its production. Based on quantum physics, Barad [25, 28, 62] argues that knowledge production is not only about epistemology but also about ontology [63]. Hence, the researcher, researched and research apparatuses "cut-together apart", defining each other and making an impact in the world [27].

Agential realism's consideration of knowledge production as an onto-epistemological phenomenon challenges longstanding traditions in studying the production of knowledge, including research knowledge. Indeed, it challenges the current epistemological focus of knowledge production in research and instead invites new types of methodologies that account for differences in an onto-epistemological view. In this sense, Stumpf [64] argues that "behaviours, just as thoughts, ... exist only in relationship to other behaviours, the process of observing them or sharing ideas introduces a new relationship – hence the observed behaviour or shared idea is different from its unobserved counterpart" [64, p. 41].

In information systems, the traditional science is considered ingrained in the scientific community [65]. This is challenging for IS researchers who adopt contemporary feminist theorization including agential realism. They need to navigate a way to present research based on new science to a research community guided by traditional science rules. Believed to be inescapable, Baskerville and Pries-Heje introduced the notion of "wrapper" to bridge between the knowledge production of new science and the demands of old science for representation [65]. However, wrapping the propositions and theoretical stance of new science in an old science disguise could miss out the richness and value of the new science and produce research that is of less value. In contrast to this view, contemporary feminist theorists and researchers have taken the concept of intra-action seriously and experimented with the diffraction methodology as a way to effect change in research processes and outcomes. Diffraction was introduced as an innovative research methodology that allows for intra-action during the research process, thus giving way to new ideas, possibilities and transformations [25]. It works against the wisdom of traditional science in terms of having defined entities to be observed. Adopting diffraction means that the researcher is focusing on the intra-action through which entities are defined and are being defined. This does not reject the notion of entities and having distinctions between them but it rejects fixed pre-assumed agencies and relationships outside of the intra-action [63, pp. 253–254]. The following section elaborates on the diffraction methodology as presented by contemporary feminist theorists.

4   Taking Research Intra-action Seriously: The Diffraction Methodology

Haraway has highlighted the problematic nature of reflection as a pervasive trope of knowing, the parallel notion of reflexivity as a method or theory of self-accounting, and hence the problems of taking account of the effect of the theory or the researcher on the investigation [25 p. 72]. She found the epistemological practices of reflexivity anchored in representation to be dissatisfying and consequently critically assessed its theoretical assumptions and consequences. She coined the metaphor and concept of diffraction by proposing the notion as an alternative to reflexivity. Diffraction refers to various phenomena that occur when waves meet a barrier such as an obstacle or a slit. These waves bend and spread out in the area beyond the barrier or slit producing a new pattern. There are many different ways for diffraction to occur depending on the phenomenon such as light or water, the nature of the barrier including slits or rocks and the size of the barrier. Haraway argues that:

> "[r]eflexivity is a bad trope for escaping the false choice between realism and relativism in thinking about strong objectivity and situated knowledges in technoscientific knowledge. What we need is to make a difference in material-semiotic apparatuses, to diffract the rays of technoscience so that we get more promising interference patterns on the recording films of our lives and bodies" [35, p. 16].

Haraway's point is that the methodology of reflexivity mirrors the geometrical optics of reflection, and that all the focus on reflexivity as a critical method of self-positioning remains caught up in geometries of sameness. In contrast, diffraction conveys our knowledge-production practices and the differences that they make on the world. Hence, it recognises that knowledge production is not a linear process that travels in direct line. It is rather an infusion of ideas, phenomenon, technology and researchers that intra-act to produce the research.

Diffraction also recognises multiplicity and that different effect of a phenomenon could occur depending on the intra-acting matters. Hence, diffraction shifts the research's focus towards how differentiation is made and where the effect of difference appear [42]. In the context of gender, Haraway clarifies that "[g]ender is always a relationship, not a performed category of beings or a possession that one can have. Gender does not pertain more to women than to men. Gender is the relations between variously constituted categories of men and women (and variously arrayed tropes), differentiated by nation, generation, class, lineage, color, and much else" [35, p. 28]. In the same vein, we can think of our IS phenomenon. Systems users for example is also a relationship not a fixed category of users and non-users. This opens the space for us to understand multiplicity and differences of use and how they come about.

Haraway's notion of diffraction was subsequently adopted and further developed by Barad [25, 27, 63, 66]. Barad agrees with Haraway that diffraction could serve as a counterpoint to reflection and reflexivity. While both are optical phenomenon and metaphors, reflection indicates mirroring and sameness whereas diffraction indicates patterns of difference. Barad goes a step further to elaborate on the notion of diffraction as "a tool of analysis for attending and responding to the effects of differences" [25, p. 72]. In this sense, it is the duty of the researcher to report on how the effects of these differences occur and matter. For Barad, diffraction is also "a method and practice that pays attention to material engagement with data and the "relations of difference and how they matter" [25, p. 71, 67]. Barad conceptualizes diffraction not as opposed to sameness, but as a dynamism where intra-actions between entities enact agential cuts that do not produce absolute separations but rather cut "together-apart" [27, p. 168].

To sum, diffraction is both a subject of research and a research practice. As a subject for research, Haraway asserts that "[d]iffraction is a narrative, graphic, psychological, spiritual, and political technology for making consequential meanings" [35, p. 273]. As a research practice, the diffraction methodology is concerned with exposing, making and practising diffraction as part of adopting contemporary feminist theorization [68] as the following section explains.

5 Diffraction: Changing Waves and Making a Difference in IS Research

Diffraction is concerned with differentiation and the creation of the new from the existing. As a research methodology, it has been adopted in different disciplines including education [67, 69], contemporary feminist studies [27, 70], arts [71, 72], philosophy [73], psychology [72, 74], and humanities [75, 76]. This section presents the application of the diffraction methodology throughout the re process.

5.1   Diffractive Reading of Literature (Diffractive Literature Review)

A diffractive literature review seeks to bring literature from different traditions together and read the texts through a lens to establish how their differences and similarities could give rise to something new. It does not aim to identify gaps in the literature and position the research as filling this gap but rather aims to create another layer for reading. This layer of reading does not simply aim to close areas where a plethora of research exists and instead uncover areas where research is needed or categorize and establish binaries between school of thoughts [77]. Rather, it is a positive approach to reading previous research from a particular position or theoretical lens to see what new understanding could emerge and what new questions and issues we face. Thus, a diffractive reading of literature "allows their insights to strengthen, challenge and articulate one another" [78, p. 190].

Diffractive literature review provides positive reading and critiquing of literature. It "… breaks through the academic habit of criticism and works along affirmative lines" [73, p. 22]. Affirmative reading involves "a mode of assenting to rather than dissenting from those 'primary' texts" while engaging with critique and involving the reader in the transformation of the literature towards a new avenue [79, p. 3]. While criticism of previous work is seen as a form of dismissal and boundary creation, reading diffractively involves working towards "more promising interference patterns" [35, p. 16]. It entails reading important insights from different strands, schools of thought or disciplines and reworking concepts. In doing so, it allows us to affirm and strengthen links between strands of literature and school of thoughts.

Diffractive reading is emergent and unfolding. Barad further elaborates on the diffractive literature review saying:

> "diffraction does not fix what is the object and what is the subject in advance, and so, unlike methods of reading one text or set of ideas against another where one set serves as a fixed frame of reference, diffraction involves reading insights through one another in ways that help illuminate differences as they emerge: how different differences get made, what gets excluded, and how these exclusions matter." [25, p. 30].

5.2   Diffractive Data Collection: Reading Data Through One Another

Barad [25, 39] argues that the technologies of observation not only cannot be separated from what is observed, but that they will always be intra-acting with (affecting and interfering with) the phenomenon under study. In this regard, it consider data collection as an onto-epistemological space of encounter [80]. Viewing data collection as an encounter focuses attention on the ongoing intra-active processes through which phenomenon and involved players are being produced. In this regard, researchers are invited not to have preconceptions and a priori assumptions that fix entities. Instead, they are encouraged to have an open encounter that allow for entities to be "more mobile, intra-active and multiple than our modes of enunciation normally suggest" [74, p. 3]. The task of the research when adopting diffractive data collection "is not to tell of something that exists independent of the research encounter, but to open up an immanent truth – to access that which is becoming true, ontologically *and* epistemologically, in the moment of the research encounter" [74]. A research encounter in this sense is experimental – the researcher does not know in advance what onto-epistemological knowledge will emerge from it [32, 38].

As researchers, we are largely influenced by Western philosophy that has long-privileged a view that begins with distinctions and clear boundaries. In contrast, agential realism unsettles boundaries and position the very making of boundaries as the subject of investigations. Hence, a question on impact of technology on people and organization cannot be answered using agential realism. Indeed, agential realism is "unsuitable to studying the "impacts" of technology or how technology "inscribes" aspects of social structure" [26, p. 77]. This is because a question on 'impact' assumes the existence of boundaries, distinct entities, and determinate relationship. The question in agential realism will be about how agential cuts occur and differences are being made. Diffractive data collection does not place the object or the subject in the center of data collection, attempt to predefine entities and their relationship, or gloss over one for the benefit of other. Instead, the researcher focuses on the phenomenon and the intra-acting elements that produce it. The researcher is no longer an outsider tasked with observing and collecting data about an external phenomenon but rather part of the phenomenon that they produce.

In terms of data collection methods, agential realism is open to all data collection method. It should be noted here that Barad resides to historical analysis of experiments in physics, other researchers adopt interviews, participant observation, or participative co-production methods as ways for collecting data.

5.3   Diffractive Analysis: Finding How Differences Are Being Made

In line with contemporary feminist theorization, diffraction supports critical inquiries and analysis as it foregrounds differentiality [76]. A diffraction pattern does not map where differences appear, but rather maps where the effects of difference appear [42, p. 300]. As a result, diffractive analysis focuses on the phenomenon and the effects of intra-action on the phenomenon. The central project for contemporary feminist theorization has been "to avoid the interpretive question 'what does it mean?' when reading theory or analysing data, and instead ask: 'how does it work?' and 'what does this text or data produce?'" [32, p. 268].

Diffractive reading of data is unlike interpretation. In interpretation, there is the interpreter (researcher), the interpreted and the interpretation that mediates between them. This thinking is binary where the researcher is seen as external to the phenomenon; "unaffected by and external to the interpretive process" reflecting the illusion of a detached researcher who at best reflects on his/her practices [81]. Analysis following the diffraction methodology is more concerned with making waves and "experimenting with different patterns of relationality … to see how the patterns shift" [82]. As diffraction goes beyond reflection and production of sameness and mirroring, diffractive data analysis goes beyond coding as coding tend to produce what is known and repetitive [83]. In diffraction, the researchers create waves of intra-actions between different data sets and between data and theories where their analysis moves from one state to another. Diffraction, as an analytical way for thinking, "does not try to fix those processes so that they can be turned into a methodic set of steps to be followed. Rather, it opens the possibility of seeing how something different comes to matter, not only in the world that we observe, but also in our research practice" [80, p. 3]. In this case, the research questions emerge with its data and analysis and advances with the researchers' own changes and transformation. In documenting her experience, Palmer reports that "the data did not only transform the kind of knowledge that was produced by the analytical work; it also transformed me as researcher" [69]. In Palmer's case, the researcher's intra-action and evolvement is part of the story. Barad explains the entanglement of the research, saying: "So while it is true that diffraction apparatuses [of physics] measure the effects of difference, even more profoundly they highlight, exhibit, and make evident the entangled structure of the changing and contingent ontology of the world, including the ontology of knowing. In fact, diffraction not only brings the reality of entanglements to light, it is itself an entangled phenomenon" [25, p. 73].

Davies [74] elegantly comments on her analytical practices, saying that: "I cannot simply reflect on my analytic practice as if it were an observable entity. It is a series of movements, affected already by the choice to see them as diffractive, and to think about them diffractively. And if analysis is a set of encounters among meaning, matter and ethics, as Barad suggests, those encounters are always already affecting and being affected by the meanings and mattering that I am analysing. This should not be read as weakness of qualitative work, but rather, in Barad's terms, a means of getting closer to the "fundamental constituents that make up the world" [25, p. 72]. Davies describes here research encounter saying: "The stories I tell and the analytic work I do with them are an entanglement of intra-acting encounters, and the very act of writing about them is one further element in a complex array of entangled movements" [74, p. 4]

Diffractive analysis opens up space for the encounter; firstly, in terms of those who we encounter as researchers and secondly, by being open to being changed by each encounter [84]. In sum, it focuses on difference: difference the research makes, difference the researchers' make, differences that subject-object intra-action make. Binary differences are not a starting point for research. Rather, the difference of the phenomenon is what matters. The resulting explanation of how differences are created is core, not the description of how an object was constructed or how a subject interacts with it. Instead, diffractive analysis focuses on how they come together to make a difference in terms of subject, object and instrument.

As a methodology of contemporary feminist theorization, diffraction focuses its attention on the phenomenon and how it emerges through intra-action. Chia has previously drawn the attention of the Organization Studies' community to the ontological character of reflexivity, suggesting the recognition of "the primacy of a becoming-realism in which the processual becoming of things is given a fundamental role in the explanatory schema" [85, p. 31]. He also draws attention to process-philosophy and the impact of its adoption in Organization Studies [86]. Cecez-Kecmanovic argues that adopting a process-philosophy in IS goes beyond established traditions of interpretivism and hence presents a fundamental challenge to researchers in its adoption [87].

Indeed, like Chia's and other process-philosophers' approaches, diffractive analysis shares a concern with 'How' and the impact on the phenomenon under study. However, diffraction holds a distinctive view on reflexivity as it replaces the usual concept and practice in qualitative research and the inherent assumptions of representations and independence of the researcher's gaze [32, 88–90]. Reflected in the research practices, researchers need to consider the encounter along with the phenomenon, the material apparatuses of research, and the knowledge-producing practices as entangled aspects of research. They need to recognize that all the entities involved in their research are constituted in the action of knowledge production, not before the action starts [35].

5.4 Diffraction in Research Output: Making a Difference

Diffraction is concerned with making a difference, including making a difference through the research. Haraway and Barad developed diffraction to move our ideas of scientific knowledge from reflective, disinterested judgment to mattering and embedded involvement [76]. Research is then seen as an intervention in the world. Diffraction is part of contemporary feminist theorization which holds strong concerns on ethics, liberty, freedom, equality, human rights and environmental issues [31]. Diffraction calls for spelling out these concerns through research. Research adopting agential realism and other contemporary feminist theorization, including the associated methodology of diffraction, should then be a call to arms, a voice of freedom, liberation, equality, ethics that calls for change, transformation and arms to action. For example, research on ultrasound scanners and 3D medical imagery has produced detailed analysis on agency and relationships of the foetus, scan technology, medical practices, mothers, family and surrounding societal images. It draws attention to the critical question of human rights and has contributed significantly to the debate on women's and foetus rights. Most IS research adopting agential realism and other contemporary feminist theorization engages with different strength on how a phenomenon is produced whilst paying less attention to why the phenomenon matters [58]. The latter is in the heart of contemporary feminist theorization, including agential realism and should be part and parcel of adopting such a theoretical lens [91–93].

To sum, the value of contemporary feminist theorization and its associated diffraction methodology lies in its purpose and mission. This is of particular interest to IS research that "has focused almost the entirety of its resources on theoretical and technical knowledge, ignoring ethical and applicative knowledge" [94, p. 268]. It also brings about a much-needed perspective regarding ethics which is currently "underrepresented in IS" [95].

6 Discussion and Concluding Remarks

Information systems' researchers adopting the sociomateriality theoretical lens of agential realism have reported difficulty in designing research, collecting data, and reporting on the non-human when adopting contemporary feminist theorizations. This paper argues that understanding and eventually resolving the methodological difficulty requires deep understanding of the theoretical foundation of agential realism and its mission. The paper unravels one of the core foundation of agential realism in contemporary feminist theorization and discusses its purpose and mission. It also shows that contemporary feminist theorization holds strong views opposing binaries and boundary creation and hence has a long tradition of deconstructing and understanding how differences come about. Furthermore, the paper also demonstrates that contemporary feminist theorization share with its predecessor feminism an interest to critically engage with phenomenon calling for transformation and change.

In this light, the paper discusses few of the roots to our methodological difficulty when applying agential realism as research tends to overlook the fundamental views of intra-activity, ontological primacy to phenomenon and difference-making that this theoretical lens holds. Consequently, the paper positions agential realism and contemporary feminist theorisation in 'new science' that attends to complexity, indeterminate encounters, fluid ontology and intra-action and which accepts and account for multiplicity and stands firmly against having a universal truth. In terms of the methodological difficulty experienced by IS researchers, this paper suggests that this difficulty stems from three main points. Firstly, the adoption of agential realism and contemporary feminist theorization as part of Science and Technology Studies. It showed how this misconception prevented IS researchers from understanding the "thick legacy" of feminist theorization and its purpose [27]. Secondly, a further methodological challenge can be observed because contemporary feminist theorization, including agential realism, presents new science whereas IS researchers tend to be more immersed in old science techniques. This could explain the struggle of IS researchers trying to present new science in an old science format [65]. Finally, using data collection methods that center the subject creates a methodological problem in analytically decentering the subject following agential realism and other contemporary feminist theorization. This creates the reported research dilemma of how "to keep the material in the storyline without falling from one side to another", resulting in "either leaving the material realm unexamined, or emphasizing the agency of the material at the determinant of understanding the entangled practice" [10, pp. 292–293].

The paper discusses the notion and methodology of diffraction that contemporary feminist theorists developed [25, 27, 28, 35, 42]. It discusses how diffraction could benefit the research process including conducting literature reviews, data collection and data analyses. In doing so, it responds to Walsham's call for IS researchers to engage, influence and make a difference in the world that they study [96].

In conclusion, contemporary feminist theorization and the associated methodology of diffraction could be fruitful avenue for IS research to explore as it enters into examining unbounded and indeterminate phenomenon that go well beyond the traditional confinement. This paper provides a start for a diffractive discussion where the new could be conceived and developed.

References

1. Orlikowski, W.J., Scott, S.V.: 10 sociomateriality: challenging the separation of technology, work and organization. Acad. Manag. Ann. **2**(1), 433–474 (2008)
2. Orlikowski, W.J.: Sociomaterial practices: exploring technology at work. Org. Stud. **28**(9), 1435–1448 (2007)
3. Robey, D., Anderson, C., Raymond, B.: Information technology, materiality, and organizational change: a professional odyssey. J. Assoc. Inf. Syst. **14**(7), 379 (2013)

4. Leonardi, P.M.: Car Crashes Without Cars: Lessons about Simulation Technology and Organizational Change from Automotive Design. MIT Press, Cambridge (2012)
5. Leonardi, P.M.: When flexible routines meet flexible technologies: Affordance, constraint, and the imbrication of human and material agencies. MIS Q. **35**, 147–167 (2011)
6. Whyte, J.: Beyond the computer: changing medium from digital to physical. Inf. Org. **23**(1), 41–57 (2013)
7. Almklov, P.G., Østerlie, T., Haavik, T.K.: Situated with infrastructures: interactivity and entanglement in sensor data interpretation. J. Assoc. Inf. Syst. **15**, 263 (2014)
8. Pentland, B.T., Singh, H.: Materiality: what are the consequences? In: Paul, M. Leonardi, B. A., Nardi, J.K. (eds.) Materiality and Organizing, pp. 287–295. Oxford University Press, Oxford (2012)
9. Majchrzak, A., Markus, M.L.: Technology affordances and constraints in management information systems (MIS) (2012)
10. Wagner, E.L., Newell, S., Piccoli, G.: Understanding project survival in an ES environment: a sociomaterial practice perspective. J. Assoc. Inf. Syst. **11**(5), 276–297 (2010)
11. de Albuquerque, J.P., Christ, M.: The tension between business process modelling and flexibility: revealing multiple dimensions with a sociomaterial approach. J. Strateg. Inf. Syst. **24**(3), 189–202 (2015)
12. Dery, K., et al.: Lost in translation? An actor-network approach to HRIS implementation. J. Strateg. Inf. Syst. **22**(3), 225–237 (2013)
13. Quattrone, P., Hopper, T.: What is IT?: SAP, accounting, and visibility in a multinational organisation. Inf. Organ. **16**(3), 212–250 (2006)
14. Cecez-Kecmanovic, D., Kautz, K., Abrahall, R.: Reframing success and failure of information systems: a performative perspective. MIS Q. **38**(2), 561–588 (2014)
15. Østerlie, T., Almklov, P.G., Hepsø, V.: Dual materiality and knowing in petroleum production. Inf. Org. **22**(2), 85–105 (2012)
16. Orlikowski, W.J., Scott, S.V.: What happens when evaluation goes online? Exploring apparatuses of valuation in the travel sector. Org. Sci. **25**(3), 868–891 (2014)
17. Orlikowski, W.J., Scott, S.V.: The algorithm and the crowd: considering the materiality of service innovation. MIS Q. **39**(1), 201–216 (2015)
18. Leonardi, P.M.: Materiality, sociomateriality, and socio-technical systems: what do these terms mean? How are they related? Do we need them? In: Materiality and Organizing: Social Interaction in a Technological World, pp. 25–48 (2012)
19. Cecez-Kecmanovic, D., et al.: The sociomateriality of information systems: current status, future directions. MIS Q. **38**(3), 809–830 (2014)
20. Elbanna, A.: Doing 'sociomateriality' research in information systems. Data Base Adv. Inf. Syst. **47**, 84–92 (2016)
21. Constantinides, P., Barrett, M.: A narrative networks approach to understanding coordination practices in emergency response. Inf. Org. **22**(4), 273–294 (2012)
22. Johri, A.: Sociomaterial bricolage: the creation of location-spanning work practices by global software developers. Inf. Softw. Technol. **53**(9), 955–968 (2011)
23. Faulkner, P., Runde, J.: On sociomateriality. In: Leonardi, P.M., Nardi, B.A., Kallinikos, J. (eds.) Materiality and Organizing: Social Interaction in a Technological World. Oxford University Press on Demand, pp. 49–66 (2012)
24. Jarzabkowski, P., Pinch, T.: Sociomateriality is 'the New Black': accomplishing repurposing, reinscripting and repairing in context. M@ n@ gement **16**(5), 579–592 (2013)
25. Barad, K.: Meeting the Universe Halfway: Quantum Physics and the Entanglement of Matter and Meaning. Duke University Press, Durham (2007)
26. Scott, S.V., Orlikowski, W.J.: Sociomateriality—taking the wrong turning? A response to Mutch. Inf. Org. **23**(2), 77–80 (2013)

27. Barad, K.: Diffracting diffraction: cutting together-apart. Parallax **20**(3), 168–187 (2014)
28. Barad, K.: Getting real: technoscientific practices and the materialization of reality. Differ. J. Feminist Cult. Stud. **10**(2), 87–91 (1998)
29. Alaimo, S., Hekman, S.: Introduction: emerging models of materiality in feminist theory. In: Alaimo, S., Hekman, S. (eds.) Material Feminisms. Indiana University Press, Bloomington, IN (2008)
30. Alaimo, S.: Material Feminisms. Indiana University Press, Bloomington (2008)
31. Lykke, N.: Feminist Studies: A Guide to Intersectional Theory, Methodology and Writing. Routledge, Abingdon (2010)
32. Taguchi, H.L.: A diffractive and Deleuzian approach to analysing interview data. Feminist Theory **13**(3), 265–281 (2012)
33. Butler, J.: Bodies that Matter: on the Discursive Limits of Sex, 1st edn. Taylor & Francis, Didcot (1993)
34. Haraway, D.: Simians, cyborgs, and women. Univ. PA Law Rev. **154**(3), 477 (1991)
35. Haraway, D.J.: Modest_Witness@ Second_Millennium. FemaleMan_Meets_OncoMouse: Feminism and Technoscience. Psychology Press, New York (1997)
36. Lykke, N.: Intersectional analysis: black box or useful critical feminist thinking technology. In: Framing Intersectionality: Debates on a Multi-faceted Concept in Gender Studies (2011)
37. Taguchi, H.L.: Going Beyond the Theory/Practice Divide in Early Childhood Education: Introducing an Intra-active Pedagogy. Routledge, Abingdon (2010)
38. Hultman, K., Taguchi, H.L.: Challenging anthropocentric analysis of visual data: a relational materialist methodological approach to educational research. Int. J. Qual. Stud. Educ. **23**(5), 525–542 (2010)
39. Barad, K.: Posthumanist performativity: toward an understanding of how matter comes to matter. Signs **28**(3), 801–831 (2003)
40. Barad, K.: A feminist approach to teaching quantum physics. In: Teaching the Majority: Breaking the Gender Barrier in Science, Mathematics, and Engineering, pp. 43–75 (1995)
41. Barad, K.: Agential Realism: Feminist Interventions in Understanding Scientific Practices. The Science Studies Reader, pp. 1–11 (1999)
42. Haraway, D.: The promises of monsters: a regenerative politics for inappropriate/d others. In: Grossberg, L., Nelson, C., Treichler, P. (eds.) Cultural Studies, pp. 295–337. Routledge, New York (1992)
43. Kruks, S.: Gender and subjectivity: Simone de beauvoir and contemporary feminism. Signs **18**(1), 89–110 (1992)
44. Gibson-Graham, J.-K.: 'Stuffed if i know!': reflections on post-modern feminist social research. Gend. Place Cult. J. Feminist Geogr. **1**(2), 205–224 (1994)
45. Parpart, J.L.: Who is the 'Other'?: a postmodern feminist critique of women and development theory and practice. Dev. Change **24**(3), 439–464 (1993)
46. Friedman, S.S.: Mappings: Feminism and the Cultural Geographies of Encounter. Princeton University Press, Princeton (1998)
47. Eschle, C.: Feminist studies of globalisation: beyond gender, beyond economism? Glob. Soc. **18**(2), 97–125 (2004)
48. Ferber, M.A., Nelson, J.A.: Beyond Economic Man: Feminist Theory and Economics. University of Chicago Press, Chicago (2009)
49. Eschle, C.: Global Democracy, Social Movements, and Feminism. Westview Press Inc., Boulder (2001)
50. Pollock, G.: Generations and Geographies in the Visual Arts: Feminist Readings. Routledge, Abingdon (2005)
51. Silvey, R.: Power, difference and mobility: feminist advances in migration studies. Prog. Hum. Geogr. **28**(4), 490–506 (2004)

52. Elwood, S.: Volunteered geographic information: future research directions motivated by critical, participatory, and feminist GIS. GeoJournal **72**(3–4), 173–183 (2008)
53. Erevelles, N.: Disability and Difference in Global Contexts: Enabling a Transformative Body Politic. Springer, Heidelberg (2011). https://doi.org/10.1057/9781137001184
54. Mol, A.: The Body Multiple: Ontology in Medical Practice. Duke University Press, Durham (2002)
55. Mol, A.: Ontological politics. A word and some questions. Sociol. Rev. **47**(S1), 74–89 (1999)
56. Mol, A.: The Logic of Care: Health and the Problem of Patient Choice. Routledge, Abingdon (2008)
57. Mol, A., Law, J.: Regions, networks and fluids: anaemia and social topology. Soc. Stud. Sci. **24**(4), 641–671 (1994)
58. Suchman, L.: Agencies in technology design: Feminist reconfigurations (2007). https://www.researchgate.net/profile/Lucy_Suchman/publication/27336947_Agencies_in_Technology_Design_Feminist_Reconfigurations/links/00b7d520038ad34bcc000000.pdf
59. Suchman, L.: Located accountabilities in technology production. Scand. J. Inf. Syst. **14**(2), 7 (2002)
60. Suchman, L.: Feminist STS and the Sciences of the Artificial, pp. 139–164. The MIT Press, Cambridge (2008)
61. Jones, M.: A matter of life and death: exploring conceptualizations of sociomateriality in the context of critical care. MIS Q. **38**(3), 895–925 (2014)
62. Barad, K.: Erasers and erasures: Pinch's unfortunate 'uncertainty principle'. Soc. Stud. Sc. (2011). https://doi.org/10.1177/0306312711406317
63. Barad, K.: Quantum entanglements and hauntological relations of inheritance: Dis/continuities, spacetime enfoldings, and justice-to-come. Derrida Today **3**(2), 240–268 (2010)
64. Stumpf, S.A.: Applying new science theories in leadership development activities. J. Manag. Dev. **14**(5), 39–49 (1995)
65. Baskerville, R., Pries-Heje, J.: Discovering the significance of scientific design practice: new science wrapped in old science. In: Proceedings of the IT Artefact Design & Work Practice Intervention Workshop, Tilberg, Netherlands (2016)
66. Barad, K.: TransMaterialities trans*/matter/realities and queer political imaginings. GLQ J. Lesbian Gay Stud. **21**(2), 387–422 (2015)
67. Bozalek, V., Zembylas, M.: Diffraction or reflection? Sketching the contours of two methodologies in educational research. Int. J. Qual. Stud. Educ. **30**(2), 111–127 (2017)
68. Van der Tuin, I.: Diffraction as a methodology for feminist onto-epistemology: on encountering Chantal Chawaf and posthuman interpellation. Parallax **20**(3), 231–244 (2014)
69. Palmer, A.: "How many sums can I do"?: performative strategies and diffractive thinking as methodological tools for rethinking mathematical subjectivity. Reconceptualizing Educ. Res. Methodol. (RERM) **1**(1), 3–18 (2011)
70. Sehgal, M.: Diffractive propositions: reading Alfred North Whitehead with Donna Haraway and Karen Barad. Parallax **20**(3), 188–201 (2014)
71. Butler, M.L.: Making waves. In: Women's Studies International Forum, Elsevier (2001)
72. Allegranti, B.: The politics of becoming bodies: sex, gender and intersubjectivity in motion. Arts Psychother. **40**(4), 394–403 (2013)
73. Van der Tuin, I.: A different starting point, a different metaphysics: reading Bergson and Barad diffractively. Hypatia **26**(1), 22–42 (2011)
74. Davies, B.: Reading anger in early childhood intra-actions: a diffractive analysis. Qual. Inq. **20**(6), 734–741 (2014)
75. Edmond, J.: Diffracted waves and world literature. Parallax **20**(3), 245–257 (2014)

76. Kaiser, B.M., Thiele, K.: Diffraction: onto-epistemology, quantum physics and the critical humanities. Parallax **20**(3), 165–167 (2014)
77. Webster, J., Watson, R.T.: Analyzing the past to prepare for the future: writing a literature review. MIS Q. **26**, xiii–xxiii (2002)
78. Hoel, A.S., Van der Tuin, I.: The ontological force of technicity: Reading Cassirer and Simondon diffractively. Philos. Technol. **26**(2), 187–202 (2013)
79. Grosz, E.: Time Travels: Feminism, Nature. Power. Duke University Press, Durham (2005)
80. Davies, B.: Listening to Children: Being and Becoming. Routledge, Abingdon (2014)
81. Schwandt, T.A.: Three epistemological stances for qualitative inquiry. In: Handbook of Qualitative Research, vol. 2, no. 2, pp. 189–213 (2000)
82. Kleinman, A.: "Intra-action" - Interview With Karen Barad. Mousse, vol. 34, pp. 76–81 (2012). (http://johannesk.com/posthumanist/readings/barad-mousse.pdf)
83. Mazzei, L.A.: Beyond an easy sense: a diffractive analysis. Qual. Inq. **20**(6), 742–746 (2014)
84. Berlant, L.: Cruel optimism. In: Gregg, M., Seigworth, G.J. (eds.) The Affect Theory Reader. Duke University Press, London (2010)
85. Chia, R.: The problem of reflexivity in organizational research: towards a postmodern science of organization. Organization **3**(1), 31–59 (1996)
86. Chia, R.: Reflections: in praise of silent transformation–allowing change through 'letting happen'. J. Change Manag. **14**(1), 8–27 (2014)
87. Cecez-Kecmanovic, D.: From substantialist to process metaphysics–exploring shifts in IS research. In: Introna, L., Kavanagh, D., Kelly, S., Orlikowski, W., Scott, S. (eds.) Beyond Interpretivism? New Encounters with Technology and Organization: IFIP WG 8.2 Working Conference on Information Systems and Organizations. Springer, Dublin (2016). https://doi.org/10.1007/978-3-319-49733-4_3
88. Davies, B., et al.: The ambivalent practices of reflexivity. Qual. Inq. **10**(3), 360–389 (2004)
89. Taguchi, H.L., Palmer, A.: A diffractive methodology to 'disclose' possible realities of girls' material-discursive health/'wellbeing' in school-settings. Gend. Educ. **25**(6), 671–687 (2013)
90. Taguchi, H.L., Palmer, A.: A more 'livable'school? A diffractive analysis of the performative enactments of girls' ill-/well-being with (in) school environments. Gend. Educ. **25**(6), 671–687 (2013)
91. Heywood, L., Drake, J.: Third Wave Agenda: Being Feminist, Doing Feminism. University of Minnesota Press, Minneapolis (1997)
92. Gillis, S., Howie, G., Munford, R.: Third Wave Feminism. Springer, London (2004). https://doi.org/10.1057/9780230523173
93. Butler, J., Scott, J.W.: Feminists Theorize the Political. Routledge, Abingdon (2013)
94. Hirschheim, R., Klein, H.K.: Crisis in the IS Field? A critical reflection on the state of the discipline. J. Assoc. Inf. Syst. **4**(1), 10 (2003)
95. Mingers, J., Walsham, G.: Toward ethical information systems: the contribution of discourse ethics. MIS Q. **34**(4), 833–854 (2010)
96. Walsham, G.: Are we making a better world with ICTs? Reflections on a future agenda for the IS field. J. Inf. Technol. **27**(2), 87–93 (2012)

Living with Monsters

Thinking with Monsters

Dirk S. Hovorka$^{(\boxtimes)}$ (ID) and Sandra Peter (ID)

University of Sydney, Sydney, Australia
Dirk.Hovorka@sydney.edu.au

Abstract. Optimistic instrumentalism dominates the narratives and discourse(s) that attend recent technology advances. Most future-studies methods in current use depend on projecting properties, processes, facts or conditions of the present into the future. Absent is substantive engagement with the human condition and day-to-day life such technological futures entail. To critique the dominant discourse on future worlds, we offer *thinking with monsters* to disclose 'living-with-technologies' and the social, political, and economic alternatives to the optimism that pervades our rational instrumentalism. We argue that shifting the focus away from facts and towards *matters of concern* engenders a critical voice that enables participation in research that produces the (future) worlds that we seek to explain and understand.

Keywords: Future(s) · Monsters · Socio-technical · Matters of concern

Three Laws of Robotics

1. A robot may not injure a human being or, through inaction, allow a human being to come to harm.
2. A robot must obey orders given it by human beings except where such orders would conflict with the First Law.
3. A robot must protect its own existence as long as such protection does not conflict with the First or Second Law.

1   Introduction

Asimov's Three Laws of Robotics are a science fiction staple and shape modern narrative expectations of robot behavior. The Laws of Robotics (written in 1942, well before the phrase Artificial Intelligence was coined at Dartmouth College[1]), conjure intelligent robots into societies in the Future. Asimov did not predict robot behavior based on existing knowledge, but rather imagined what the lived-world would be like if such technologies permeated everyday life. In imagining distant and unknowable

---

[1] https://www.dartmouth.edu/~ai50/homepage.html.

© IFIP International Federation for Information Processing 2018
Published by Springer Nature Switzerland AG 2018. All Rights Reserved
U. Schultze et al. (Eds.): IS&O 2018, IFIP AICT 543, pp. 159–176, 2018.
https://doi.org/10.1007/978-3-030-04091-8_12

worlds, Asimov articulated new social, political and legal assemblages in which Robotics would make sense. He illustrated what dwelling in the world would feel like by narratively removing/collapsing the unknowns and uncertainties of the future world.

Through hundreds of novels and short stories, the socio-technical-political world of robots and humans illustrate and explore the dynamics of new social orders. At the time of publication, these visions of a pervasive penetration of inscrutable technologies unsettled people by articulating future states of affairs in constant motion, constantly becoming [1] rather than predictably extending the present. New actors, neither solely organic nor solely technological, but rather cyborgs and positronic hybrids inhabited the future. Asimov's Laws of Robotics reflect the recognition that during large-scale technological shifts, "that which appears for the first time and, consequently, is not yet recognized" will co-construct substantive cultural changes. In addressing living-with-technologies [2], the Robotics narratives echo Derrida's exhortation on cultural change to "prepare yourself to experience the future and welcome the monster" [3, p. 385].

Some imaginary futures, such as Asimov's Robot Series and Philip K Dick's "Minority Report", exposed the tensions and tradeoffs between that which we believe we control and that which is Other. In doing so they recognize that a "figure of the monster ... surfaces, in one form or another, *in any attempt to imagine worlds radically different* from those that look threatening in the present" [italics added: 4, p. 325]. These authors disclose day-to-day life in new world(s) where cultural changes produce destabilizing versions of the future. In some instances, embedded technologies are implicated in morally repugnant or monstrous manipulations of society and humanity.

Interestingly, many of the social dynamics in those stories are now an unnoticed condition of present social life. Was the undesirable lived-world (e.g. ubiquitous surveillance, denial of human rights; lack of "being left alone") of those futures not sufficiently of concern to avoid? We see with frequency "the futures we are getting hardly seem like the ones we explicitly decide on; they are more like the messed-up ones we are drifting unwittingly and implacably into" [5, p. 170]. We posit that alternative discourses can provide "intellectual structures from which IS research can respond to the needs of our future society... we must then ask whether and how our approaches to inquiry can affect our ability to do so" [6, p. 1]. In becoming sensitive to the disharmonies of living with technologies we can reveal further work to be done.

The Laws of Robotics underlie a broad narrative that encodes future artificial intelligence(s) as being predictable, subject to rules, and thus controllable and benign. The imagined social order became the background against which to explore and express what it means to be human, or machine, or Other and to interrogate the implications of such technologically saturated worlds The present-day deployment of potentially world-altering technologies including autonomous vehicles, Artificial Intelligence(s), nanotechnology, and the Internet of Things, is largely viewed as beneficial and non-problematic [7]. Like Asimov's robots, the implications of these technologies are worthy of concern for those interested in social and environmental well-being. The unavoidability of some future state of affairs (even stasis) would suggest that intending to influence, shape, or create a desirable future would be an area of concern for individuals, business, and society.

While Asimov and Dick wrote in the science fiction genre, the range of future-studies spans predictions, scenarios, foresight, science fiction, artifacts from the future and other techniques through which academics and practitioners can engage with futures. Yet researchers frequently conceptualize future(s) as a continuation of the present and amenable to rational inquiry. Consequently, IS and management oriented academic literature which focus on 'scientific' techniques do so through:

> *"Omission and simplification [to] help us to understand – but help us, in many cases, to understand the wrong thing; for our comprehension may be only of the abbreviator's neatly formulated notions, not of the vast, ramifying reality from which these notions have been so arbitrarily abstracted" [8, p. xxi].*

One such omission is the role of current research as actively creating value-laden technological change. Instead, corporate entities, celebrities, cultural gurus, online-bots, and algorithmic influences shape the dominant narratives about the world we can have and should desire.

Regarding the role of critique, Latour suggests that perhaps in the world of academics the wrong questions are being asked:

> *"My worry is that it might not be aiming at the right target. [...] Generals have always been accused of being on the ready one war late..... Would it be so surprising, after all, if intellectuals were also one war late, one critique late..... It has been a long time, after all, since intellectuals were in the vanguard" [9, p. 224].*

In this essay, we present a means of critically interrogating the societies, culture(s) and peoples' relationality with technologies in future worlds through material and discursive engagements in the present. We do not focus attention on technologies *per se*, but rather on disclosing future world(s) of embedded technology. We look to literatures and research practices which can mobilize future research by making the familiar strange, yet connected to our present day. We can engage the future(s) by *thinking with monsters*.

2   *The Thing*: A Focus on Matters of Concern

Current narratives, both academic and industry-based, predominantly articulate 'the future' in a very optimistic manner in which technologies play a determining role as objects and tools of the world. The future itself is conceived as a continuation of the past/present, which we must prepare for and adapt to through a variety of discovery techniques.

If we instead consider future(s) as produced by social, cultural, and technological activity, not merely as a container for such activity, we can look to Latour's "celebrated *Thing*" (2004) as a gathering; a focusing of attention. Latour cites the example of the 2003 televised hearings which "assembled to try to coalesce, to gather in one decision, one object, one projection of force: a military strike against Iraq. ... it was an assembly where matters of great concern were debated and proven – except there was much puzzlement about which type of proofs should be given and how accurate they were" (2004, p. 235). The *Thing* provides a metaphor for grounding research on the assembling of networks of participants, values, materials, and actions in - future -

technologically saturated world(s). From this perspective, researchers are offered an arena of activity and discourse to disclose future world(s) from multiple perspectives.

In many areas of inquiry, including science, when members of a community agree on the (temporary) stability of certain facts, basic concepts, interpretations, and modes of reasoning, they simultaneously mark off zones of ignorance and uncertainty. Common future-studies approaches including predictions, scenarios, and forecasting, treat the future as knowable, at least in part, but do so by restricting the world to a zone of extrapolation from known facts. These techniques largely render hidden the very every-dayness of the world of people who dwell. Yet living with technologies [2] and the worlds in which such technologies exist and make sense is notably absent. For example, novels and novellas based on the Three Laws of Robotics made visible the ethical dilemmas created when action is dictated by computational logics and questioned human treatment of 'intelligent' and empathetic beings.

The field of IS is oriented to change, novelty and innovation. But the practices, laws, social norms, and institutions which underpin the experience of living in a technological future are performed, not given, and are not of necessity positive changes. We need not accept socio-technical futures as a question of facts or as resistant to research concerns. Some aspects of research "must of necessity rest on elements of reality (concepts, proposals, matchings up, results…) which are considered irrefutable and firmly established" [10, p. 206]. Matters of concern happen when researchers shift attention to the actors, assumptions, processes, and unknowns upon which irrefutable facts are agreed. As in the discussions about going to war in Iraq, the potentials and the scope of many current technologies to reshape societies invite alternative perspectives, values, and voices by which to illuminate the coordination of action and how objects, environments, technologies and people may become meaningful – in the future.

In providing alternative access to the future, we seek to develop researchers' ability to know how, and when to think differently instead of assuming continuation of what is already known. Problematizing [10–12] the concerns of the futures "would require that all entities, including computers, cease to be objects defined simply by their inputs and outputs and become again things, mediating, assembling, gathering …" [9, p. 246] and include the rich abundance of everyday experience which comprise future worlds [13].

Futures are "unpredictable, uncertain, and often unknowable, the outcome of many known and especially 'unknown unknowns'" [14, p. 1] and simultaneously essential for all individuals, organizations, and societies to consider. What the future is and who gets to define it a contested space that has garnered much attention throughout history [14–16]. Many future-studies approaches uncritically accept the facts, mechanisms and processes used in predictions, scenarios, forecasts, and similar techniques as stable and unproblematic. Latour offers the example of the Columbia explosion as the "transformation of a completely mastered, perfectly understood, quite forgotten by the media, taken-for-granted, matter-of-factual projectile" [9] into a gathering of media, volunteers, scientists, engineers, experiments, and locations – a matter of intense focus and concern. In reframing our consideration of the future as matters of concern we emphasize that our research orientations regarding future(s) may also embrace the highly complex, future-situated experience of living with technology. *Thinking with monsters* does not draw back a metaphorical curtain to reveal a future that already

exists but instead responds to the idea that "our research practices are performative....
and produce the very world(s) that we seek to describe and explain" [17, p. 64].

2.1 The Monster

Monsters have long featured in the stories of humanity. Used as objects of heroic deeds
(in Greek myths), for illustrating the hubris of Man in grasping life-giving powers [18],
or for demonstrating how Minotaur-like hybrids reveal our own hidden intentions and
unspoken desires [19, 20], monsters hold a grip on our imagination. Foucault's characterized the Monster as combining the impossible and the forbidden and that "its
existence and form is not only a violation of the laws of society but also a violation of
the laws of nature" [21, p. 55]. Monstrosity arrives through a variety of means and
serves multiple functions. Monsters can be physical entities terrifying and manifest –
somehow solid and of this world. As compound beings, or Others, distinct yet akin to
us, monsters are menacing, unknown, uncontrollable and can serve to unite us against a
common foe.

But monsters in literature can also reflect anxieties of our own humanity – they
serve as a mirror to our own fears of unknowns by opening space in which to see
ourselves and the Other as reciprocally constitutive [22]. Monsters can "demonstrate,
monsters alert us, … monsters act as a moral compass" [23] to show us something
unseen and alert us to values and concerns to which we have not attended. A monster
can be unnamable and when we speak of it, "it becomes slippery, heterogonous, and
nebulous; it evades, but it also invades the imagination as a valuable experience of
absolute Otherness" [22, p. xii] thus inciting consideration of something we should
know - but do not. In this sense, the strange familiarity of technologically saturated
future(s) are monstrous. They are unsettling: the inscrutability of motivations, unease
about the futures imminent arrival, and our inability to predict, foresee or control what
is about to happen.

Many of the concerns which have emerged in our present world around fairness,
morality, and life/death decisions made by robotic algorithms [24], featured promi-
nently in Asimov's fictions. From this view we see Asimov's Three Laws of Robotics
as stabilizing the unknowns of something that did not yet exist, thus enabling concerns
only noticed in 'making the familiar strange' to be voiced. He echoes Derrida's sense
of monsters which "shows itself in something that is not yet shown …. it strikes the
eye, it frightens precisely because no anticipation had prepared one to identify this
figure" [3, p. 386]. Asimov's Robots Series discloses how people and machines coexist and meanings change. Robots exist in a contested space and enact different
realities. At the same time his future(s), while uneasy, enables us to enroll in research
concerns and value identification in our own time.

2.2 Historical Futures

Concern with the future is as old as humankind itself. What fearsome animal may lurk
on the path ahead, what foods may be found along the way, what conditions may arrive
with those dark clouds, were likely issues for hunter-gatherers. Oracles, prophecies,
divinations and various forms of future-telling have been prevalent across historical

societies and still capture the common imagination. From throwing bones to reading palms, from automatons to planetary alignments, and from tea leaves to goat entrails, humans have sought to know and perhaps control avoidable histories [25–27].

Numerous metaphors for the future underlie and shape the epistemic stance of the variety of future-studies. The future has been likened to a foreign country in which we are always arriving but never sure where we are. It is sometimes compared to a book yet to be written, or a journey we must navigate [28]. Others maintain the future is existential making, in which materialities push back on human intentions in the co-constitution of a world [29]. The epistemic stance revealed by these metaphors directs researchers' approach to futures as predicted, discovered, created/built, or socially imagined. What is consistent is that individuals, institutions, businesses, and governments all anticipate, plan for, and pursue the future as a mainstay of their varied agendas.

Modern future-studies on the West can be divided into three periods [16]: (1) the advent of rationalism and technological forecasting and the growth of professionalism of future and systematic development of alternative futures (1945–1960's); (2) institutionalization and industrialization of worldwide futures discourse, and normative futures involving business communities and decision-making processes (1960's–80's); and (3) risk-society discourses, with a narrowing and fragmentation of efforts emphasizing foresight for specific companies and technologies and a focus on strategic planning.

This historical account reveals that people previously engaged vigorously with techniques to interrogate the implications of futures based on what action possibilities were observed in the present time. Large institutions (e.g. The Intergovernmental Panel on Climate Change, the European Strategy and Policy Analysis System), the RAND Corporation, and governments have developed and continue to successfully deploy a subset of future-studies methods which provide exemplars of how seeing the future(s) in alternative configurations reveals contested space (e.g. [30–32]).

In general, future-studies focus on specific technological aspects and abstractions of what is to come. For example, authors have focused on the philosophy of technology to examine how IS research might inform future-studies [33], the destructive capacity in algorithmic decisions [24], and on methods of future-studies [2, 14, 28, 34]. In other streams of inquiry, the future is contested, agential, and orchestrated, with a greater focus on the role(s) of actors and metaphor [35]. There are few instances [24, 36] in which academics expand the typical range of future-studies to disclose aspects of living-with-technologies which are often absent in traditional research.

This disengagement raises the question of who owns the future? The narratives about futures are rife with consulting firms offering to future-proof companies, techniques intended to help executives navigate the unknown, and governments and militaries looking at risks and opportunities with scenario planning. Businesses take a dominating role in the development and implementation of ubiquitous and often invisible technologies and forms of organizing. The intellectual situation is analogous to arguments by Vannevar Bush, as head of wartime research at the end of World War II, who articulated the need for scientific knowledge production to remain independent of government control [4]. The monster he deployed was the shadow of Soviet Lysenkoism as political interference in the realm of science, a "disturbing image that challenge[d] and threaten[ed] the performance and reaffirmation of desired social order" (ibid, p. 56).

3 Future-Studies: A Categorization

Dozens of techniques have been developed to apprehend futures. Research in mega-trends [37, 38] and socio-technical innovation [39–42] indicate that historicity and path-dependencies have a strong influence on possible futures. The future is not an empty context-free place for exploitation. Numerous factors, including the materialities of infrastructure and information [43], technologies [44], organizational routines [45], and social structures [46] impose constraints on what can change, how fast change can occur and for whom change occurs. Different configurations, goals and values of 'the present' in locales and societies influence the potentialities of different futures.

The techniques of explanatory theory, prediction, foresight, and scenario-building lock our inquiry into specific ontological assumptions of the world and how the world becomes known. They privilege the empirical and the external, are locked into the dominant cultural assumptions and obscure imagination and social innovation [47]. Many future(s) research techniques build in assumptions of stability and the continuity of the present (e.g. a state of the future is determined by a state in the present). But futures are not value free [33, 44] and the values we aspire to create possible, plausible, and preferable futures.

Latour's [48, p. 156] suggestive metaphor: "Scientific facts are like trains, they do not work off their rails. You can extend the rails and connect them but you cannot drive a locomotive through a field" illustrate the challenges of researching future(s). Our scientific episteme break an immensely complex world into manageable parts [12]. But living in a world with new forms of organizing, work, medicine, and government is located in the metaphorical fields between the rails. In disclosing future world(s) we must loosen the grip of our episteme as the only methods by which to create and evaluate knowledge. Researching the complex futures involving Artificial Intelligence (s), global climate change, genetically modified organisms or nano-technology involves an examination across multiple unknown fields, not just where the various scientific 'rails' run. This is particularly crucial when we are interested in the human experience and the attendant policy, regulation, and social implications of future world(s).

The uncertainty in our knowing is a direct result of holding tightly to our scientific episteme. Entering the spaces between the rails requires us to enter zones of unknowns and uncertainties. Research which discloses futures through critical interpretation of technological and policy innovation narratives [2, 33] can challenge the underpinning of technological rationality. The pathways to these futures are neither linear nor determinant and multiple interventions, social and biophysical conditions and values will shape the realization of future(s). These zones of uncertainty – the present and future(s) beyond our epistemological mapping are precisely where social imaginaries [4, 49, 50]; design anthropology [51–53], and science fictions [54–56] and artifacts from the future [57] are revelatory. They disclose new worlds by collapsing uncertainties (of the future) while maintaining a reflective continuity with our empirical experience based on the slowly or non-changing aspects of the durable present [2]. The imaginative visions of the future, while not definitive of what will occur, supports discourse on what society desires in futures.

The wide range of futures studies techniques do not disclose worlds or sustain discourse equally. We cluster them (Table 1) based on the extent to which they allow epistemic distancing from our tightly held assumptions of where the future lies.

These categories are not exhaustive but are sufficient to illustrate that a variety of futures studies approaches in different fields have fruitfully engaged in discourses and

Table 1. Categories of future-studies methods by epistemic distancing.

	Assumptions	Method	Epistemic function
A	The future exists and can be discovered The future is an extension/extrapolation of the present/past; current explanations of phenomenon are stable; provide prediction and normative guidance	Prediction/forecasting Best practice Delphi studies Scenario thinking Fringe sketching	Reliant on the acceptance of one (or few) factors which are determinate the future. Often focus on outcomes regarding specific technologies, companies or sectors
B	The future is created through choice and action Challenges current social and technological trajectories through speculative design; human-oriented interventions to address ill-defined, 'wicked' problems; challenge current knowledge as "it could be otherwise"	Design anthropology Thought experiments Antagonistic scenarios/war gaming	Reliant on assumed fundamental aspects of human, social and/or physical science principles (e.g. markets, technological scalability, rationality) rather than specific determinant factors; Focus includes a variety of social, political or economic outcomes
C	The future is actively imagined and socially accepted; encode what is possible through technology, business and shared social vision; connects innovation in science and technology to power, social orders and justice	Socio-technical imaginaries Speculative design Artifacts from the future	Epistemic distancing through active imaginative work to disclose assumptions underlying socio-technical assemblages and normative order. Reinterprets/challenges existing normative values to highlight dis-harmonies
D	Radical extrapolation (Reductio ad absurdum) or vivid imagination to expose values in the present Highlights ideals and values as enacted in perfect worlds (/ or the opposite – anti perfect worlds)	Science fiction Utopia/dystopia fictions	Value-laden depictions reveal discontents and the conditions people seek to obtain/avoid. Epistemic radicalism; purchase on the dynamism of social change challenges the assumptions of institutional, knowledge, political, and social structures

practices. It is beyond the scope of this essay to review each of these techniques/methods. But while it is possible to find academic research using techniques in categories A-B, there are few examples that draw on the speculative and imaginative techniques in C-D. Given what is at stake we suggest that "technologies, like the people who use them, have social lives and so one must imagine the social futures as well as improvements..." [28, p. 14]. Narratively removing/collapsing uncertainties, can ground and sustain discourses regarding what worlds allow these technologies to be enacted and values we are deliberately or unwittingly creating. In addition to techniques which identify non-changing aspects of the durable present [2] we need discourses about what is at stake and who we, as a society want to become.

4   Thinking with Monsters

In presenting 'the monster' as the unease produced by realistic accounts of future worlds with which we are both familiar and estranged, we open a critical orientation to our current research practices. The monster surfaces when imagined worlds challenge our accepted material, social, and intellectual categories which can no longer be taken for granted. The monstrosity of Victor Frankenstein's experiment was not the creation of an embodied being but the challenge to the triumph of science at the time, condensed into the problem of life itself.

Thinking with monsters is a research orientation that embraces the unknowns between the rails of our episteme to ground a critical discourse. This orientation temporarily collapses what cannot be known (the social, economic, political aspects of the future) into discernable narratives, artifacts, or richly described social worlds. This stands in contrast to the epistemic probabilities of prediction, forecast, scenarios and similar techniques which discard, obscure, and leave unattended and unvoiced) the very matters of every-day living with technology.

The use of social imaginaries, science fictions, and artifacts from the future can expose social/political norms, conventions, and values that might 'break' or become unrecognizable in a world where a powerful technology has become the background of everyday life. Richly describing the lived-world of future(s) can 'make the familiar strange' in ways that challenge our assumptions of continuity across past-present-future. This estrangement or distancing effect is attributed to Bertolt Brecht and can produce a critical framing of technologies and systems [58]. Estrangement is perceived as an alienation from what would be a seemingly familiar empirical environment. Analogous to entering a familiar room where all the furniture has been rearranged, we recognize the broad outlines but struggle with an undefined Otherness. The effectiveness of thinking with monsters resides in the dialectic of familiarity with an [alternative] mundane technologically rich environment and the estranging sense of Otherness. This orientation enables critical reexamination of the configurations, relationships, and practices of our world. Foregrounding these aspects of social/political/economic/environmental life enables research which focuses on "what is not said, what matters are rendered hidden, what grievances never get formed" [59, p. 4] in many of the future-studies approaches.

Our initial example from Asimov illustrates the monstrosity of a [future]-everyday inhabited by those things "born perhaps slightly before their time; when it is not known if the environment is quite ready for them" [60, p. 71]. Such a fictional imaginary is based on a cognitive continuum with the scientific understanding of the day and is thus distinguished from fantastical worlds or folktales. But the narratives are not about science or technology but rather the social conditions which enable the technologies to flourish.

We highlight here the manner through by categories C-D of futures-studies (Table 1) can disclose the unsettling conditions for which we are not yet prepared. For example, science fiction worlds [56], social imaginaries [4, 50], and world disclosing [61], can estrange us from our everyday practices through imaginative illustration of 'it could be otherwise' overlain on our empirical experience. The seeming ordinariness of a future for which we are not ready creates a "monster [that] violates the law by its very existence, it triggers [a] response of something quite different from the law itself" [21, p. 56]. This violation of what we expect triggers a critical interrogation of our knowledge, beliefs, and values and may challenge both our optimism and our instrumental narratives.

4.1 Monstrous Futures

We offer an example of how the monster surfaces when imagined worlds challenge our assumptions of how technologies enter our collective lives. Steven Spielberg's 2002 movie Minority Report (loosely based on Dick's short story of the same title [62]), focused on how technology reconstructs society:

> *"Imagine, a world without, murder. Six years ago, the homicidal rates had reached epidemic proportions. It seemed that only a miracle could stop the bloodshed.... Within three months of the pre-crime program, the homicidal rates in the District of Columbia had reduced 90 percent."*

The original story and the subsequent screen adaptation were written well before current ubiquitous data collection practices, the use of algorithms and machine learning to enable policing and sentencing programs, and a range of government and corporate platforms to track and influence our social, material, political, and economic lives.

In the imagined world of Minority Report, the institutional, legal, and social acceptance of predictive algorithmic technology disclosed a style of governance and social interaction. Shops identify customers through face/retinal scans and manipulate people through predictive marketing, while the government's capability for constant tracking and surveillance is background state of affairs.

Minority Report allows us to inhabit the trade-offs and the morality of an interconnected surveillance state and geographical targeted advertising through face/retinal scans. Its familiar yet strange world surfaces the tensions between the individuals' sense of being stalked and the societal need for safety, security, and a market economy. The story enabled a critical examination of such tradeoffs and foregrounded many of the tensions and social implications of the present-day world of smart phones, machine learning, workplace analytics, alongside the ubiquity of data collection through platforms like Amazon and Facebook. It crystallized the interconnectedness of social constructions and technological capabilities.

More than decade after the movie, researchers raised concerns regarding economic and societal transformations due to the "the blurring of long-established social and institutional divisions … organizations and their relations to individuals qua users…" in a landscape where data is a core component of commercial strategies", [63] cited in [64, p. 76]. Inspired, in part, by a 2009 interview revealing that Google retained individual search histories that could be made available to state authorities and law enforcement agencies, Zuboff [64] articulated the incipient production, circulation and distribution of power in this new world – 'surveillance capitalism'. By disclosing emergent logics of accumulation, and experimentations in a world of surveillance and attendant economic incentives and structures, she gathers researchers to an agenda requiring careful analysis and theorization.

Thus Zuboff has grounded a substantive gathering, matter of concern and emphasizes that the "trajectory of this narrative depends in no small measure on the scholars drawn to this frontier project" (2015, p. 86). But, the practices associated with capitalizing on (big) data and the challenges to privacy and self-determination that Zuboff calls attention are the very ones that were laid bare in Minority Report more than a decade earlier.

4.2 Bringing Out the Monsters

Many of today's technical and scientific advances (e.g. synthetic biology, planetary-scale systems, large scale social engineering, virtual and augmented reality) challenge our factual understanding of how technologies fit into our organizations and processes, our global society or even our physical selves. When focusing on the social and material conditions of people, social imaginaries, science fictions, and artifacts from the future enable us to consider emergent roles and relationships when living with these technologies has become "every-day". Approaches that (temporarily) collapse the unknowns in monstrous futures enable researchers to join the vanguard of research which creates those futures.

For example, emerging technologies that will soon be able to create realistic avatars – animated hyper-realistic human characters, that look, behave and sound like real people [65]. Such 'digital humans' are already being deployed as digital assistants, models for fashion houses, clones of deceased artists or fake versions of heads of state. The speed with which digital humans may enter our lives conceals the uncertainties about how, where, and what is at stake as they do so. What grand challenges will they help address and what problems will they create?

We illustrate this with an "artifact from a future" where digital humans are part of the furniture of the world. A (futuristic) employment separation letter (Fig. 1) specifies departure terms for an employee by reminding them that their personal digital avatar – a realistic avatar that can be puppeteered in real time for teaching apart from them – will remain at the company's discretion for 20 years.

The letter raises concerns regarding power, identity, authenticity, and deception in a landscape infused by digital humans. It triggers a critical interrogation of what values, copyright and legal issues, and social norms might be challenged and allows us to

Private and confidential

Walt Gregorovich
Executive Director, Business Education
27 July 2021

Sandra, Peter
133 Castlereagh
Sydney, NSW 2000

Dear Dr Peter,

I am writing to you about the conclusion of your employment with The University of Sydney Business School on 30 July 2021.

This letter seeks to clarify your departure terms as discussed in our face-to-face meeting.

Your personal digital avatar will remain at the University's discretion as per the terms of your employment for 20 years. We wish to remind you at this point that you will be contacted for consent for any physical alterations of your avatar, and we may deploy/ or retire your digital avatar without notice.

Whilst you are not obliged to do so, you may wish to notify us of any changes that are pertinent to your digital avatar in the coming years.

You will receive your final pay check on July 31.

Finally, if you wish to take part in an exit interview with HR for internal data purposes, it would be greatly appreciated, though you are in no way obliged to do so.

Thank you for your service to the University of Sydney. We look forward to your digital self remaining in the lives of our students for many years to come.

Yours sincerely,

Walt Gregorovich
Executive Director, Business Education

PLEASE KEEP A COPY OF THIS LETTER FOR YOUR RECORDS

Fig. 1. Artifact from the future: employment separation letter

articulate potential research agendas. Other imagined artifacts might include obituaries of "AI personalities", news articles or policy documents concerning working would autonomous agents.

5   Discussion

Future-studies methods has been the subject of a rich body of work in other subject areas (e.g. political science, philosophy, Future studies, and literary studies) where fictional realities allow researchers to access, inhabit, and explore the possibilities of divergent tomorrows. We orient these ideas to envision the every-day living with those technologies that were 'born before their time'. This Thinking with Monsters discloses how worlds would re-arrange (or not) around new tools, technologies or the practices which include them. By collapsing future(s) into a (temporarily) stable form we may engage rationally with technologies' functions and properties but also create a different quality of engagement, which highlights meanings and the practices that implicate technologies. Thinking with monsters offers a new "way of seeing" by reconsidering the assumptions and asking questions regarding the future(s) our technologies create. What are their implications for the values we pursue, our ways if interaction, and our social lives? Who is responsible (and in what way are they responsible) for understanding technological futures and mitigating their unintended and often undesirable consequences. Thinking with monsters discloses new territories and thus enable research that allows us to ask different kinds of questions. It offers a provocative approach to interrogating the possible, desirable, or regrettable implications of technology deployment and to explore what we value today and how imagined tomorrows can be obtained or avoided. Thinking with Monsters shifts the discourse to questioning the lived experience of humans in the world.

These imaginaries can be revelatory. For example, the universal translator described in Murray Leinster's 1945 novella 'First Contact' [66], and explored in science fiction from Star Trek to Doctor Who, is now proposed to support conversations in 40 languages with Google's new headphones. In a world where machine learning is poised to provide us such advances, Star Trek and Doctor Who not only inspire us to build a universal translator, but also reveal that word translation itself cannot resolve conflict or overcome differences in culture. These human issues must be worked through carefully to create a livable future [28].

At the time Asimov imagined the Three Laws of Robotics, robots were figurative, not real - plausible, perhaps possible, both attractive and repellent. The challenges these narratives surfaced regarding ethics, intelligence, autonomy and consciousness continue a research discourse regarding the social implications living with such robots would require. A similar discourse is ongoing with Zuboff, O'Neill and others prompting concerns regarding the (Big) Otherness of corporate power, what constitutes privacy under conditions of surveillance, and justice and fairness of broadly deployed algorithmic decision making. This research is an important response to observed technological and social effects in the world. Equally important is proactive critical engagement with the social-political and economic implications yet to come surrounding numerous technologies, which will co-constitute likely and maybe even desirable futures. Imaginative research grounded can help establish current research concerns and critically identify the tradeoffs being made as our research performs our future(s). In this view, the monster has shifted from a manifest and threating technology artifact to our own existential ambiguity of a lived present and our anticipated, but uncertain future. Through imagining the activities of people in the presence of new technology, the social world and the cultural expressions important to both the present and the future are revealed. Acts of imagination can work to (temporarily) collapse the uncertainties of the future into a focus for discourse, research, and action.

6   Conclusion

We have argued that thinking with monsters provides academics a critical voice, to paraphrase Aristotle's Rhetoric, "into the things about which we make decisions, and into which we therefore inquire [and] present us with alternative possibilities". This voice is crucial in shaping research *matters of concern* in reframing and recalibrating current technology implementations and attendant policies that constitute futures and the articulation of values in the present. Scholars involved in the development and deployment of technologies that co-constitute organizational and social life can utilize novel and bold ways to engage with futures and provide alternatives to the dominant future(s) discourses. Catalyzing public and business engagement regarding highly impactful technologies is crucial as they become increasingly and inexorably involved in the way we live and work.

The academic discourses revolving around technological changes have been largely concerned with the qualities, inputs, and outputs of the technologies and closely related business or economic interests. Alarms have been raised, and concerns voiced, but usually as autopsies of events – to the facts of the Challenger spacecraft accident [9] or to Cambridge Analytica's revelation of mass data exposure. This form of post hoc analysis of conceals questions of values and politics: "Who gets to decide on the agenda for scientific research and development? Who gets to say what problems or grand challenges we try to solve? Who gets to say how we solve them (or resolve them or muddle through them)? Who gets to partake in those benefits, and are they the same people put at risk by our attempts to solve the problems at stake?" [18, p. xvii]. *Thinking with monsters* discloses the social-political-technological worlds in which technologies make sense in the everyday and brings into focus the world from within. The emergence of research concerns thus provides a critical narrative to the development and deployment of powerful technologies of enormous consequence. This enables an intention to build a future to dwell in, founded on the premise that "the forms humans build, whether in the imagination or on the ground, arise within the currents of their involved activity, in the specific relational contexts of their practical engagement with their surroundings" [67, p. 10]. By working imaginatively with technology and researching social life with the Other, we can augment current research activity on immediate factual matters with attention on the meanings and aspirations which accompany our technological assemblages.

Our current research activity on immediate factual matters will unwittingly become our future, for better or worse, if we do not focus attention on the meanings which accompany our gadgets and gods. At the 200th anniversary of Shelley's "Frankenstein", it is valuable to be reminded that it was not the monstrous being who was of concern but the "social consequence of that science…a being rejected by his creator who eventually turns to violence…he is an embodiment of social pathology" [68, p. 65].

Shelley reflected on the inability of humanity to identify and reflect on the social products and consequences of science and technology. This is critical at our current time as widely implemented technologies become inscrutable even to those who design them, as we lose sight of who and what is controlled by those technologies, and as businesses take a greater role in organizing our lives and shaping our knowledge and preferences. *Thinking with monsters* enables us to gather attention on concerns and values which we want to inhabit. As Latour [9] suggests, a Future that is always being built as an ongoing construction, is in need of great caution and care.

References

1. Haraway, D.: The promises of monsters: a regenerative politics for inappropriate/d others. In: Grossberg, L., Nelson, C., Treichler, P.A. (eds.) Cultural Studies, pp. 295–337. Routledge, New York (1992)
2. Aanestad, M.: Information systems innovation research: between novel futures and durable presents. In: Chiasson, M., Henfridsson, O., Karsten, H., DeGross, J.I. (eds.) Researching the Future in Information Systems. IFIPAICT, vol. 356, pp. 27–41. Springer, Heidelberg (2011). https://doi.org/10.1007/978-3-642-21364-9_3
3. Derrida, J.: Passages—From traumatism to promise. In: Weber, E. (ed.) Points…: Interviews, 1974–1994, pp. 372–395. Stanford University Press, Stanford (1995)
4. Jasanoff, S., Kim, S.-H.: Dreamscapes of Modernity: Sociotechnical Imaginaries and the Fabrication of Power. University of Chicago Press, Chicago (2015)
5. Tonkinwise, C.: How we intend to future: review of Anthony Dunne and Fiona Raby, speculative everything: design, fiction, and social dreaming. Des. Philos. Pap. **12**(2), 169–187 (2014)
6. Chiasson, M., Henfridsson, O., Karsten, H., DeGross, J.I. (eds.): Researching the Future in Information Systems. IFIPAICT, vol. 356. Springer, Heidelberg (2011)
7. Murphy, R., Woods, D.D.: Beyond Asimov: the three laws of responsible robotics. IEEE Intell. Syst. **24**(4), 14–20 (2009)
8. Huxley, A.: Brave New World Revisited. Harper & Brothers, New York (1958)
9. Latour, B.: Why has critique run out of steam? From matters of fact to matters of concern. Crit. Inq. **30**(2), 225–248 (2004)
10. Callon, M.: Struggles and negotiations to define what is problematic and what is not. In: Knorr, K.D., Krohn, R., Whitley, R. (eds.) The Social Process of Scientific Investigation. SOSC, vol. 4, pp. 197–219. Springer, Dordrecht (1980). https://doi.org/10.1007/978-94-009-9109-5_8
11. Bacchi, C.: Why study problematizations? Making politics visible. Open J. Polit. Sci. **2**(01), 1 (2012)
12. Carolan, M.S.: Ontological politics: mapping a complex environmental problem. Environ. Values **13**, 497–522 (2004)
13. Stahl, B.C.: What does the future hold? A critical view of emerging information and communication technologies and their social consequences. In: Chiasson, M., Henfridsson, O., Karsten, H., DeGross, J.I. (eds.) Researching the Future in Information Systems. IFIPAICT, vol. 356, pp. 59–76. Springer, Heidelberg (2011). https://doi.org/10.1007/978-3-642-21364-9_5
14. Urry, J.: What is the Future?. Wiley, Hoboken (2016)
15. Slaughter, R.A.: Futures studies as an intellectual and applied discipline. Am. Behav. Sci. **42**(3), 372–385 (1998)

16. Son, H.: The history of Western futures studies: an exploration of the intellectual traditions and three-phase periodization. Futures **66**, 120–137 (2015)
17. Schultze, U.: What kind of world do we want to help make with our theories? Inf. Organ. **27** (1), 60–66 (2017)
18. Shelley, M., et al.: Frankenstein: Annotated for Scientists, Engineers, and Creators of All Kinds. MIT Press, Cambridge (2017)
19. Crook, S.: Minotaurs and other monsters: 'Everyday life' in recent social theory. Sociology **32**(3), 523–540 (1998)
20. Haraway, D.: Simians, Cyborgs, and Women. The Reinvention of Nature. Free Association Books, London (1991)
21. Foucault, M.: Abnormal: Lectures at the College de France (1974–1975). Verso, London (2003). Davidson, A.I., et al. (eds.)
22. Beville, M.: The Unnameable Monster in Literature and Film. Routledge, Abingdon (2013)
23. Warner, M.: Monsters, magic and miracles. In: The Times Literary Supplement (2012)
24. O'Neil, C.: Weapons of Math Destruction: How Big Data Increases Inequality and Threatens Democracy. Broadway Books, New York City (2017)
25. Burnett, C.: Magic and Divination in the Middle Ages: Texts and Techniques in the Islamic and Christian Worlds, vol. 557. Variorum Publishing, Kettering (1996)
26. Freidel, D.A., Schele, L., Parker, J.: Maya Cosmos Three Thousand Years on the Shaman's Path. William Morrow Paperbacks, New York City (1993)
27. Rochberg, F.: The Heavenly Writing: Divination, Horoscopy, and Astronomy in Mesopotamian Culture. Cambridge University Press, Cambridge (2004)
28. Montfort, N.: The Future MIT Press Essential Knowledge Series. MIT Press, Cambridge (2017)
29. Ingold, T.: Making: Anthropology, Archaeology, Art and Architecture. Routledge, Abingdon (2013)
30. IPoCC: Climate Change 2014: Mitigation of Climate Change, vol. 3. Cambridge University Press, Cambridge (2015)
31. Garnett, K., et al.: Delivering sustainable river basin management: plausible future scenarios for the water environment to 2030 and 2050. Report B (2017)
32. Australian Government: Future Cities: Planning for our growing population. Infrastructure Australia (2018)
33. Chiasson, M., Davidson, E., Winter, J.: Philosophical foundations for informing the future (S) through IS research. Eur. J. Inf. Syst. **27**(3), 367–379 (2018)
34. Bauman, Z.: Utopia with no Topos. Hist. Hum. Sci. **16**(1), 11–25 (2003)
35. Brown, N., Rappert, B.: Contested Futures: A Sociology of Prospective Techno-Science. Routledge, Abingdon (2017)
36. Lichtner, V., Venters, W.: Journey to DOR: a retro science-fiction story on researching ePrescribing. In: Chiasson, M., Henfridsson, O., Karsten, H., DeGross, J.I. (eds.) Researching the Future in Information Systems. IFIPAICT, vol. 356, pp. 151–161. Springer, Heidelberg (2011). https://doi.org/10.1007/978-3-642-21364-9_10
37. Naisbitt, J., Cracknell, J.: Megatrends: Ten New Directions Transforming Our Lives. Warner Books, New York (1984)
38. Vielmetter, G., Sell, Y.: Leadership 2030: The Six Megatrends You Need to Understand to Lead Your Company into the Future. AMACOM, Nashville (2014)
39. Bijker, W.E.: Of Bicycles, Bakelites, and Bulbs: Toward a Theory of Sociotechnical Change. MIT Press, Cambridge (1997)
40. Feenberg, A.: Critical Theory of Technology. Oxford University Press, Oxford (1991)
41. Geels, F.W.: Processes and patterns in transitions and system innovations: refining the co-evolutionary multi-level perspective. Technol. Forecast. Soc. Change **72**, 681–696 (2005)

42. Pickering, A.: The Mangle of Practice: Time, Agency, and Science. University of Chicago Press, Chicago (1995)
43. Dourish, P.: The Stuff of Bits: An Essay on the Materialities of Information. MIT Press, Cambridge (2017)
44. Feenberg, A., Callon, M.: Between Reason and Experience: Essays in Technology and Modernity. MIT Press, Cambridge (2010)
45. Pentland, B.T., Feldman, M.S.: Designing routines: on the folly of designing artifacts, while hoping for patterns of action. Inf. Org. **18**(4), 235–250 (2008)
46. Lee, A.S.: Thinking about social theory and philosophy for information systems. In: Mingers, J., Willcocks, L. (eds.) Social Theory and Philosophy for Information Systems, pp. 1–26. Wiley, Hoboken (2004)
47. Inayatullah, S.: From 'who am I?' to 'when am I?': framing the shape and time of the future. Futures **25**(3), 235–253 (1993)
48. Latour, B.: Give me a laboratory and I will raise the world. In: Knorr-Cetina, K.D., Mulkay, M. (eds.) Science Observed: Perspectives on the Social Study of Science, pp. 141–170. Sage, London (1983)
49. Robinson, K.S.: New York 2140. Fanucci, Rome (2017)
50. Taylor, C.: Modern Social Imaginaries. Duke University Press, Durham (2004)
51. Gunn, W., Otto, T., Smith, R.C.: Design Anthropology: Theory and Practice. A&C Black, London (2013)
52. Hunt, J.: Prototyping the social: temporality and speculative futures at the intersection of design and culture. In: Clarke, A.J. (ed.) Design Anthropology. EDITION, pp. 33–44. Springer, Vienna (2011). https://doi.org/10.1007/978-3-7091-0234-3_3
53. Ballard, J.G.: The Drowned World: A Novel, vol. 17. WW Norton & Company, New York City (2012)
54. Bell, F., et al.: Science fiction prototypes: visionary technology narratives between futures. Futures **50**, 5–14 (2013)
55. Forster, E.: The machine stops. In: Burton, S.H. (ed.) Longman Heritage of Literature Series. Longman Group Ltd., Great Britain (1965)
56. Freedman, C.: Critical Theory and Science Fiction. Wesleyan University Press, Middletown (2000)
57. Dunne, A., Raby, F.: Speculative Everything: Design, Fiction, and Social Dreaming. MIT Press, Cambridge (2013)
58. Suvin, D.: Metamorphoses of Science Fiction: On the Poetics and History of a Literary Genre. Yale University Press, New Haven (1979)
59. Rappert, B.: sensing absence: how to see what isn't there in the study of science and security. In: Rappert, B., Balmer, B. (eds.) Absence in Science, Security and Policy. GIS, pp. 3–33. Springer, Heidelberg (2015). https://doi.org/10.1057/9781137493736_1
60. Mosley, N.: Hopeful Monsters. A&C Black, London (2012)
61. Spinosa, C., Flores, F., Dreyfus, H.L.: Disclosing New Worlds: Entrepreneurship, Democratic action, and the Cultivation of Solidarity. MIT Press, Cambridge (1999)
62. Dick, P.K.: Minority report. Fantast. Universe **4**(6) (1956)
63. Constantiou, I.D., Kallinikos, J.: New games, new rules: big data and the changing context of strategy. J. Inf. Technol. **30**(1), 44–57 (2015)
64. Zuboff, S.: Big other: surveillance capitalism and the prospects of an information civilization. J. Inf. Technol. **30**(1), 75–89 (2015)
65. Seymour, M., Riemer, K.: Agents, avatars, and actors: potentials and implications of natural face technology for the creation of realistic visual presence. J. Assoc. Inf. Syst. (forthcoming)

66. Leinster, M.: First Contact. The Science Fiction Hall of Fame: Volume One, 1929–1964. Tor, New York (1945)
67. Ingold, T.: Being Alive: Essays on Movement, Knowledge and Description. Routledge, London (2011)
68. Cranny-Francis, A.: The 'Science' of Science Fiction. Reading Science. Critical and Functional Perspectives on Discourses of Science. Routledge, London (1998). Martin, I., Veel, R. (eds.)

A Bestiary of Digital Monsters

Rachel Douglas-Jones(✉) ⓘ, John Mark Burnett ⓘ, Marisa Cohn,
Christopher Gad, Michael Hockenhull ⓘ, Bastian Jørgensen,
James Maguire, Mace Ojala ⓘ, and Brit Ross Winthereik ⓘ

IT University of Copenhagen, Rued Langaards Vej 7,
2300 Copenhagen, Denmark
{rdoj,jmbu,mcoh,chga,michh,bmjo,jmag,maco,
brwi}@itu.dk

Abstract. This article puts forward a bestiary of digital monsters. By bringing into dialogue scholarship in monster theory with that in science and technology studies, we develop the idea of the bestiary as a way of exploring sites where digital monsters are made. We discuss the role of bestiaries in narrating anxieties about the present. We proceed to populate our bestiary with various sociotechnical 'beasts' arising in collaborative research project on new data relations in Denmark. The paper argues for the place of the ever-incomplete bestiary in understanding digital monsters, for the bestiary's role as gathering point within our project, and for its capacities to speak beyond a single research setting. Through the bestiary, we look toward the ways we already live with monsters and to the forms of analysis available for describing the beasts in our midst.

Keywords: Bestiary · Digital · Monster

1 Introduction

Today's digital monsters can be loud, crashing through headlines and twitter storms shrouded in the armor of controversy, revelation and shock value. They can also become virtually undetectable, creeping into our lives unnoticed. Moments of exposure highlight their monstrous contours: a technology previously benign flips and is suddenly problematic. Seen as though for the first time, monstrous beings are 'not yet recognized' [7: 386], existing at the edge of the known, on the cusp of the future. In moments of revelation, devices, platforms or softwares we have welcomed into our lives are suddenly distant. As digital technologies continuously transform who we are, including what we perceive as our needs, the sense is that they are always lurking around with their potential and unpredictable effects. We never know exactly when and where they may unnerve or even terrify us. In this way, they defy the border between real and imaginary.

In this article, we put forward a bestiary of digital monsters as a way of relating to the digital monstrous. Borrowing from early ways of identifying and telling stories about the things in our worlds with which we must live and learn to relate, the bestiary offers us a 'thought device' [10] through which the technological monstrous can be

U. Schultze et al. (Eds.): IS&O 2018, IFIP AICT 543, pp. 177–190, 2018.
https://doi.org/10.1007/978-3-030-04091-8_13

understood. In a series of collected interviews discussing the character of the future, the French philosopher Jacques Derrida argues that to be open to the future is to 'welcome the monstrous arrivant, to welcome it, that is, to accord hospitality to that which is absolutely foreign or strange' [7: 387]. As scholars studying acts that claim to bring the future into being, our task then, is necessarily one of living with monsters. We know that technological futures are themselves imaginative figurings [4, 8], making us careful about the devices we as analysts use in narration. Within this contemporary bestiary, therefore, the monstrous is not a property of an entity nor something inherently good 'gone wrong'. Instead, it emerges in a narrated relation, in which critical analysts of technology are themselves caught up [27].

The examples we put forward in the article, the 'beasts', arise in attempts to govern organizations, businesses and citizens. We are drawing on an ongoing, collective research project *Data as Relation – Governance in the Age of Big Data*. None of the beasts are technologies alone, isolated from the people who made, use, or discuss them. Instead, one of our objectives in thinking with the monster concept through a bestiary is to ensure that the concept of the monster does not 'other' the digital as untamed or alien. Our 'beasts' illustrate how that which is monstrous might emerge not as an object but as a practice, a habit, a sociotechnical assemblage. The analysis is informed by two key analytical repertoires, first, the critical theorist Jeffrey Jerome Cohen's *Seven Theses of Monster Culture* [5] and second, anthropologist and science and technology scholar Donna Haraway's work on the 'promise' of monsters [14]. In addition to work in Science and Technology Studies and Monster Theory, these two scholars in particular help us consider the 'ontological liminality' that is part of making monsters: the ongoing question, what are they? Cohen's seven foundational "breakable postulates" [5: 4] for example, range from concern with the *body* of the monster (thesis 1) to its role in bringing about category crises, or policing the 'borders of the possible' [5: 13]. His framework originates in cultural theory, marrying familiar western monsters with those of myth in his analyses of the vampire, the gargoyle, *Godzilla*, the Cyclops, *King Kong* and *Alien*. In turn, Donna Haraway, who is well known for thinking with a repertoire of figures such as the cyborg, oncomouse, or coyote, warns us against attempting to identify 'real' differences, the things that would make monsters 'other'. What she suggests instead is that we work to map some of the *effects* of difference. As she argues, the identification of 'real' differences 'invites the illusion of essential, fixed positions, while the second trains us to more subtle vision' [14: 300]. In bringing both Cohen's "breakable postulates" and Haraway's attention to the subtleties of difference-making into conversation with contemporary technologies, we develop the idea of the technological bestiary as a way of exploring the sites where the monstrous is made. The bestiary, we argue, can act as a gathering point, an object around which further communal exploration of life in the digital can take place. In what follows, we discuss the bestiary as a genre and form before going on to begin to populate our bestiary with empirically derived beasts, 'living beings' [7: 386]. From ongoing research, our aim is to make the bestiary speak beyond the examples put forward here, to be part of a conversation about the emergence of monstrosity and a reflexivity about what such descriptions mean and do.

2   A Bestiary

A bestiary is a collection of monsters, real and imagined. Medieval bestiaries were collections of drawings and fables about many fascinating creatures with various capacities, conducts and patterns of life (including a variety of rocks) and were often intended as tools of education and instruction. The kinds of creatures described in such collections ranged from locally known species, to those known but never seen, to those mentioned in travelogues, and to those in the bible. Alongside these images and accounts were stories, moral tales that gave bestiaries a social role comparable with that of the fairytale. In contrast to later zoology handbooks, in a bestiary both 'known' and 'imaginary' monsters could cross species boundaries, taking on features and elements of other entities. Some bestiaries contained observations about species, subsequently refuted by natural philosophers, only to be later deemed real by modern science. Thus, these early books of beasts fulfilled a range of social and intellectual functions, acting not as imprecise zoology textbooks or religious texts, "but also a description of the world as it was known" [3]. They were multimedia devices that aimed to make the world known.

Creating a bestiary is also a work of describing the world. It is good to think with. While sources for thinking the monstrous change over time, our bestiary borrows from the characteristics of the medieval book, describing the emergent monster and telling stories about its everyday life and way of being. However, it also makes a number of liberal interpretive departures from the medieval style, working inventively with the genre to bring monsters (with and without bodies) to the fore, reflexively inserting the role of the analyst in their making and description. Crucially, digital monsters are both identified by field informants, objects of anxiety or unease, as well as by the authors as analysts and participants in ongoing studies. We have included beasts according to four guiding ideas.

First, rather than pointing to the physical form of objects in the world, the monsters that gain a place in the bestiary are visible through the effects of the differences that they make. Haraway describes the appearance of the effects of difference as a 'diffraction pattern' [14: 300], a technique of attending to difference through its effects rather than through essentializing. As noted above, our collective curiosity hinges on newly emerging relations made through data, this attention to the effects of difference allows us to bring forward the power of the imaginary in shaping and re-shaping futures as digitization projects are born, gather pace, or evaporate.

Second, in line with this descriptive spirit, the work of a present-day bestiary is the work of figuring out what is monstrous, rather than simply identifying monsters [5]. The distinction is important: Including something in the bestiary is a move of calling forth, rather than calling out. Description is participation in the work of analysis. To name a beast is a domesticating move, which allows us disempower the potential threat posed by the undiagnosed and the unknown. It is also to make a value judgement, to diagnose its characteristics, and some normative work in deciding what is monstrous in our midst. Entries contain a critique of the making-monstrous, since the starting point is that the monstrous is neither a property of the research site, nor of the thing itself. The bestiary becomes a site to study potential, aftermath and description itself, bringing monsters into being in a way that does not parallel the revelatory mode of the news cycle, but is a more careful critique of those of us who, living in close analytical proximity with them, could make them accountable.

Third, we attend to monsters whose monstrosity is not merely given through appearance. In his analysis of Invisible Monsters, the literature scholar Jeffrey Weinstock describes a 'decoupling of monstrosity from appearance', with the monstrous 'reconfigured as a kind of invisible disease that eats away at the body and the body politic' [28: 275]. He is thinking here of monsters that live amongst us undetected, forces that find their way into the 'crevices of everyday life' and the silent infiltrations that give rise to unease [28: 276]. Weinstock's analysis of figures such as the psychopath, the terrorist, the faceless corporation or government agency draws out a contemporary monstrosity manifest in invisibility and potential ubiquity [28: 276]. For our purposes, might Weinstock's attention to 'silent infiltration' help us handle the sense of creepiness that lingers around questions of privacy, data transfer or algorithmic processing? Before they become the 'loud' monsters that take up headline space in the latest data scandal, indeed, if they ever do, the undetected ubiquity of contemporary digital worlds should give us pause.

Finally, as with prior attempts to catalogue the monstrous, 'total inclusivity would not be possible' [23: 9, 26]. The bestiary, following this line of thinking, is put forward as an expandable exercise, yet one that is inherently incomplete. What a bestiary does is provide us with a space in which we can explore the capacities of description in our ethnographic narration, and remain open to bringing forward further monsters that emerge from observations made by those in the field and from our own senses of unease. The beasts of the bestiary thus exist in lateral relation to each other [12, 22], an analytical choice which refuses to privilege the position of the analyst or observer.

In this sense, the bestiary performs the messy work of the list, the gathering up of figures for the telling of stories that can 'stay with the trouble' [15]. The calling forth of monsters is not meant to fix their identity, but to work *with* the power of naming, to how we can work with these emerging forms of monstrosity, and consider the care, caution or antagonism with which they ought to be handled. The bestiary wards against a totalizing idea of the "digital monstrosity". As in a medieval bestiary, these beasts are not fixed, because our accounts are necessarily incomplete. As a lateral rather than taxonomic exercise, some beasts are hybridized from disparate accounts, others may turn out to be an exotification of the unknown mixed in with the real. We hope they may find recognition in the research of others. Regardless, the work that they do is to sit side by side, an interspecies gathering of descriptions where they might breed or even feast upon each other. We introduce the empirical descriptions that follow with a contextualization of the setting from which they are drawn, and we follow these narrated beasts with a section on bestiary analytics that aims to draw out the effects such juxtapositions can produce.

3 Beasts

As noted above, the beasts of our Bestiary come from all arise within a single research project, Data as Relation, with distinct research sites across the Danish public and private sectors. The potential role for digital data is a topic of high interest in Denmark, which as a nation state is already highly invested in and vocal about digitization processes, expressed in a series of Digital Strategies since 2001 [1, 9]. As colleagues within the project have pointed out, transformations in state practices deeply implicate citizens, and both political and institutional work is required to make citizens 'digital' [24]. Our research project's point of departure is that the use of big data and digitization in the public sector is not merely a technical upgrade of existing infrastructures, but implies a reinvention of societal relations[1]. The five beasts presented below are drawn from the subprojects within Data as Relation where research is currently being undertaken by the 14 strong research team.

The authors are exploring sites where the promises of data are being worked with in practice, with fieldworkers entering spaces where contracts are negotiated, technological solutions proposed, potentials weighed and softwares proffered. These are spaces of government administrations, digitization agencies, international data center agreements and health data negotiations. Each of the five illustrations below has a distinct style in thinking through the bestiary as a common project for the collaboration, yet together we have challenged ourselves to use it to pinpoint moments of unease, moments of observation and questions without resolution, which act as analytic openings for keeping the problematic in view. The final beast is focused on the sites where social science research methods are intertwined with the methodological techniques at play in the fieldsites under study: it provides a reflexive commentary on living with the potential for monstrosity within our own fields. What they share is attentiveness to the relations being forged through data practices, and the meeting of the human and the technical. Offered foremost as empirical vignettes, the beasts presented are important for their capacity to surface the concerns or anxieties of those with whom we work, which are sidelined by deadlines, silenced in momentum, or made ephemeral by the affect of rapid transformation. In some cases, this is simply the work of the analyst, in making the familiar strange.

3.1   Codice Crepitus

Our first beast is a breed between the software engineering practice 'DevOps' and a large Danish public administration, which we will here call the Processing Authority. 'DevOps' combines the two words 'development' and 'operations', expressing the vision that these should be unified. At a conference in Copenhagen in 2017, advocates for DevOps suggested that DevOps does not only require "cultural change", but the use of software in every step of software development. These advocates projected an image of the so-called "DevOps Metro Map" with approximately 145 'stops', each related to particular pieces of software, and the "Periodic Table of DevOps Tools" with about 120 suggestions for software to use. One advocate claimed, that if one area was in real need of a digital transformation, it is software development itself. He referred to an article published in the Wall Street Journal in 2011: "Why Software Is Eating the World" [2]. Here venture capitalist Andreessen, prompts his readers to accept that software companies are an inevitable part of the future:

---

[1] See Data as Relation homepage at www.dar.itu.dk.

... new software ideas will result in the rise of new Silicon Valley-style start-ups that invade existing industries with impunity. Over the next 10 years, the battles between incumbents and software-powered insurgents will be epic. Joseph Schumpeter, the economist who coined the term "creative destruction," would be proud [2].

The idea of "software eating the world" is presented as a good thing, and the enthusiasm with which it is presented resonates with ethnographic experiences. The DevOps work was encountered by Jørgensen during his ethnography of IT projects in the Processing Authority, which is currently developing its own new data platform to share data with other public organizations. This is a change from how the Processing Authority has managed its data: at present, an external consultancy company is in charge, a configuration which does not afford the Processing Authority control of their own data. As a customer rather than an owner, the Processing Authority's command and authority over their systems was troubled, as well as their ability to make further efficiency savings required by ambitious State financial plans. DevOps was not only a methodological principle in this IT project, it was also the name of a new department. DevOps was related to the administration being "in the midst of building an internal IT organization in order to take home a series of the organizations critical IT system" [2].

To an observer the combination of DevOps and the Danish Processing Authority seems like a strange beast. On the one hand, we see a wish to become less dependent on external actors – to build the capacity to 'take home' critical systems. On the other hand, the tools considered to do so create new global dependencies. At project meetings, it was not unusual to discuss five or more different software programs of which at least one would be new: Jira, Confluence, Github, Travis, Appdynamics, Redmine are but a few examples of names tossed around. The constant effort to bring new software into the process disconcerted Jørgensen; How could he or his interlocutors ever know any of these programs well enough to decide which ones to include, or how they would work together? And how would the people in the room look back in 5 or 10 years on these new dependencies?

Is it the case, as Andreessen argues, that software is currently "eating the world"? Or is it the hybrid beast of DevOps and the Danish Processing Authority that 'eats' software? One thing seems clear: In the Processing Authority's attempt to get rid of old software dependencies and take home data, the beast simultaneously has to 'swallow' new ones which connects its 'home' to multiple elsewheres.

Viewed through Cohen's breakable postulates, this software story concerns the monstrous problem of excess, of failed containment, a monstrosity that escapes or explodes.

3.2   Digitalis Dementore

Our second beast emerges in the meeting of the public and private sectors and their intertwined race to digitalize and become "data-driven". It exists in the proximal future, a data economy that is not yet here, yet somehow already exists. In a subproject focused on how digitalization efforts change the internal constitution of the Danish public sector, author Hockenhull examines the role of private sector actors within this process, and examines how futures are summoned into being. Ethnography for the subproject takes place at conferences, workshops and seminars concerned with digital and data-oriented technologies, and over the course of the first year of fieldwork, Hockenhull has become embedded within a public organization currently implementing several strategies to become more "data-driven". From these environs, we detect the contours of a beast lurking behind the scenes, a dampening of the spirit stalking from site to site.

The form of this beast is hard to describe: when first noted, it is innocuous, even common, to the untrained eye. Yet we were alerted to it by the repetition of certain phrases, scenarios and predictions. By the veritable chanting iteration of certain futures, and the interconnection of everything digital. Throughout fieldwork it became apparent that there are startlingly *few* different imaginaries of what the future of the digital might hold, and that these are repeated across sites; in the form of notions of exponential growth, disruption, unicorn stories and anecdotes about pregnancy tests bought in Target. This is the wraithlike form of the *Digitalis Dementore*, a gestalt composed of a highly limited set of sociotechnical imaginaries that haunt the dreams and nightmares alike of cutting-edge innovators.

The effects produced by this beast are those of continued sameness and uniformity of thought. Digital technologies and data are presented as both the cataclysmic purveyors of disruptive demise, and as the potential saviors of everything from a company's bottom-line to the cure for all social ills. However most of these imaginaries are frighteningly uniform, dreary and drained of any creative spark or warmth, unsettlingly homogeneous. They postulate worlds of brimming and vibrant Smartness, worlds made commensurable, made manageable, yet inevitably they produce the same "stupid city" [13] and the same business-oriented output.

Describing the *Digitalis Dementore* is itself a fraught venture, not because its composite imaginaries in themselves are dangerous. Instead, the mere invoking of the beast risks summoning it whilst simultaneously hiding it in plain common-sense sight. Obvious stories, hard to argue against, make themselves at home in confident rhetoric and slick powerpoint slides, becoming impossible to resist. Always its persuasive power is put to work in the service of similar solutions to diverse problems, purchased at a premium from actors who are difficult to hold accountable to their promises.

To describe the *Digitalis Dementore* is difficult for the above reasons, but it is also the way forward towards learning to live with it. The description itself relies on merriment at the expense of the beast, seeing and repeating its own repetitions in order to show it in a different light. To point out the self-important certainty with which futures are presented, is an attempt to wedge in the possibility that things might be otherwise.

3.3 Data Delere

Our third beast stands at the border of what will be permitted to exist and what will not: a monster of Cohen's 'category crisis' [5]. It emerges from the health data sector, where anxieties around access to data have inherited more explicit and sometimes more stringent biomedical models of consent and privacy. Nonetheless, in the autumn of 2014, a mundane technology designed to automate the collection of primary care data and improve the treatment in Danish General Practices rose to public notoriety in Denmark [19]. The data collection project had previously initially been approved for four chronic diseases, yet when the Danish national press broke the story, they revealed that the data collection technology had unlawfully gathered sensitive data from all patient consultations, dating as far back as 2007. No explicit consent had been obtained from the patients and general practitioners, from whom this data had been acquired, who then claimed to be ill-informed about their contribution. The contentious data was stored in a national database. Contentious though it was perceived as invaluable due to its unprecedented detail about primary care and its patients. With interests high and varied, this "golden egg" became the object of a fierce political struggle.

Narrating the controversy is an empirical challenge: it has many twists and turns. Newspapers pursued quotes voraciously and antagonistic formations gathered on new media platforms: the discussion moved on from questions of consent to that of 'what should be done'? As the months passed, public pressure rose, with eventual calls to delete the database. Yet deletion itself proved challenging. And it is here the beast of deletion begins to become visible. In the aftermath of scandal and the technicalities of handling contested data resources, a host of questions were posed to which answers have had to be found. Basic questions were difficult to answer: Where actually was the data? Who had the right to delete it? Under whose domain did it fall? And whose job was it to decide? For months, authorities argued over what should be done, and what was acceptable. Even as government ministries discussed, the National Archives stepped in as an attempt to preserve what was felt as the inherent potential of the data. When the database was eventually deleted, the case became narrative within the landscape of Danish medical data development, continuing to haunt conferences for years afterwards.

In the tussle over normative values placed on patient data, author Burnett found that the tension focused in on the contested database. The monster *Data Delere* arose not from revelation and loud controversy about a data scandal, but instead the political, institutional and technical intricacies of how a distributed dataset could be *deleted*. While the work of naming the monstrous in this case came about through news media controversy, it is through following, drawing out the narrative, that the many-headed monster of un-delete-able data becomes visible. Not the monster of breached data rights or of infringed privacy, but of those intricate sociotechnical knots, the tying of which will vary across legal and political regimes [17].

3.4   A Mithe: Occultis Aperta

Hidden in plain sight, this fourth beast takes its bestiality from scale, secrecy and concealment. It is the offspring of many different possible futures, of negotiations and promises between alluring tech companies and small municipalities. It concerns the material infrastructure of the data sector: data centers. Spoken of variously as "Engines of the cloud," "brains of the network," "archives of digital capitalism," or "factories of the 21st century;" data centers can be conceptualized in many ways. As machine-like interventions into physical, social, and political landscapes, they are both utterly located; megaprojects that devour land, energy and resources, and entirely distributed; part of planetary wide computational infrastructures. Such doubleness provides openings for productive ambiguity in how data centres take up residency within specific landscapes.

Take the rise of the Big-Tech's (Apple, Facebook, Google) hyper scale data centres. As Europe welcomes Big-Tech's data with open arms, northern states have emerged as the location of choice. The windy landscapes of Denmark are particularly attractive to electricity hungry server farms as they buzz and hum with the acoustics of alternating green electric current. A cool northerly climate, excellent English, a highly organized bureaucracy, and well-developed wind energy infrastructures are some of the things that make the union between the data center industry and the Danish investment sector seem ideal, facilitating technology companies in parading the green credentials of their new European storage and analytics facilities. In turn, Denmark bolsters its credentials as a hyper digitalized state, a place where new forms of digital governance await inception. But the encounter between these large tech corporations and small energy rich welfare states is far from frictionless, as new arrangements of culture and power emerge within it. Such small states do energy collectively, pushing the frontiers of science and innovation to generate phalanxes of wind turbines - on land and sea - in the service of a particular vision of welfarism. And is this welfarism that Big-Tech appropriates in making a home for itself within these landscapes.

While a range of media outlets, experts, and politicians conjure Big-Tech as purveyors of hopeful, promising futures, lurking within such speculative tales is the doubleness that Big-tech's infrastructural composition affords; both here, yet not, resident, yet strange. In appropriating particular strands of Danish state welfarism, the emissaries of hope render Big-Tech as harbingers of future welfare security, bringing to the next generation what prior generations have lost; jobs, opportunities, and infrastructure. So what are the differences that are made? As the emerging, diffractive effects of this encounter begin to unfold - abolishing green taxes, non-green energy, shrouding negotiations in secrecy, silencing participants with non-disclosure agreements – we are beginning to see that the scale of Big-tech's needs (a possible twelve data centers) might just be too much for a small nation state to contain. The energy they consume threatens to outstrip the wind's capacity to provide (and the windmill's capacity to collect) and the process they invoke threatens to outflank the democratic norms of the state.

A creeping sense of discomfort is emerging as the potential monstrosity of this relationship becomes more palpable. In the same way that the state is struggling to contain the voraciousness of Big-Tech, the opacity of the political form which has given rise to these server farms is struggling to contain an architectural form which has until now, kept them hidden in plain sight.

3.5 Instrumentua

Our fifth beast is the offspring of an infatuation with instrumentation, an infatuation that effects ethnographic imaginaries. It comes of a cross-cutting, reflexive component of project work, which is concerned with drawing out relations between *Data as Relation* subprojects, and with designing research methods tools that will enable this kind of collaborative ethnography. Within an imaginary where instrumentation meets the digital, ethnographic material can only come to terms with datafication through the clarification, beautification and amplification offered in the use of computational data analytics. The vision goes like this: already datafied sites are best ventured into with the assistance of a tolerant beast native to those worlds, an informant which might be persuaded to lend its capacities of alien vision and reasoning. To summon it, the ethnographers need only to make a very careful whisper in the language of Python.

The emergence of this beast is not unique to our project. The competitive social science grant will often include this beast because it is seen to provide an innovative edge. It promises to 'scale up' the ways a project can speak, travel, and garner publics. It promises to transfer mathodological [sic.] learnings of one grant to the next. The hope is that by embracing data analytics systems, a project can materially participate in and interrupt the logics of data. Dressed up ethnography lures funds and new collaborators, new interest. But there is also the lure of the virtualization of ethnography, that by utilizing new platforms to gather, compare, visualize ethnographic material we might achieve parity with the power, legitimacy and futures of the practices we study. That our ethnographic insights could scale, loom larger in the minds of those to whom we might wish to speak. It lures the ethnographer into counterfactual sites, that release the imagination from limitations of the "field", that attempts to crawl, cache, scrape, remember its way into differently bounded analysis, promising field-sites that are unhinged from locale but become increasingly monolithic.

Intimate engagement might train the ethnographer for new ways of seeing and dreaming. And the creature too perhaps learns and takes something back to the data worlds from these border encounters as it travels across sites. Yet this beast can be devouring in its instrumentality: It demands that ethnographic material behave as data, to be "switchable" [18] across different forms of containment in databases for field notes, images, blogs or visualizations. In exchange, it suggests re-adoptability by the ethnographer and their peers. A likeness to tools; lendable, tradable, durable and affordable. Yet, this monster stands at the threshold to becoming [5] stretching out its digits toward the handy ethnographer, as if it already acknowledged how readily it may yet again be abandoned, discarded after completing the tasks asked of it [6]. What inheres in this relation? Could an ethnographer be reasonably trusted to pick bugs crawling off its skin, a care without which this creature would be doomed to the absence of convivial companionship?

4   Bestiary Analytics

If change is inherently the site of the monstrous, a world where 'humanity has to grasp its future' [16: 196], the sites where people go about explicitly bringing the future into being are the sites to view the difference those monsters make. Yet of course each of these manifests in distinct forms. Bringing beasts together in a bestiary foregrounds acts of noticing, analysis of making, and objectification. As much as attending to those things which get called out as monstrous (a way of 'reading cultures from the monsters they engender' [5: 3]) we attend to monsters in the making. In a departure from cultural theory's engagements with the beasts of popular culture, our bestiary carries an ethnographic sensibility, calling us as analysts to account for what we describe into being.

In the cases described above, monstrosity emerges through narration, seeing, and engagement. The beasts we describe emerge from the specificity of our Danish research settings, yet we suspect that beasts of these types can be described across research site boundaries. Digital ubiquity poses a certain methodological challenge to scholars of data and its lives, and as researchers, we carry expectations about the capacity to bound our fields of study, to organize analytically what will fall within and outwith those worlds. Yet through a bestiary of digital monsters, we would hope to bring out some of the observations both of those with whom we work (such as software engineers, data center designers, or platform builders) and of our own as researchers. For example, we could probably fill an entire shelf of bestiaries with cousins of *Codice Crepitus*, a series of tales whereby the lives of outsourced projects and the lure of in-house data analytics advantages are giving rise to disconnects between software development styles and management practices: in these muddles, those with whom we work find monstrous tangles, and our descriptions can give voice to this complexity. *Digitalis Demontore* is similarly visible only through long term immersion in the sites that characterize themselves as the forefront of change. Sited within the spaces where those whose visions seek practical instantiations and technical skills, repeated slides and phrases that work, but lose meaning. The patient and attentive ear can begin to hear the murmurings of a monster that is the opposite of what it claims: imaginaries that compose *Digitalis Demontore* are themselves everyday, contestable, but it is their uniformity and per-suasive power and the downstream effects of buying into these that are monstrous.

Through its form of narrative juxtaposition, the bestiary allows us to attend to the politics of our analyses, and the language of description we use. Levina and Bui argue that monstrosity has "transcended its status as a metaphor and has indeed become a necessary condition of our existence in the twenty-first century" [20: 2], both producing and representing the changes of twenty-first technological "monster culture" [5]. A similar move takes place for information technologies, which—in the words of the conference call—'no longer merely represent the world, but also produce it'. Taking this performativity seriously, the digital cannot be considered 'other' to 'the human' nor as a metaphor for human life. We should not describe it as such. In response to the present-day ubiquity of digital endeavors, this kind of analysis allows us to find "a way of staying in the same plane of knowing" as those whom our stories about monstrosity are about [26], a practice known as laterality [11, 12, 19]. Defying the boundary between emic and etic, laterality is a move that refuses the privileging of an academic, theoretical perspective over that of interlocutors or collaborators. In the juxtaposition of the beasts above, we can see stories of frustrations, fears and forms of anger brought about by technological changes. Data, not least its concomitant sense of possibility and volume, brings people and technologies into new relations around future-making. Would a fuller, richer bestiary inspire new ways of deliberating and conversing about or even laugh about monstrous, digital technologies?

Above all, in its inherent refusal of totality the bestiary makes different kinds of cuts in analytical fields. More than ever before, field connections are partial [25]. We envision, for one thing, that the bestiary opens up for participation. As much as our project has benefited from the work of describing technological anxieties that take monstrous form, so might other common projects. A bestiary can travel: in this case, through publication. In continuity with bestiaries of old, fables of the monstrous technological present resonate with fables of the medieval bestiary in their capacity to inspire analogical learning. For early bestiaries, the moral question was precisely about thinking across the different 'species': What could be learned about human ways of life from various depictions of the worlds of creatures? If today, living with the techno-logically monstrous is part of the human condition, perhaps the question is not so much a matter of analogical learning across species, as it is about finding and depicting monstrosity in specific encounters. Or, as MacCormack puts it (in the spirit of the project from which these cases emerge) in the 'study of relation more than of an object' [21: 305].

5 Conclusion

In a moment which feels full of the monstrous, we argue that it is necessary to describe the monsters we encounter in our research with care. Rather than reveling in the reveal and staying within its shock value, monstrosity can be approached as a revelatory way of knowing the technologies that traverse disparate systems of value. Cohen tells us that the monster 'always escapes' [5] and the impossibility of knowing it in its entirety is part of what makes it monstrous. In using the monstrous as a construct through which to understand our present moment of technological anxiety, we have worked through a series of cases from an emergent bestiary. Asking about the kind of relations are possible with monsters necessitates an enquiry into what makes monsters monstrous. Although we have named our beasts, our Bestiary is more focused on the processes of technological making that bring about moments of unease, and the role of description in drawing the eye to the monstrous, than the satisfactions offered by taxonomies. They demonstrate moments of breach in the making of contemporary technological realities, resonances with earlier monsters, and worlds of monsterly haunting. Yet like Borges' Celestial Emporium of Benevolent Knowledge, the monsters of our bestiary illustrate the limits of classificatory schema upon the monstrous, recalling Foucault's laughter upon reading Borges's list, which for him, 'shattered... all the familiar landmarks of thought—our thought, the thought that bears the stamp of our age and our geography—breaking up all the ordered surfaces and all the planes with which we are accustomed to tame the wild profusion of existing things' [10: 1]. Analysis may seek this accustomed taming, but, it may sometimes need to encounter such a break with the familiar landmarks of thought that taming ceases to be the objective. Keeping both forms of monstrosity in sight is the task of a reflexive critical analysis, and perhaps, a bestiary analytics.

Acknowledgement. With thanks to the Data as Relation research group, particularly Jannick Schou whose monster appeared in earlier versions of this paper. The draft paper was presented at the second seminar of the Research Network for the Anthropology of Technology in Copen-hagen, September 2018 and we thank participants for their constructive comments. The project is funded by the Villum Fonden, Denmark, under grant agreement 12823.

References

1. Agency for Digitisation: A Stronger and More Secure Digital Denmark: The Digital Strategy 2016–2020 (2016)
2. Andreessen, M.: Why software is eating the world. Wall Street J. (2011). https://www.wsj.com/articles/SB10001424053111903480904576512250915629460 or https://a16z.com/2016/08/20/why-software-is-eating-the-world/
3. Badke, D.: Introduction. The Medieval Bestiary. http://bestiary.ca/intro.htm. Accessed 30 May 2018
4. Biles, J.: Monstrous technologies and the telepathology of everyday life. In: Levina, M., Bui, D-M.T. (eds.) Monster Culture in the 21st Century, pp. 147–162. Bloomsbury, London (2013)
5. Cohen, J.J.: Monster culture: seven theses. In: Cohen, J.J. (ed.) Monster Theory, pp. 3–26. Minnesota University Press, Minneapolis (1996)
6. Cohen, J.J.: Postscript: the promise of monsters. In: Mittman, A.S., Dendle, P.J. (eds.) Ashgate Research Companion to Monsters and the Monstrous, pp. 449–464. Ashgate, London (2012)
7. Derrida, J., Weber, E.: Points…: Interviews, 1974–1994. Stanford University Press, Stanford (1995)
8. Dourish, P., Bell, G.: Divining a Digital Future. MIT Press, Boston (2011)
9. Dunleavy, P., Margetts, H., Bastow, C., Tinkler, J.: Digital Era Governance: IT Corporations, the State and E-Government. Oxford University Press, New York (2006)
10. Foucault, M.: On the Order of Things. Routledge, London (2005)
11. Gad, C., Jensen, C.B., Winthereik, B.R.: Practical ontology: worlds in STS and anthropology. Nat. Cult. 3, 67–86 (2015)
12. Gad, C., Bruun-Jensen, C.: Lateral concepts. Engag. Sci. Technol. Soc. 2, 3–12 (2016). https://doi.org/10.17351/ests2016.77
13. Greenfield, A.: Against the Smart City. Do Projects, New York (2013)
14. Haraway, D.: The promises of monsters: a regenerative politics for inappropriate/d others. In: Grossberg, L., Nelson, C., Treichler, P. (eds.) Cultural Studies, pp. 295–337. Routledge, New York (1992)
15. Haraway, D.: Staying with the Trouble. Duke University Press, Durham (2016)
16. Hardt, M., Negri, A.: Multitude: War and Democracy in the Age of Empire. Penguin Press, New York (2004)
17. Jasanoff, S.: Designs on Nature: Science and Democracy in Europe and the United States. Princeton University Press, Princeton (2005)
18. Kittler, F.: Realtime analysis, time axis manipulation. Publ. Cult. 13(1), 1–18 (2017)
19. Langhoff, T.O., Amstrup, M.H., Mørck, P., Bjørn, P.: Infrastructures for healthcare: from synergy to reverse synergy. Health Inform. J. 24(1), 43–53 (2016)
20. Levina, M., Bui, D.-M.T.: Introduction. In: Levina, M., Bui, D.-M.T. (eds.) Monster Culture in the 21st Century, pp. 1–14. Bloomsbury, London (2013)
21. MacCormack, P.: Posthuman teratology. In: Mittman, A.S., Dendle, P.J. (eds.) The Ashgate Research Companion to Monsters and the Monstrous, pp. 293–309. Ashgate, London (2013)
22. Maurer, B.: Mutual Life, Limited: Islamic Banking, Alternative Currencies. Lateral Reason. Princeton University Press, Princeton (2005)
23. Mittman, A.S.: Introduction: the impact of monsters and Monster Studies. In: Mittman, A.S., Dendle, P.J. (eds.) The Ashgate Research Companion to Monsters and the Monstrous, pp. 1–16. Ashgate, London (2012)

24. Schou, J., Hjelholt, M.: Digital citizenship and neoliberalization: governing digital citizens in Denmark. Citizensh. Stud. **22**(5), 507–522 (2018)
25. Strathern, M.: Partial Connections. Rowman & Littlefield, London (2004)
26. Verran, H.: Working with those who think otherwise. Common Knowl. **20**(3), 527–539 (2014)
27. Winthereik, B., Verran, H.: Ethnographic stories as generalisations that intervene. Sci. Stud. **25**(1), 37–51 (2012)
28. Weinstock, J.A.: Invisible monsters: vision, horror and contemporary culture. In: Mittman, A.S., Dendle, P.J. (eds.) Ashgate Research Companion to Monsters and the Monstrous, pp. 275–292. Ashgate, London (2013)

Frankenstein's Monster as Mythical Mattering: Rethinking the Creator-Creation Technology Relationship

Natalie Hardwicke(✉)

The University of Sydney, Sydney, Australia
business.infosystems@sydney.edu.au

Abstract. The mythical tale of Frankenstein portrays a certain pursuit of knowledge as being the monster. By drawing parallels between Frankenstein's tale and aspects of both Martin Heidegger's and Marshall McLuhan's work, this paper foregrounds what ontologically needs to "matter" for us to "love" our technological creations. Creator-creation modes of being are problematized in relation to the pursuit of knowledge, suggesting an organic view of being is needed. What this view highlights is an important knowledge-identity dichotomy; one which plays an irrevocable role in our understanding of the people-technology relationship.

Keywords: Knowledge · Myth · Sociomateriality · Technology
Identity

1 Introduction

This year's conference theme, "living with monsters", coincides with the 200-year anniversary of the mythical tale of Frankenstein. Since its publication, the tale has been metaphorically used to discuss various aspects of modern social life, such as the potential repercussions we face for how we treat our artificial (technological) creations [1]. As the conference calls for papers that encourage "rethinking" about our so-called technological "monsters", this paper heeds the call by problematizing a key aspect of scholarly practice.

Scholars arguably play a privileged role in commenting on, as well as influencing and educating others about, our increasingly ubiquitous technological world. However, as part of this pursuit, scholars can also be seen as embodying the same monster that is depicted in the fictitious tale of Frankenstein. The monster portrayed in the tale is not, as Latour [2] suggests, the act of creature abandonment, but rather an individual's pursuit of knowledge. Stated by Frankenstein to Captain Walton [3]:

> Learn from me, if not by my precepts, at least by my example, how dangerous is the acquirement of knowledge, and how much happier that man is who believes his native town to be the world, than he who aspires to become greater than his nature will allow (p. 42).

It seems fitting to explore what Frankenstein meant by such a statement, especially given that debates have emerged in the sociomateriality literature for how matter comes

U. Schultze et al. (Eds.): IS&O 2018, IFIP AICT 543, pp. 191–197, 2018.
https://doi.org/10.1007/978-3-030-04091-8_14

to "matter" [4]; and suggestions have also been made urging scholars to build an ontological foundation for strengthening the sociomaterial stance [5]. To build such a foundation, some have turned to the philosophies of Martin Heidegger [6] and Marshall McLuhan [7]. Fittingly, aspects of what "mattered" [8] in Heidegger's *Being and Time* [9] and McLuhan's *The Extensions of Man* [10], offer striking parallels to Frankenstein's cautionary tale; a tale that directly discusses problems of *being* that we encounter in relation to the natural world, other people, and the material entities we create.

For example, Heidegger's "Dasein" shows that the meaning we derive from our being-in-the-world comes from the encounters we have with others and things that are not-of-the-self. This is how Frankenstein's creature comes to identify as being foreign, as he is rejected by the world he finds himself in. Similarly, McLuhan saw our technological evolution as the iterative imitation of the human body – that we ourselves are already a version of Frankenstein. For example, McLuhan viewed the wheel as an extension of the foot, whilst artificial intelligence (AI) could be viewed as an extension of human thought or cognition.

By exploring the role of myth in relation to Frankenstein and aspects of Heidegger's and McLuhan's work, this short paper aims to foreground a knowledge-identity dichotomy; one that stands at the ontological helm of our empirical technological focus. What this paper suggests is that to "love" our technologies requires us to understand what Heidegger meant by the "authentic self".

2   Technology as Myth

The role that myth plays in our lives is well-established. Since Ancient Greece, for example, creative artistic works have functioned as societal disguises; of cloaking messages as stories in order to explore the nature of existence and reveal aspects of ourselves to ourselves [11]. According to Campbell and Moyers [12], mythical stories depict the same central message; one that sees the hero, or the protagonist, experience a type of metaphysical awakening.

In the referenced philosophies of Heidegger and McLuhan, they too acknowledged the powerful role of art and myth in this regard. Heidegger saw artistic works as the conveyor of truth and as the goal of philosophy – that art conveys the *meaning* of being to us, which in essence delivers a form of technological insight. Otherwise known as "enframing", this insight sees technology as revealing something about us that is nontechnical in nature. The message of seemingly "monstrous" technology would, in Heidegger's view, be seen not as something to do with the technologies themselves, but something that resides in the essence of man – of our failure to see a truth revealed via our technological enframing, in which what we *do* with technology reveals the nature of our being to us.

Similarly, McLuhan believed that we live our lives "mythically", in which our technological progressions symbolically reveal our own nature to us. He also saw art as an avenue for us to convey meaning to ourselves in an electronic age of information overload. Part of McLuhan's analysis of seeing technology as the mythical message for our being human was his turn towards the work of Carl Jung; referencing Jung's concept of "shadow". In this vein, the idea of a monster would be viewed from the perspective of technologies reflecting our unconscious – of us manifesting into being that which we need to be made consciously aware of [13].

What Heidegger and McLuhan both allude to is that our technologies become something that require our conscious attention and questioning for the role they play in our lives. The creation of an artificial construct, and the subsequent role that construct plays in the creator's life, is the essence of the Frankenstein tale.

3   The Tale of Frankenstein

As the tale goes, the scientist Victor Frankenstein harvests body parts from a graveyard, stitches pieces together, and creates a pseudo man. When Frankenstein "zaps" his creature to life, he is however horrified at the sight of his own creation – fleeing in terror and remorse. Left alone, the creature begins to contemplate its existence and attempts to fit-in with society, but is rejected and condemned. The creature then commits acts of murder, against those held near and dear by Frankenstein, in a plight of revenge against his creator. Frankenstein then sees himself as having no other option but to dedicate the rest of his life in the pursuit of destroying his creation; atoning for the destruction caused. This relationship that creator and creation come to have is hinged on their respective pursuits of knowledge.

Such pursuit, however, begins with Captain Walton – the explorer who Frankenstein recounts his tale to. At the time he meets Frankenstein, Walton is on an expedition seeking to navigate to unknown lands; to obtain knowledge not yet possessed by any man on earth, even stating that the cost of a crew member's life was worth paying if it meant acquiring the knowledge he sought. Walton's character is seen as a version of Frankenstein on the cusp of making the same mistake, or he can choose to change his course after hearing Frankenstein's cautionary tale.

In his recount of such a tale, Frankenstein reveals what he originally desired in wanting to create his creature, which was to obtain, "The secrets to heaven and earth" (p.33) to learn the metaphysical and physical wonders of the world. In turn, Frankenstein's creature seeks knowledge about what makes us human – specifically wanting to know why it was he was made, but also why he was abandoned by his creator and then condemned by society.

In this vein, the creature can be seen as seeking knowledge of his identity and reason for existence, whereas Walton seeks novelty in knowledge, and Frankenstein seeks mastery of it. Arguably, this thirst for knowledge, as portrayed by these three characters, lies at the center of what has become known in our own social context as "The Frankenstein Problem" [14]. By discussing this problem, the monster of knowledge becomes evident when we falsely believe we exist as separate selves.

4   The Frankenstein Problem and Revelations of Being

The Frankenstein problem explores the conundrum we face when we view our existence from one of two perspectives regarding the creator-creation relationship, as portrayed in the tale. From a religious standpoint, existence is seen as a ceramic model, in which God is the craftsman who, similar to Frankenstein, has used certain material and moulded us into being. This view sees the world as an artefact that we have been "thrown into", yet much like Frankenstein's creature, we do not understand why.

In the second, scientific view, existence is seen as a mechanical construct. We have stumbled upon the laws of nature and, just as Frankenstein did, have substituted ourselves for being in the position of God-on-earth; creators of artificial life as expressed via our technology. However, a God complex ensues. We can explain and imitate the "machine" of life, but we still cannot explain ourselves as the metaphorical ghost trapped inside [15].

What the religious and scientific views foreground are a sense of alienation and foreignness; that we are either the victims of life, much like the creature, or we seek to control our own fate, much like Frankenstein. Yet if we take Frankenstein as an example, he saw himself as standing apart, separate from the natural world, desiring power and control over its secrets. In turn, however, Frankenstein becomes the victim of having his creature lord that same power and control over his being, with the creature at one point saying to Frankenstein, "You are my creator, but I am your master; obey!" (p. 205).

In McLuhan's view, our western technological pursuits have the same outcome, in which the technologies we mould and create in turn end up shaping and controlling our actions. McLuhan also noted that death-oriented myths, of which Frankenstein is an example, are often associated with this technological know-how; that they try to warn us against our desire to imitate life as a form of mechanical automation, rather than recognising life's organic origins. This warning stems from our desire to divide and control, which in turn promotes the illusion of separateness between man and nature, and man and machine.

In Heidegger's view, this desire for separateness, as embodied by our technology, derives from a false sense of self, based on an existential conundrum. For Heidegger, human beings are the only creature whose existence is an issue for it, which stems from the knowledge of our inevitable death. Yet for the most part we live our lives in denial, born out of fear of this inevitability, immersing ourselves in worldly activities.

The religious and scientific views associated with the Frankenstein problem can be seen as embodying the same fear, disguised by immortality. Arguably, religion seeks to displace the fear of death by promising immortality in heaven, so long as we behave in certain ways on earth; whereas science seeks to delay death, even eradicate it entirely, as suggested by our technological advancements where we substitute organic matter with artificial means.

Yet as we know from Frankenstein's tale, the desire to capture life, defy death, or see one's identity as being separate to everything else, leads us towards a pathway of destruction. In hindsight, Frankenstein tells Walton that his scientific desire was a type of "madness", especially when he realized that what he actually lived for, and what he cared most about, were the people he loved – the same people killed as a result of his knowledge pursuit and subsequent creation.

The same lack of contemplation is also true of Frankenstein's creature in his attempt to be accepted by society. McLuhan saw our individual quest for identity similar to the creature's – as violent and tribal, seeing any attempt to fit-in with the status quo as both binding and blinding us from questioning our own consciousness.

The journey and the conflict that is told between Frankenstein and his creature alludes us to two observations. Firstly, that they each needed to experience their respective journeys in order to reflect, and then subsequently regret, their actions in hindsight; and secondly, the knowledge they each sought to gain was not the knowledge they needed to obtain.

In other words, the message of Frankenstein, along with Heidegger and McLuhan's ideas, foregrounds a third, organic model of existence; one that transcends and liberates the self from the false dualism of self and other (creator and creation), being and non-being (life and death). Although a similar claim has been made by the ontological inseparability argument [6], which is the view that we cannot divorce people from technology, the organic model illuminates the "authentic self" which outlines why this inseparability is the case.

5 Foregrounding the Organic Model

In Heidegger's view, one finds one's authentic self by first living in, and then overcoming, a world of experienced "facticity". It is the idea of being-in a world of imposed parameters, a social world always-already given to, and made for us by others ('the one'), offering 'inauthentic' experiences, and then precisely to overcome them. In other words, Heidegger suggested that all schemas of the world are inherently hermeneutic, meaning that such truth can only be realized *by* one's self first living through the inauthentic experience, and in accepting death, that we do not stand over or against the world, merely reflecting on it, but rather are part of the natural world which expresses itself in finite cycles of life and death, living our lives in our own-most ways. Similarly, McLuhan saw learning as something that takes place after-the-fact, in which we as individuals have to experience, but then also have to abandon, that which we perceived to be "reality".

When Frankenstein's loved ones die at the hand of his creation, he must come to realize that their deaths were the result of his unquestioned pursuit of technological knowledge. In atoning for their deaths, Frankenstein renounces himself and his own separate desires. Similarly, the creature comes to the same realization, but only after Frankenstein dies. The creature realizes he too will one day face the same fate as his creator, and therefore acknowledges his need to find happiness in the knowledge of death.

Furthermore, the creature reflects in hindsight and realizes that the happiest he felt was when he was first in nature and did not think, at the time, to question his reason for being. It was only by being-in a social context with others that the creature came to believe that he did not "belong". If we refer back to Frankenstein's warning to Walton, the same message is portrayed – that man's existence is already the highest and ultimate form of being, as it exists in-line with the natural world. This realization is part of the authentic self-claim. The conundrum, however, is that one must first live through the inauthentic experience in order to find their authentic self.

In the tale, Frankenstein and his creature have already sealed their own fate upon such realization, but it is Walton who learns from their mistakes; abandoning his own quest, yet disliking the feeling that resulted – that he had to sacrifice his individualism for reasons that were greater than his own knowledge pursuit.

In this light, interpreting the tale of Frankenstein as one that warns against the abandonment of our own technological creations would be missing the point. Although there is merit in suggesting we should love our creations rather than abandon them [2], our ability to do so requires us to first realize what the actual abandonment message is in the tale - that we must abandon our belief in the separate self.

To put this another way, our created technologies only become "monstrous" in the first place when we falsely believe we exist separately from nature or from one another [16]. To love our technologies means only having technology that aligns us with the world, not technology where we attempt, like Frankenstein, to impose our will over nature, or the world more broadly, as a result of seeing ourselves as being separate from it, or expecting to find answers to life via our individualistic knowledge pursuits. The technology we need would allow us to be with our loved ones, not technology that destroys, or is pursued at the cost of people's lives or wellbeing, or at the cost of destroying nature.

6   Conclusion

What this paper has done is use the role of myth to suggest a need for technological reflection at an ontological level. As suggested by the tale of Frankenstein, and supported by the works of both Heidegger and McLuhan, this can only be achieved through individual contemplation and introspection. What this requires is re-evaluation for how we as individuals perceive the creator-creation relationship; of needing to overcome the dichotomous view of self and other, being and non-being. It is not our technologies that we need to love, but rather, it is the authentic self we each need to find.

References

1. Baldick, C.: In Frankenstein's Shadow: Myth, Monstrosity, and Nineteenth-Century Writing. OUP, Oxford (1990)
2. Latour, B.: Love your monsters. Breakthrough J. 2(11), 21–28 (2011)
3. Shelley, M.: Frankenstein. England, London (1818)
4. Orlikowski, W.J., Scott, S.V.: Sociomateriality: challenging the separation of technology, work and organization. Acad. Manag. Ann. 2(1), 433–474 (2008)
5. Ou Yang, S.: Returning to the philosophical roots of sociomateriality: how M. Heidegger and M. Mcluhan questioned information communication technology. ACM 47(4), 93–105 (2016)
6. Riemer, K., Johnston, R.B.: Clarifying ontological inseparability with Heidegger's analysis of equipment. MIS Q. 41(4) (2017)
7. Utesheva, A., Boell, S.: Theorizing society and technology in information systems research. ACM SIGMIS Database: DATABASE for Adv. Inf. Syst. 47(4), 106–110 (2016)

8. Barad, K.: Posthumanist performativity: toward an understanding of how matter comes to matter. Signs **28**(3), 801–831 (2003)
9. Heidegger, M.: Being and Time: A Translation of sein Und Zeit. SUNY press, Albany (1996)
10. McLuhan, M.: The Extensions of Man, New York (1964)
11. Woodard, R.D.: The Cambridge Companion to Greek Mythology. Cambridge University Press, Cambridge (2007)
12. Campbell, J., Moyers, B.: The Power of Myth. Anchor, New York City (2011)
13. Glick, M.A.: Symbol and artifact: Jungian dynamics at McLuhan's technological interface (1976)
14. Wilson, J.: The frankenstein problem. Philosophy **39**(149), 223–232 (1964)
15. Koestler, A.: The Ghost in the Machine. Macmillan, Oxford (1968)
16. Allen, B.: A dao of technology? Dao **9**(2), 151–160 (2010)

Author Index

Zeitfracht Medien GmbH
Ferdinand-Jühlke-Straße 7
99095 Erfurt, Deutschland
produktsicherheit@kolibri360.de